HANS REICHENBACH

THE RISE OF
SCIENTIFIC
PHILOSOPHY

UNIVERSITY OF CALIFORNIA PRESS
BERKELEY AND LOS ANGELES · 1968

UNIVERSITY OF CALIFORNIA PRESS
Berkeley and Los Angeles
CAMBRIDGE UNIVERSITY PRESS
London, England

◆

Copyright, 1951, by
The Regents of the University of California

THIRTEENTH PRINTING, 1968

Manufactured in the United States of America

THE RISE OF
SCIENTIFIC PHILOSOPHY

Contents

v

211405

Preface

Philosophy is regarded by many as inseparable from speculation. They believe that the philosopher cannot use methods which establish knowledge, be it knowledge of facts or of logical relations; that he must speak a language which is not accessible to verification—in short, that philosophy is not a science. The present book is intended to establish the contrary thesis. It maintains that philosophic speculation is a passing stage, occurring when philosophic problems are raised at a time which does not possess the logical means to solve them. It claims that there is, and always has been, a scientific approach to philosophy. And it wishes to show that from this ground has sprung a scientific philosophy which, in the science of our time, has found the tools to solve those problems that in earlier times have been the subject of guesswork only. To put it briefly: this book is written with the intention of showing that philosophy has proceeded from speculation to science.

A presentation of this kind is necessarily critical in its analysis of earlier phases of philosophy. In its first part, therefore, this book is concerned with an examination of the shortcomings of traditional philosophy. This part of the inquiry is directed toward the psychological roots from which speculative philosophy has grown. It thus assumes the form of an attack upon what Francis Bacon has called "the idols of the theater". The power of these idols, of the philosophic systems of the past, is still great enough to challenge critique three centuries after Bacon's death. The second part of this book turns to an exposition of modern scientific philosophy. It attempts to collect the philosophic results that have been developed through the analysis of modern science and the use of symbolic logic.

Though concerned with philosophic systems and scientific thought, this book is not written on the assumption that the reader has a technical knowledge of its subject matter. The philosophical concepts and doctrines referred to are always explained along with the criticism to which they are subjected. And though the book deals with the logical analysis of modern mathematics and physics, it does not presuppose that the reader is a mathematician or a physicist. If he has common sense enough to wish to learn more than common sense can teach him, the reader is well prepared to follow the arguments of the book.

Thus this book may be used as an introduction to philosophy, and in particular, to scientific philosophy. Yet it is not intended to give a so-called "objective" presentation of traditional philosophical material. No attempt is made to expound philosophical systems with the attitude of the interpreter, who wishes to find some truth in every philosophy and hopes to make his readers believe that every philosophical doctrine can be understood. This way of teaching philosophy is none too successful. Many of those who were once willing to study philosophy from presentations purporting to be objective have found that philosophical doctrines remained incomprehensible to them. Others have tried to understand philosophical systems as best they could and to combine philosophical results with those of science, but have discovered that they were unable to unite science with philosophy. Now, if philosophy appears incomprehensible to unprejudiced thought or incompatible with modern science, the fault must be on the philosopher's side. He has too often sacrificed truth to the desire to give answers, and clarity to the temptation of speaking in pictures; and his language has lacked the precision which is the scientist's compass in escaping the reefs of error.

PREFACE

If a presentation of philosophy is to be objective, it should therefore be objective in the standards of its critique rather than in the sense of a philosophic relativism. The investigations of this book are intended to be objective in this sense. This presentation is written for the many who have read books on philosophy and science and were not satisfied; who have tried to find meanings but got stuck in a barrage of words; yet who have not abandoned hope that some day philosophy will become as cogent and as powerful as science.

That such a scientific philosophy is already in existence is not yet sufficiently known. As a remnant of the philosophy of speculation, a haze of vagueness still screens off philosophic knowledge from the eyes of those who were not trained in the methods of logical analysis. In the hope that this haze will evaporate in the fresh air of clear meanings, the present study was undertaken. This book is meant to inquire into the roots of philosophical error and to present the evidence that philosophy has risen from error to truth.

HANS REICHENBACH

University of California, Los Angeles

Acknowledgement

In the final wording of the manuscript, valuable help as to content and expression was given to me by Dr. Wesley Robson, Los Angeles; Dr. William Holther, Berkeley; Professor Herbert Feigl, Minneapolis; Mr. John Kirk, Los Angeles; and Mr. Stillman Drake, Piedmont, California.

My greatest indebtedness for help in writing this book goes to my wife, Maria Reichenbach. Her untiring interest, her ready advice, and her uncompromising critique have greatly contributed to making ideas clear which, I hope, deserve to be presented to a wider public than the two of us.

H. R.

PART ONE

The Roots of Speculative Philosophy

1.

The Question

HERE IS A passage taken from the writings of a
famous philosopher: "Reason is substance,
as well as infinite power, its own infinite
material underlying all the natural and
spiritual life; as also the infinite form, that which sets the
material in motion. Reason is the substance from which
all things derive their being."

Many a reader has no patience with linguistic products
of this brand. Failing to see any meaning in them, he may
feel inclined to throw the book into the fire. In order to
progress from this emotional response to logical critique,
such a reader is invited to study so-called philosophical
language with the attitude of the neutral observer, as the
naturalist studies a rare specimen of beetle. Analysis of
error begins with analysis of language.

The student of philosophy usually is not irritated by
obscure formulations. On the contrary, reading the
quoted passage he would presumably be convinced that
it must be his fault if he does not understand it. He therefore would read it again and again and thus would eventually reach a stage in which he thinks he has understood
it. At this point it would appear quite obvious to him that
reason consists of an infinite material which underlies all
natural and spiritual life and is therefore the substance
of all things. He has been so conditioned to this way of

talking as to forget all criticisms which a less "educated" man would make.

Now consider a scientist trained to use his words in such a way that every sentence has a meaning. His statements are so phrased that he is always able to prove their truth. He does not mind if long chains of thought are involved in the proof; he is not afraid of abstract reasoning. But he demands that somehow the abstract thought be connected with what his eyes see and his ears hear and his fingers feel. What would such a man say if he read the quoted passage?

The words "material" and "substance" are no strangers to him. He has applied them in his description of many an experiment; he has learned to measure the weight and the solidity of a material or a substance. He knows that a material may consist of several substances, each of which may look very different from the material. So these words do not offer any difficulty in themselves.

But what kind of material is that which underlies life? One would like to assume that it is the substance of which our bodies are made. How then can it be identical with reason? Reason is an abstract capacity of human beings, manifesting itself in their behavior, or to be modest, in parts of their behavior. Does the philosopher quoted wish to say that our bodies are made of an abstract capacity of themselves?

Even a philosopher cannot mean such an absurdity. What then does he mean? Presumably he means to say that all happenings in the universe are so arranged that they serve a reasonable purpose. That is a questionable assumption, but at least a comprehensible one. Yet if it is all the philosopher wants to say, why must he say it in a cryptic way?

That is the question I wish to answer before I can say what philosophy is, and what it should be.

4

2.

The Search for Generality
and the Pseudo Explanation

THE SEARCH for knowledge is as old as the history of mankind. With the beginning of social grouping and the use of tools for a richer satisfaction of daily needs the *desire to know* arose, since knowledge is indispensable for control of the objects of our environment so as to make them our servants.

The essence of knowledge is *generalization*. That fire can be produced by rubbing wood in a certain way is a knowledge derived by generalization from individual experiences; the statement means that rubbing wood in this way will *always* produce fire. The art of discovery is therefore the art of correct generalization. What is irrelevant, such as the particular shape or size of the piece of wood used, is to be excluded from the generalization; what is relevant, for example, the dryness of the wood, is to be included in it. The meaning of the term "relevant" can thus be defined: that is relevant which must be mentioned for the generalization to be valid. The separation of relevant from irrelevant factors is the beginning of knowledge.

Generalization, therefore, is the origin of science. The science of the ancients is expressed in the many techniques of civilization they possessed: building houses and weaving cloth and forging arms and sailing ships and cultivating the soil. It is embodied in a more pronounced form in their physics and astronomy and mathematics. What entitles us to speak of an ancient science is the fact that the ancients had succeeded in establishing quite a few generalizations of a rather comprehensive kind: they knew laws of geometry, which hold for all parts of space without exceptions; laws of astronomy, which govern time; and a number of physical and chemical laws, such as the laws of the lever and the laws relating heat to melting. All these laws are generalizations; they say that a certain implication holds for all things of a specified kind. In other words, they are *if-then always* statements. The example "if a metal is sufficiently heated, then it always melts", is of this kind.

Generalization, furthermore, is the very nature of explanation. What we mean by explaining an observed fact is incorporating that fact into a general law. We observe that as the day progresses a wind begins to blow from the sea to the land; we explain this fact by incorporating it into the general law that heated bodies expand and thus become lighter with respect to equal volumes. We then see how this law applies in the example considered: the sun heats the land more strongly than the water so that the air over the land becomes warm and rises, thus leaving its place to an air current from the sea. We observe that living organisms need food in order to exist; we explain this fact by incorporating it into the general law of the conservation of energy. The energy which the organisms spend in their activities must be replaced from the calories of the food. We observe that bodies fall down when not supported; we explain this fact by incorporating it into the general law that masses attract each other. The great mass of the earth pulls the small masses toward its surface.

The words "attract" and "pull", which we used in the

last example, are dangerous words. They suggest an analogy with certain psychological experiences. We are attracted by objects we desire, like food or a late-model car; and we like to imagine the attraction of bodies by the earth as the satisfaction of a sort of desire, at least on the side of the earth. But such an interpretation would be what the logician calls an *anthropomorphism,* that is, the assignment of human qualities to physical objects. It is obvious that no explanation is supplied by a parallelism between natural events and human concerns. When we say that Newton's law of attraction explains the falling of bodies, we mean that the movement of bodies toward the earth is incorporated into a general law according to which all bodies move toward each other. The word "attraction" as employed by Newton means no more than such a movement of bodies toward each other. The explanatory power of Newton's law derives from its generality, not from its superficial analogy with psychological experiences. Explanation is generalization.

Sometimes explanation is achieved by assuming some fact that is not or cannot be observed. For instance, the barking of a dog might be explained by the assumption that a stranger is approaching the house; and the occurrence of marine fossils in mountains is explained by assuming that the ground was at some time at a lower level and covered by the ocean. But the unobserved fact is explanatory only because it shows the observed fact to be the manifestation of a general law: dogs bark when strangers approach, marine animals do not live on the land. General laws thus can be used for inferences uncovering new facts, and explanation becomes an instrument for supplementing the world of direct experience with inferred objects and occurrences.

No wonder that the successful explanation of many natural phenomena developed in the human mind an urge toward ever greater generality. The multitude of observed facts could not satisfy the desire to know; the quest for knowledge transcended observation and demanded generality. Yet it is an unfortunate matter of fact that human beings are inclined to give answers even when they do not have the means to find correct answers. Scientific explanation demands ample observation and critical thought; the higher the generality aspired to, the greater must be the mass of observational material, and the more critical the thought. Where scientific explanation failed because the knowledge of the time was insufficient to provide the right generalization, imagination took its place and supplied a kind of explanation which appealed to the urge for generality by satisfying it with naïve parallelisms. Superficial analogies, particularly analogies with human experiences, were confused with generalizations and taken to be explanations. The search for generality was appeased by the *pseudo explanation*. It is from this ground that philosophy sprang.

Such an origin does not make for a good record. But I am not writing a letter of recommendation for philosophy. I wish to explain its existence and its nature. And it is a fact that both its weakness and its strength can be accounted for by its origin on so dubious a base.

Let me illustrate what I mean by a pseudo explanation. The desire to understand the physical world has at all times led to the question of how the world began. The mythologies of all peoples include primitive versions of the origin of the universe. The best known story of creation, a product of the Hebrew imaginative spirit, is given in the Bible and dates about the ninth century B.C. It explains the world as the creation of God. Its explanation is of the naïve type that satisfies a primitive mind, or a childlike mind, proceeding by anthropomorphic analogies: as humans make homes and tools and gardens, God made the world. One of the most general and fundamental questions, that of the genesis of the physical world, is answered by an analogy with experiences of the daily environment. That pictures of this kind do not constitute an explanation, that, if they were true, they would make the problem of an explanation only more difficult to solve, has often been rightly argued. The story of creation is a pseudo explanation.

And yet—what a suggestive power lives in it! The Jewish people, then still in a primitive stage, gave the world a narrative so vivid as to have fascinated all readers down to our day. Our imagination is held in thrall by the awe-inspiring picture of a god whose spirit moved upon the face of the waters and who set all the world into being by a few commands. Deep innate desires for a powerful father are satisfied by this brilliant antique fiction. The satisfaction of psychological desires, however, is not explanation. Philosophy has always been impaired by a confusion of logic with poetry, of rational explanation with imagery, of generality with analogy. Many a philosophical system is like the Bible, a masterpiece of poetry, abundant in pictures that stimulate our imagination, but devoid of the power of clarification that issues from scientific explanation.

There are some Greek cosmogonies which differ from the Jewish story of the origin of the world in that they assume an evolution, not a creation. In this respect they are more scientific; but they offer no scientific explanation in the modern sense, for they too are constructed by primitive generalizations from daily experience. Anaximander, who lived about 600 B.C., believed that the world evolved from an infinite substance, which he called *apeiron*. First the warm separated from the cold, which became the earth; the warm fire surrounded the cold earth and was then caught in wheel-like hoses of air.

There it still is; the fire is visible through the holes in the hoses, which appear to us as the sun, the moon, and the stars. Living beings evolved from the moisture surrounding the earth and began as lower forms; even human beings started as fishes. The philosopher who gave us these fanciful pictures of the origin of the world took analogy to be explanation. And yet, his pseudo explanations are not entirely futile, being at least a sort of step in the right direction. They are primitive scientific theories and, if employed as directives for further observation and analysis, might eventually have led to better explanations. For instance, Anaximander's wheel-like hoses are attempts at explaining the circular paths of the stars.

There are two kinds of false generalization, which can be classified as innocuous and pernicious forms of error. The first, often found among empirically minded philosophers, lend themselves rather easily to correction and improvement in the light of further experience. The second, which consist in analogies and pseudo explanations, lead to empty verbalisms and dangerous dogmatism. Generalizations of this kind seem to pervade the work of speculative philosophers.

As an instance of a pernicious generalization, which uses a superficial analogy with the intention of constructing a universal law, consider the philosophic passage quoted in the introduction. The observation on which the statement is based is the fact that reason in large measure controls human actions and thus determines, at least partly, social developments. Looking for an explanation the philosopher regards reason as analogous to a substance that determines the properties of the objects which are composed of it. For instance, the substance iron determines the properties of a bridge built of it. Obviously, the analogy is pretty bad. Iron is the same kind of stuff as the bridge; but reason is not a stuff like human bodies and cannot be the material carrier of human actions. When Thales, who about 600 B.C. acquired fame as the "sage of Miletus", put forth the theory that water is the substance of all things, he made a false generalization; the observation that water is contained in many materials, as in the soil, or in living organisms, was falsely extrapolated to the assumption that water is contained in every object. Thales' theory, however, is sensible in so far as it makes one physical substance the building block for all the others; it is at least a generalization, though a false one, and not an analogy. How much superior is Thales' language to that of the quoted passage!

The trouble with loose language is that it creates false ideas, and the comparison of reason with a substance offers a good illustration for this fact. The philosopher who wrote this passage would strongly object to the interpretation of his statement as a mere analogy. He would claim that he had found the real substance of all things and would ridicule an insistence on physical substance. He would maintain that there is a "deeper" meaning of substance, of which physical substance is but a special case. Translated into comprehensible language this would mean that the relation between the happenings in the universe and reason is the same as the relation between the bridge and the iron out of which it is made. But this comparison is obviously untenable, and the translation shows that any serious interpretation of the analogy would lead to logical blunder. Calling reason a substance may produce some images in the listener; but in further application such word combinations mislead the philosopher to jump to conclusions which logic cannot warrant. Pernicious errors through false analogies have been the philosopher's disease at all times.

The fallacy committed in this analogy is an example

of a kind of mistake called the *substantialization of abstracta*. An abstract noun, like "reason", is treated as though it refers to some thing-like entity. There is a classic illustration of this kind of fallacy in the philosophy of Aristotle (384–322 B.C.), where he treats of form and matter.

Geometrical objects present the aspect of a form as distinct from the matter of which they are built; the form can change while the matter remains the same. This simple daily experience has become the source of a chapter of philosophy which is as obscure as it is influential and which is made possible only by the misuse of an analogy. The form of the future statue, Aristotle argues, must be in the block of wood before it is carved, otherwise it would not be there later; all becoming, likewise, consists in the process of matter taking on form. Form, therefore, must be a something. It is obvious that this inference can only be made by the help of a vague usage of words. To say that the form of the statue is in the wood before the sculptor has shaped it, means that it is possible for us to define inside the block of wood, or "see" into it, a surface which is identical with the later surface of the statue. Reading Aristotle, one sometimes has the feeling that he really means only this trivial fact. But clear and reasonable passages in his writings are followed by obscure language; he says such things as that one makes a brazen sphere out of bronze and sphere by putting the form into this material, and arrives at regarding form as a substance which exists perpetually without change.

A figure of speech has thus become the root of a philosophical discipline, which is called *ontology,* and which is supposed to deal with the ultimate grounds of being. The phrase "ultimate grounds of being" is itself a figure of speech; I may be pardoned if I use metaphysical language without further explanation and merely add the statement that for Aristotle form and matter are such ultimate grounds of being. Form is actual reality and matter is potential reality, because matter is capable of taking on many different forms. Furthermore, the relation of form and matter is regarded as lurking behind many other relations. In the scheme of the universe, the upper and the lower spheres and elements, the soul and the body, the male and the female, stand to one another in the same relation as form and matter. Aristotle evidently believes that these other relations are explained by the strained comparison with the fundamental relation of form and matter. A literal interpretation of analogy thus supplies a pseudo explanation, which by the uncritical use of a picture brings many different phenomena together under one label.

I will admit that Aristotle's historical significance must not be judged by a scale of criticism which is the product of modern scientific thought. But measured even by the scientific standards of his time, or of his own achievements in the fields of biology and logic, his metaphysics is not knowledge, not explanation, but *analogism*, that is, an escape into picture language. The urge to discover generalities makes the philosopher forget the very principles he applies successfully in more limited fields of inquiry, and makes him drift away on words where knowledge is not yet available. Here is the psychological root of the strange mixture of observation and metaphysics, which makes this outstanding collector of empirical material a dogmatic theorist, who satisfies his desire for explanation by coining words and setting up principles that are not translatable into verifiable experiences.

What Aristotle knew about the structure of the universe, or about the biological function of the male and female, was not enough to admit of a generalization. His astronomy was that of the geocentric system, for which the earth is the center of the universe; and his knowledge of the mechanism of reproduction did not include what is an elementary fact for modern biology: he did not know that the male spermatozoön and the female ovum unite in the generation of a new individual. Nobody would reproach him for not knowing results that could not be discovered without the telescope or the microscope. But in the absence of knowledge it was a weakness of his to mistake poor analogies for explanation. For instance, in speaking about reproduction he says that the male individual merely impresses a form upon the biological substance of the female. Misleading even as a figure of speech, this vague assertion cannot be regarded as the first step on a path toward sounder ways of thought. It has been the tragic result of such analogism that philosophic systems, instead of gradually preparing an approach to a scientific philosophy, have actually barred its development. Aristotle's metaphysics has influenced the thought of two thousand years and is still admired by many a philosopher of our time.

It is true that modern historians of philosophy permit themselves occasional criticisms within the frame of the usual veneration of Aristotle, pretending to discriminate between his philosophical insights and those parts of his system which they regard as the product of the imperfections of his time. But what is presented to us as philosophical insight is too often empty verbalism filled with meanings the author had never thought of. The relation of form and matter lends itself to many analogies, without supplying explanation. Apologetic interpretation is not the means to overcome the deeply rooted mistakes of a philosopher. It does not promote philosophic research if the errors of great men are given meanings so twisted as to become divinatory guesses of what men in later times had the resources to prove. The history of philosophy would advance much faster if its progress were not so often delayed by those who have made the history of philosophy the subject of their research.

I have used Aristotle's doctrine of form and matter as an illustration of what I have called a pseudo explanation. Ancient philosophy supplies us with another instance of this unfortunate form of reasoning—the philosophy of Plato. Since Aristotle was once Plato's student, one might even believe that he was disposed to his way of thinking by the plentiful use his teacher made of picture language and analogism. But I will rather examine Plato's philosophy without reference to its effects on Aristotle, which have often been analyzed. Its influence can be traced through a great variety of philosophical systems, reason enough to study its logical origin in more detail.

The philosophy of Plato (427–347 B.C.) is based on one of the strangest and yet most influential philosophical doctrines—his theory of ideas. The theory of ideas, so much admired and so intrinsically antilogical, arose from the attempt to give an account for the possibility of mathematical knowledge as well as of moral conduct. I shall discuss the latter root of the theory in Chapter 4 and restrict my present remarks to the first root.

Mathematical demonstration has always been regarded as a method of knowledge satisfying the highest standards of truth, and Plato certainly emphasized the superiority of mathematics to all other forms of knowledge. But the study of mathematics leads to certain logical difficulties when undertaken with the critical attitude of the philosopher. This applies, in particular, to geometry, a discipline which stood in the foreground of the investigations of Greek mathematicians. I will explain these difficulties in the logical form and the terminology in which we would present them today and then discuss the solution offered by Plato.

A short excursion into logic will be helpful to make the problem clear. The logician distinguishes between *universal* statements and *particular* statements. Universal statements are all-statements; they have the form "all things of a certain kind have a certain property". They are also called *general implications,* because they state that the condition laid down implies having the property. As an example consider the statement "all heated metals expand". It can be phrased: "if a metal is heated, it expands". When we want to apply such an implication to a particular object, we must make sure that the object satisfies the condition laid down; then we can infer that it has the property stated. For instance, we observe that a certain metal is heated; we then proceed to say that it expands. The statement "this heated metal expands" is a particular statement.

The theorems of geometry have the form of universal statements, or general implications. As an illustration, consider the theorem "all triangles have an angular sum of 180 degrees", or Pythagoras' theorem "in all right triangles the square of the hypotenuse equals the sum of the squares of the two sides". When we wish to apply such theorems, we must make sure that the condition laid down is satisfied. For instance, when we have drawn a triangle on the ground, we must check by the help of taut strings whether its sides are straight; we then may assert that its angles will add up to 180 degrees.

General implications of this kind are very useful; they allow us to make predictions. For instance, the implication about heated bodies allows us to predict that railroad tracks will expand in the sun. The implication about triangles foretells what results we shall find when we proceed to measuring the angles of a triangle marked by three towers. Such statements are called *synthetic*, an expression which may be translated as *informative*.

There is another kind of general implication. Consider the statement "all bachelors are unmarried". This statement is not very useful. If we wish to know whether a certain man is a bachelor, we must first know whether he is unmarried; and once we know it, the statement does not tell us anything else. The implication does not add anything to the condition laid down by it. Statements of this kind are empty; they are called *analytic*, an expression which may be translated as *self-explanatory*.

We must now discuss the question how we can find out whether a general implication is true. For analytic implications this question is easily answered; the implication "all bachelors are unmarried" follows from the meaning of the word "bachelor". It is different with synthetic implications. The meaning of the words "metal" and "heated" does not include any reference to "expanding". The implication can therefore be verified only through observation. We have found in all our past experiences that heated metals expand; therefore we feel entitled to set up the general implication.

This explanation, however, appears to break down for geometrical implications. Did we learn from past experiences that the angles of a triangle add up to 180 degrees? Some reflection on geometrical method speaks against an affirmative answer. We know that the mathematician has a proof for the theorem of the angular sum. For this proof, he draws lines on paper and explains to us certain relations with reference to the diagram, but does not measure angles. He appeals to certain general truths called *axioms*, from which he derives the theorem logically; for instance, he refers to the axiom that given a straight line and a point outside it, there is one and only one parallel to that line through this point. This axiom is illustrated in his diagram. But he does not prove it by measurements; he does not measure the distances between the lines in order to show that the lines are parallel.

In fact, he might even admit that his diagram is poorly drawn and thus supplies no good instance of a triangle and of parallels; but he would insist that his proof is strict nonetheless. Geometrical knowledge, he would argue, stems from the mind, not from observation. Triangles on paper may be helpful to make clear what we are talking about; but they do not supply the proof. Proof is a matter of reasoning, not of observation. In order to perform such reasoning, we visualize geometrical relations and "see", in some "higher" sense of the word, that the geometrical conclusion is inescapable and thus strictly true. Geometrical truth is a product of reason; that makes it superior to empirical truth, which is found through generalization of a great number of instances.

The result of this analysis is that reason appears capable of discovering general properties of physical objects. This is, in fact, an amazing consequence. There would be no problem if the truth of reason were restricted to analytic truth. That bachelors are unmarried can be known from reason alone; but since this statement is empty, it offers no philosophical problems. It is different with synthetic statements. How can reason uncover synthetic truth?

In this form the question was asked by Kant, more than two thousand years after Plato's time. Plato did not state the question so clearly, but he must have seen the problem along these lines. We infer this interpretation from the answer he gives to the question, that is, from the way he speaks about the origin of geometrical knowledge.

2. THE SEARCH FOR GENERALITY

Plato tells us that apart from physical things there exists a second kind of things, which he calls *ideas*. There exists the idea of a triangle, or of parallels, or of a circle, apart from the corresponding figures drawn on paper. The ideas are superior to physical objects; they exhibit the properties of these objects in a perfect way, and we thus learn more about physical objects by looking at their ideas than by looking at these objects themselves. What Plato means is again illustrated by reference to geometrical figures: the straight lines we draw have a certain thickness and thus are not lines in the sense of the geometrician, which have no thickness; the corners of a triangle drawn in the sand are actually small areas and are thus not ideal points. The discrepancy between the meaning of geometrical concepts and their realizations through physical objects leads Plato to the belief that there must exist ideal objects, or ideal representatives of these meanings. Plato thus arrives at a world of a higher reality than our world of physical things; the latter are said to *partake* of the ideal things in such a way that they show the properties of the ideal things in an imperfect way.

But mathematical objects are not the only things that exist in an ideal form. According to Plato, there are all kinds of ideas, such as the idea of a cat, or of a human being, or of a house. In short, every class name (a name of a kind of objects), or *universal*, indicates the existence of the corresponding idea. Like mathematical ideas, the ideas of other objects are perfect as compared with their imperfect copies in the real world. Thus the ideal cat shows all the properties of "cattiness" in a perfect form, and the ideal athlete is superior to every actual athlete in every respect; for instance, he exhibits the ideal bodily shape. Incidentally, our present use of the word "ideal" derives from Plato's theory.

19

Strange as the doctrine of ideas may appear to the modern mind, within the frame of knowledge available in Plato's time it must be regarded as an attempt at explanation, as an attempt to explain the apparently synthetic nature of mathematical truth. We see the properties of ideal things through acts of vision and thus acquire a knowledge of real things. A vision of ideas is regarded as a source of knowledge comparable to the observation of real objects, but superior to it in that it reveals *necessary* properties of its objects. Sense observation cannot tell us infallible truth, but vision can. We see through "the eye of the mind" that through a given point only one parallel line can be drawn with respect to a given line. Because this theorem appears to us as an infallible truth, it cannot be derived from empirical observations; it is dictated to us by an act of vision which we can perform even while the eyes of our bodies are closed. In this form we can express Plato's conception of geometrical knowledge. Whatever one may think of it, one must admit that it reveals a deep insight into the logical problems of geometry. It was advocated, in a somewhat improved version, by Kant; and in fact, it could not be replaced by a less mysterious conception before developments in the nineteenth century had led to new discoveries on mathematical grounds, discoveries which ruled out both Plato's and Kant's interpretation of geometry.

It must be realized that acts of vision, for Plato, can supply knowledge only because the ideal things exist. The extension of the concept of existence is indispensable for him. Since physical things exist, they can be seen; since ideas exist, they can be seen through the eye of the mind. Plato must have come to his conception through an argument of this kind, though he does not formulate the argument explicitly. Mathematical vision is construed by Plato as analogous to sense perception. Here, however, is the point where the logic of his theory is unsound, judged even by a scale of criticism adjusted to his time. An analogy takes over where an explanation is intended. And the analogy, obviously, is none too good. It erases the intrinsic difference between mathematical and empirical knowledge. It ignores the fact that "seeing" necessary relations is essentially different from seeing empirical objects. A picture is put in the place of an explanation, and a world of an independent and "higher" reality is invented because the philosopher proceeds by analogy rather than by analysis. As in the illustrations from other philosophies given above, the literal interpretation of an analogy becomes the root of a philosophical misconception. The theory of ideas, with its generalization of the concept of existence, supplies a pseudo explanation.

The Platonist might try to defend himself by an argument of the following kind. The existence of ideas, he would argue, must not be misinterpreted. Their existence need not be precisely of the same kind as that of empirical objects. Is not the philosopher allowed to use certain terms of everyday language in a somewhat wider meaning if he needs such terms?

I do not think that this argument supplies a good defense of Platonism. It is, of course, often true that terms of the language of daily life are taken over into the language of science because of their analogy to some new concepts which the scientist needs. For instance, the term "energy" is used in physics in an abstract meaning, which has some resemblance to its meaning in everyday life. Such reëmployment of terms, however, is permissible only when the new meaning is precisely defined and all further use of the term keeps strictly to its new meaning, not to its analogy with the old meaning. A

21

physicist who speaks of the energy of the radiation of the sun would not allow himself to say that the sun is energetic, like an energetic man. Such language would represent a relapse into previous meanings. Now, Plato's use of the word "existence" is not of the scientific type. If it were, the statement that ideal objects exist would have been defined in terms of other statements that do not contain such a questionable term, and would not have been used independently as having a meaning comparable to that of physical existence. We may define the existence of an ideal triangle as meaning that we can speak about triangles in terms of implications. Or, using algebra for an illustration, we may say that for every algebraic equation concerning an unknown quantity, provided it satisfies certain conditions, there exists a solution; in this usage, the word "exists" means that we know how to find the solution. Such a use of the word "existence" represents a harmless mode of speech, which in fact is often employed by mathematicians. But when Plato speaks of the existence of ideas, the phrase means much more than an expression translatable into established meanings.

What Plato wants is an explanation of the possibility of knowing mathematical truth. His theory of ideas is constructed as an explanation of such knowledge; that is, he believes the existence of ideas can explain our knowledge of mathematical objects because it makes possible a sort of perception of mathematical truth in the same sense that the existence of a tree makes possible a perception of a tree. It is obvious that the interpretation of ideal existence as a mode of speech would not help him, since it would not account for a sort of sense perception of mathematical objects. Instead, he arrives at a concept of ideal existence, which includes the properties of both physical existence and mathematical knowledge, a strange blend of two incompatible constituents which ever since has haunted philosophical language.

I said above that it is the end of science when the desire for knowledge is appeased by a pseudo explanation, by the confusion of analogy with generality, and by the use of pictures instead of well-defined concepts. Like the cosmologies of his time, Plato's theory of ideas is not science but poetry; it is a product of imagination, but not of logical analysis. In the further development of his theory, Plato does not hesitate to exhibit openly the mystical rather than logical train of his thought: he connects his theory of ideas with the conception of a migration of souls.

This turn is made in Plato's dialogue *Meno*. Socrates wishes to explain the nature of geometrical knowledge and illustrates it by an experiment with a young slave, unschooled in mathematics, from whom he appears to extract a geometrical proof. He does not explain to the boy the geometrical relations used for the solution; he makes him "see" them through asking questions, and the charming scene is used by Plato as an illustration of a rational insight into geometrical truth, of an innate knowledge not derived from experience. This interpretation, though not acceptable to modern conceptions, would have been, in Plato's time, a strong enough argument for a vision of ideas. But Plato does not content himself with such a result; he wants to carry explanation further and to explain the possibility of innate knowledge. It is in this context that Socrates maintains innate knowledge to be reminiscence, to be recollection of visions of ideas which men had in previous lives of their souls. Among these previous lives, there was a life in "the heaven which is beyond the heavens", during which the ideas were perceived. Plato thus resorts to mythology in order to "explain" a knowledge of ideas. And it is hard to see why in previous lives a vision of ideas was possible if it is impossible in our present lives—or why a theory of reminiscence is necessary if there is a vision of ideas in our present lives.

The poetic simile is not bothered by logic. In Greek mythology, the question was raised why the earth does not fall into infinite space, and the answer was given that a giant, called Atlas, carried the terrestrial globe on his shoulders. Plato's theory of reminiscence has about the same explanatory qualities as this story, in that it merely shifts the origin of a knowledge of ideas from one life to another. And Plato's cosmology, presented in the *Timaeus*, differs from such naïve fiction only by the use of abstract language. For instance, he tells us that *being* subsisted before the generation of the universe. Only the obscurity of the language persuades the philosopher to see deep wisdom in such words, which in sober examination recall the grin of the Cheshire cat that remained visible after the cat had vanished.

But I do not wish to ridicule Plato. His pictures speak the persuasive language that appeals to the imagination —only they should not be taken as explanation. It is poetry that Plato has created, and his dialogues are masterpieces of world literature. The story of Socrates who teaches young men by the method of asking questions is a beautiful example of didactic poetry, which has found a place by the side of Homer's *Iliad* and the teachings of the Prophets. We should not take too seriously what Socrates says; what matters is how he says it and how he stimulates his disciples to logical argument. Plato's philosophy is the work of a philosopher turned poet.

It seems to be an irresistible temptation to a philosopher, when he sees questions he is unable to answer, to offer picture language in place of explanation. If Plato had studied the problem of the origin of geometrical knowledge with the attitude of the scientist, his answer would have consisted in the candid admission "I do not know". The mathematician Euclid, who, a generation after Plato, constructed the axiomatic system of geometry, did not attempt to give any explanation for our knowledge of the geometrical axioms. The philosopher, in contrast, appears incapable of mastering his desire to know. Throughout the history of philosophy we find the philosophical mind associated with the imagination of the poet; where the philosopher asked, the poet answered. In reading the presentations of philosophical systems, we should therefore concentrate our attention on the questions asked rather than on the answers given. The discovery of fundamental questions is in itself an essential contribution to intellectual progress, and when the history of philosophy is conceived as a history of questions, it offers a much more fruitful aspect than when it is regarded as a history of systems. Some of these questions, reaching far back in history, have found scientific answers only in our day. One of these is the question of the origin of mathematical knowledge. Other questions having a similar history will be taken up in following chapters.

The analysis of the present chapter has been the first answer to the psychological question concerning philosophical language, which was raised in the discussion of the passage by which this book was introduced. The philosopher speaks an unscientific language because he attempts to answer questions at a time when the means to a scientific answer are not yet at hand. This historical explanation, though, is of limited validity. There are philosophers who continue to speak picture language at a time when the means for a scientific solution do exist. While the historical explanation applies to Plato, it cannot be adduced for the author of the quotation about reason being the substance of all things, who could have had the benefit of two thousand years of scientific research subsequent to Plato's time—but did not make use of it.

3.

The Search for Certainty
and the Rationalistic
Conception of Knowledge

W HAT THE preceding chapter has shown is
that the obscure conceptions of philosophical systems originate in certain
extralogical motives intervening in the
process of thought. The legitimate search for explanation in terms of generality is offered a pseudosatisfaction
through picture language. Such an intrusion of poetry
into knowledge is abetted by an urge for the construction
of an imaginary world of pictures, which can become
stronger than the quest for truth. The urge for picture-
thinking may be called an extralogical motive because it
does not represent a form of logical analysis but orig-
inates from mental needs outside the realm of logic.

There is a second extralogical motive which often in-
terferes with the process of analysis. While knowledge
acquired by sense observation is on the whole successful
in everyday life, it is early recognized as being none too
reliable. There are a few simple physical laws that seem
to hold without exception, like the law that fire is hot,
or that humans are mortal, or that unsupported bodies
fall downward; but there are too many other rules which
do have exceptions, like the rule that a seed planted in

the ground will grow, or the rules of the weather, or the rules for the cure of human diseases. And a more comprehensive observation often reveals exceptions even to the stricter laws. For instance, the fire of fireflies is not hot, at least not in the usual sense of the word "hot"; and soap bubbles may rise into the air. While these exceptions can be taken care of by a more precise wording of the law, stating the conditions of its validity and the meanings of its terms more carefully, there usually remains a doubt whether the new formulation is free from exception, whether we can be sure that later discoveries will not reveal some limitation of the improved formulation. The development of science, with its repeated elimination of older theories and their replacement by new ones, supplies good reasons for such doubt.

There is another source of doubt: it is the fact that our personal experiences divide into a world of reality and a world of dream. That such a division must be made is, historically speaking, a discovery of a rather late period of the evolution of man; we know that the primitive peoples of our day do not possess a clear delineation of the two worlds. A primitive man who dreams that another man attacks him may take his dream for reality and go and kill the other man; or when he dreams that his wife deceives him with another man he may proceed to similar acts of vengeance, or acts of justice, the terminology depending on the point of view. A psychoanalyst might be willing to excuse the man to some extent by pointing out that such dreams will not occur without grounds and may justify, if not the retribution, at least the suspicion. The primitive man, however, acts not on the basis of psychoanalytical considerations, but because he lacks a clear distinction between dream and reality. Although the common-sense man of our day usually feels comfortably immune against such confusion, a little analysis reveals that his confidence cannot claim certainty. For while we dream we do not know that we are dreaming; it is only later, after awaking, that we recognize our dream as a dream. How then can we claim that our present experiences are of a more reliable type than those of a dream? The fact that they are associated with a feeling of reality does not make them more dependable, because we have the same feeling in a dream. We cannot completely exclude the possibility that later experiences will prove that we are dreaming even now. The argument is not raised in order to dissuade the common-sense man from his trust in his experiences; it shows, however, that we cannot claim absolute reliability for such trust.

The philosopher has always been troubled by the unreliability of sense perception, which he has illustrated by considerations like the given ones; in addition, he has mentioned sense illusions in the waking state, such as the apparent bending of a stick partly immersed in water, or the mirage in the desert. He therefore rejoiced to find at least one domain of knowledge which appeared exempt from deceit: that was mathematical knowledge.

Plato, as mentioned above, regarded mathematics as the supreme form of all knowledge. His influence has greatly contributed to the widespread conception that unless knowledge is of a mathematical form it is not knowledge at all. The modern scientist, despite his use of mathematics as a powerful instrument of research, would not accept this maxim unconditionally. He would insist that observation cannot be omitted from empirical science and would leave to mathematics merely the function of establishing connections between the various results of empirical investigation. He is very willing to use these mathematical connections as a guide to new observational discoveries; but he knows that they can help him only because he starts with observational material, and he is always ready to abandon mathematical conclusions if they are not confirmed by later observation. Empirical science, in the modern sense of the phrase, is a successful combination of mathematical with observational method. Its results are regarded, not as absolutely certain, but as highly probable and sufficiently reliable for all practical purposes.

To Plato, however, the concept of empirical knowledge would have appeared an absurdity. When he identified knowledge with mathematical knowledge, he wanted to say that observation should play no part in knowledge. "Arguments from probabilities are impostors", so we learn from one of Socrates' disciples in the dialogue *Phaedo*. Plato wanted certainty, not the inductive reliability which modern physics regards as its only attainable goal.

It is true, of course, that the Greeks had no science of physics comparable to ours and that Plato did not know how much might be achieved through the combination of mathematical method with experience. Nevertheless, there was one natural science which even in Plato's day had had great success with such a combination, the science of astronomy. The mathematical laws of the revolution of the stars and planets had been uncovered, to a high degree of perfection, by skillful observation and geometrical reasoning. But Plato was not willing to admit the contribution of observation to astronomy. He insisted that astronomy was knowledge only inasmuch as the motions of the stars were "apprehended by reason and intelligence". According to him, observations of the stars could not tell us very much about the laws governing their revolution, because their actual motion is imperfect and not strictly controlled by laws. It would be absurd, says Plato, to assume that the real motions of the stars are "eternal and subject to no deviation". He makes it very clear what he thinks of the observational astronomer: "Whether a man gapes at the heavens or blinks on the ground, seeking to learn some particular of sense, I would deny that he can learn, for nothing of that sort is matter of science; his soul is looking downwards, not upwards, whether his way to knowledge is by water or by land, whether he floats, or only lies on his back". Instead of observing the stars, we should try to find the laws of their revolution through thinking. The astronomer should "let the heavens alone" and approach his subject matter by the use of "the natural gift of reason" (*Republic* VII, pp. 529–530). Empirical science could not be rejected more strongly than in these words, which express the conviction that knowledge of nature does not require observation and is attainable through reason alone.

How can this antiempirical attitude be explained psychologically? It is the search for certainty which makes the philosopher disregard the contribution of observation to knowledge. Since he wants absolutely certain knowledge, he cannot accept the results of observations; since arguments from probabilities are for him impostors, he turns to mathematics as the only admissible source of truth. The ideal of the complete mathematization of knowledge, of a physics which is of the same type as geometry and arithmetic, springs from the desire to find absolute certainty for the laws of nature. It leads to the absurd demand that the physicist forget about his observations, that the astronomer turn his eyes away from the stars.

The kind of philosophy which regards reason as a source of knowledge of the physical world has been called *rationalism*. This word and its adjective *rationalistic* must be carefully distinguished from the word *rational*. Scientific knowledge is attained by the use of rational methods, because it requires the use of reason in application to observational material. But it is not rationalistic. This predicate would apply not to scientific method, but to a philosophical method which regards reason as a source of synthetic knowledge about the world and does not require observation for the verification of such knowledge.

In philosophical literature, the name *rationalism* is often restricted to certain rationalistic systems of the modern era, from which the systems of the Platonic type are distinguished as *idealism*. In the present book the name *rationalism* will always be used in the wider sense, so as to include idealism. This notation appears justified because both kinds of philosophy are alike inasmuch as they regard reason as an independent source of knowledge of the physical world. The psychological root of all rationalism in the wider sense is an extralogical motive, that is, a motive not justifiable in terms of logic: it is the search for certainty.

Plato was not the first rationalist. His most important predecessor was the mathematician-philosopher Pythagoras (about 540 B.C.), whose doctrines greatly influenced Plato. It appears understandable that the mathematician is more likely than others to turn rationalist. Knowing the success of logical deduction in a subject matter that does not require a reference to observation, he may be inclined to believe that his methods can be extended to other subject matters. The result is a theory of knowledge in which acts of insight replace sense perception, and in which reason is believed to possess a power of its own by means of which it discovers the general laws of the physical world.

Once empirical observation is abandoned as a source of truth, it is then but a short step to mysticism. If reason can create knowledge, other creations of the human mind may appear as trustworthy as knowledge. From this conception results a strange blend of mysticism and mathematics, which has never died out since its origin in Pythagoras' philosophy. His religious veneration of number and logic led him to the statement that all things are numbers, a doctrine hardly translatable into meaningful terms. The theory of the migration of the soul, discussed above in the context of Plato's theory of ideas, was one of the chief doctrines of Pythagoras, who is assumed to have taken it over from oriental religions. We know that Plato was acquainted with this doctrine through his connection with Pythagoreans. The conception that logical insight can reveal properties of the physical world is also Pythagorean in origin. Pythagoras' followers practiced a sort of religious cult, the mystical character of which is visible in certain taboos said to have been imposed upon them by the master. For instance, they were taught that it is dangerous to leave an impress of the body on one's bed and were required to straighten out their bedclothes when they got up in the morning.

There are other forms of mysticism, which are not associated with mathematics. The mystic usually has an antirational and antilogical bias and shows contempt for the power of reason. He claims possession of some sort of supernatural experience, which presents him with infallible truth through a visionary act. This kind of mysticism is known from religious mystics. Outside the realm of religion, antirational mysticism has not played an important part, and I may omit its discussion in this book, which is concerned with the analysis of forms of philosophy that are related to scientific thought and have contributed to the great controversy between philosophy and science. Only a mathematically inclined mysticism falls into the scope of this analysis. What unites such a mathematical mysticism with nonmathematical forms is the reference to acts of supersensuous vision; what distinguishes it from those other forms is the use of vision for the establishment of intellectual truth.

Of course, rationalism is not invariably mystical. Logical analysis in itself may be employed for the establishment of a kind of knowledge which is regarded as absolutely certain and yet as connected with knowledge of everyday life or scientific knowledge. Modern times have produced various rationalist sytems of this nonmystical scientific type.

Among such systems I should like to discuss the rationalism of the French philosopher Descartes (1596–1650). In various writings he presented arguments for the uncertainty of perceptual knowledge, arguments of the kind mentioned above. It seems that he was extremely troubled by the uncertainty of all knowledge; he promised the Holy Virgin a pilgrimage to Loretto if she would illuminate his mind and help him find absolute certainty. He reports that the illumination came to him while he was living in an oven during a winter campaign in which he participated as an officer; and he expressed his gratitude to the Holy Virgin by fulfilling his vow.

Descartes' proof for absolute certainty is constructed by means of a logical trick. I can doubt everything, he argues, except one thing: that is the fact that I doubt. But when I doubt I think; and when I think I must exist. He thus claims to have proved the existence of the ego by logical reasoning; I think, therefore, I am, so goes his magical formula. When I call this inference a logical trick, I do not wish to say that Descartes intended to deceive his readers; I would rather say that he was himself deceived by this tricky form of reasoning. But logically speaking, the step from doubt to certainty performed in Descartes' inference resembles a sleight of hand—from doubting he proceeds to considering doubt as an action of an *ego,* and thus believes that he has found some fact which cannot be doubted.

Later analysis has shown the fallacy in Descartes' argument. The concept of the ego is not of so simple a nature as Descartes believed. We do not see our own selves in the way we see houses and people around us. We may perhaps speak of an observation of our acts of thought, or of doubt; they are not perceived, however, as the products of an ego, but as separate objects, as images accompanied by feelings. To say "I think" goes beyond the immediate experience in that the sentence employs the word "I". The statement "I think" represents not an observational datum, but the end of long chains of thought which uncover the existence of an ego as distinct from the ego of other persons. Descartes should have said "there is thought", thus indicating the sort of detached occurrence of the contents of thought, their emergence independent of acts of volition or other attitudes involving the ego. But then Descartes' inference could no longer be made. If the existence of the ego is not warranted by immediate awareness, its existence cannot be asserted with higher certainty than that of other objects derived by means of plausible additions to observational data.

It is scarcely necessary to go into a more detailed refutation of Descartes' inference. Even if the inference were tenable it would not prove very much and could not establish certainty of our knowledge about things other than the ego—that much is clear through the way Descartes continues the argument. He first infers that because there is an ego there must be God; or else the ego could not have the idea of an infinite being. He goes on to infer that then the things around us must also exist, since otherwise God would be an impostor. That is a theological argument, which appears strange enough

35

when offered by so eminent a mathematician as Descartes. The interesting question is: how is it possible that a logical issue, the attainability of certainty, was dealt with by a maze of arguments composed of tricks and theology, arguments that cannot be taken seriously by any scientifically trained reader of our day?

The psychology of philosophers is a problem which deserves more attention than is usually paid to it in the presentations of the history of philosophy. Its study is likely to throw more light on the meaning of philosophical systems than all attempts at a logical analysis of these systems. There is poor logic in Descartes' inference, but there is a great deal of psychological information to be gathered from it. It was the search for certainty which made this excellent mathematician drift into such muddled logic. It seems that the search for certainty can make a man blind to the postulates of logic, that the attempt to base knowledge on reason alone can make him abandon the principles of cogent reasoning.

Psychologists explain the search for certainty as the desire to return to the early days of infancy, which were not troubled by doubt and were guided by the confidence in parental wisdom. This desire is usually intensified by an education which conditions the child to regard doubt as sin and confidence as a religious command. The biographer of Descartes might attempt to combine this general explanation with the religious tinge of Descartes' doubts, his prayer for illumination and his pilgrimage, which indicate that this man needed his philosophical system in order to overcome a deeply rooted complex of uncertainty. Without entering into a specific study of Descartes' case, one may draw an important conclusion from it: if the result of a logical inquiry is determined by a preconceived aim, if logic is made the instrument of proof of a result which we wish to establish for some other reason, the logic of the argument is prone to be fallacious. Logic can thrive only in an atmosphere of perfect freedom, on a ground whose extracts do not burden it with remnants of fear and prejudice. He who inquires into the nature of knowledge should keep his eyes open and be willing to accept any result that cogent reasoning brings to light; it does not matter if the result contradicts his conception of what knowledge should be. The philosopher must not make himself the servant of his desires.

This maxim seems to be trivial, but only because we do not realize how difficult it is to follow the maxim. The search for certainty is one of the most dangerous sources of error because it is associated with the claim of a superior knowledge. The certainty of logical proof is thus regarded as the ideal of knowledge; and the requirement is introduced that all knowledge should be established by methods as reliable as logic. In order to see the consequences of this conception, let us study more closely the nature of logical proof.

Logical proof is called *deduction;* the conclusion is obtained by deducing it from other statements, called the premises of the argument. The argument is so constructed that if the premises are true the conclusion must also be true. For instance, from the two statements "all men are mortal" and "Socrates is a man", we can derive the conclusion "Socrates is mortal". The example illustrates the emptiness of deduction: the conclusion cannot state more than is said in the premises, it merely makes explicit some consequence which is contained implicitly in the premises. It unwraps, so to speak, the conclusion that was wrapped up in the premises.

The value of deduction is grounded in its emptiness. For the very reason that the deduction does not add anything to the premises, it may always be applied without a risk of leading to a failure. More precisely speaking, the conclusion is no less reliable than the premises. It is the logical function of deduction to transfer truth from given statements to other statements—but that is all it can do. It cannot establish synthetic truth unless another synthetic truth is already known.

The premises of the example, "all men are mortal" and "Socrates is a man", are both empirical truths, that is, truths derived from observation. The conclusion "Socrates is mortal", consequently, is also an empirical truth, and has no more certainty than the premises. Philosophers have always attempted to find premises of a better kind, which would not be subject to any criticism. Descartes believed that he had an unquestionable truth in his premise "I doubt". It was explained above that the term "I" in this premise can be questioned and that the inference cannot supply absolute certainty. The rationalist, however, will not give up, but will continue to look for unquestionable premises.

Now there are premises of this kind; they are given by the principles of logic. For instance: that every entity is identical with itself, and that every sentence is either true or false—the "to be or not to be" of the logician—are unquestionable premises. The trouble with them is that they, too, are empty. They state nothing about the physical world. They are rules for our description of the physical world, but do not contribute to the content of the description; they determine only its form, that is, the language of our description. The principles of logic, therefore, are *analytic*. (The term was introduced above as meaning "self-explanatory and empty".) In contrast, statements which inform us about a fact, such as observations with our eyes, are *synthetic*, that is, they add something to our knowledge. All the synthetic statements which experience presents to us, however, are subject to doubt and cannot provide us with absolutely certain knowledge.

An attempt to establish the desired certainty on an analytic premise was made in the famous *ontological* proof of God's existence, constructed by Anselm of Canterbury in the eleventh century. The demonstration begins with the definition of God as an infinitely perfect being; since such a being must have all essential properties, it must also have the property of existence. Therefore, so goes the conclusion, God exists. The premise, in fact, is analytic, because every definition is. Since the statement of God's existence is synthetic, the inference represents a trick by which a synthetic conclusion is derived from an analytic premise.

The fallacious nature of this inference is easily seen from its absurd consequences. If it is permissible to derive existence from a definition, we could demonstrate the existence of a cat with three tails by defining such an animal as a cat which has three tails and which exists. Logically speaking, the fallacy consists in a confusion of universals with particulars. From the definition we can only infer the universal statement that if something is a cat with three tails it exists, which is a true statement. But the particular statement that there is a cat with three tails cannot be derived. Similarly, we can infer from Anselm's definition only the statement that if something is an infinitely perfect being it exists, but not that there is such a being. (Anselm's confusion of universals and particulars, incidentally, is cognate to a similar confusion existing in the Aristotelian theory of the syllogism.)

It was Immanuel Kant (1724–1804) who saw that certainty of a synthetic nature cannot be derived from analytic premises but requires synthetic premises of unquestionable truth. Believing that such statements exist, he called them *synthetic a priori*. The word "a priori" means "not derived from experience", or "derived from reason and necessarily true". Kant's philosophy represents the great attempt to prove that there are synthetic a-priori truths; and historically speaking it represents the last great construction of a rationalist philosophy. He is superior to his predecessors Plato and Descartes in his avoidance of their mistakes. He does not commit himself to an existence of Platonic ideas; nor does he smuggle in a pseudonecessary premise by a trick, as Descartes does. He claims to have found the synthetic a priori in the principles of mathematics and mathematical physics. Like Plato, he starts with mathematical knowledge; he explains such knowledge, however, not by the existence of objects of a higher reality, but by an ingenious interpretation of empirical knowledge, to be discussed presently.

If progress in the history of philosophy consists in the discovery of significant questions, Kant is to be assigned a high rank because of his question concerning the existence of a synthetic a priori. Like other philosophers, however, he claims merit not for the question but for his answer to it. He even formulates the question in a somewhat different way. He is so convinced of the existence of a synthetic a priori that he regards it as hardly necessary to ask whether there is one; therefore, he poses his question in the form: how is a synthetic a priori possible? The proof of its existence, he continues, is supplied by mathematics and mathematical physics.

There is very much to be said in defense of Kant's position. That he regards the axioms of geometry as synthetic a priori bears witness to a deep insight into the peculiar problems of geometry. Kant saw that Euclid's geometry occupied a unique position in that it revealed necessary relations holding for empirical objects, relations which could not be regarded as analytic. He is much more explicit than Plato about this point. Kant knew that the strictness of mathematical proof cannot account for the empirical truth of geometrical theorems. Geometrical propositions, such as the theorem about the angular sum of a triangle, or Pythagoras' theorem, are derivable by strict logical deduction from the axioms. But these axioms themselves are not so derivable—they cannot be derivable because every derivation of synthetic conclusions has to start with synthetic premises. The truth of the axioms must therefore be established by other means than logic; they must be synthetic a priori. Once the axioms are known to be true for physical objects, the applicability of the theorems to these objects is then guaranteed by logic, since the truth of the axioms is transferred by the logical derivation to the theorems. Conversely, if one is convinced that geometrical theorems apply to physical reality, one admits belief in the truth of the axioms and therefore in a synthetic a priori. Even those persons who would not like to commit themselves openly to a synthetic a priori indicate through their behavior that they believe in it: they do not hesitate to apply the results of geometry to practical measurements. This argument, Kant maintains, proves the existence of the synthetic a priori.

Kant contends that similar arguments can be constructed from mathematical physics. Ask a physicist, he explains, what is the weight of smoke; he will ascertain it by weighing the substance before the burning and then deducting the weight of the ashes. In this determination of the weight of the smoke the assumption is expressed that mass is indestructible. The principle of the conservation of mass, Kant argues, is thus shown to be a synthetic a-priori truth, which the physicist recognizes through the method of his experiment. We know today that the computation described by Kant leads to the wrong result, because it does not take into account the weight of the oxygen which enters into a chemical combination with the burning substance. Had Kant known of this discovery of a later time, however, he would have argued that, although it modifies the mode of computation, it does not contradict the principle of the conservation of mass; this principle will supply once more the frame of the computation if the weight of the oxygen is included in the consideration.

Another synthetic a priori of the physicist, according to Kant, is the principle of causality. Although we often are unable to find the cause of an observed event, we do not assume that it occurred without a cause; we are convinced that we shall find the cause if we only go on searching for it. This conviction determines the method of scientific research and is the propelling force of every scientific experiment; if we did not believe in causality, there would be no science. As in the other arguments constructed by Kant, the existence of the synthetic a priori is here proved by reference to scientific procedure: science presupposes the synthetic a priori—this contention is the basis of Kant's philosophical system.

What makes Kant's position so strong is its scientific background. His search for certainty is not of the mystical type that appeals to an insight into a world of ideas, nor of the type that resorts to logical tricks which extract certainty from empty presuppositions, as a magician pulls a rabbit out of an empty hat. Kant mobilizes the science of his day for the proof that certainty is attainable; and he claims that the philosopher's dream of certainty is borne out by the results of science. From the appeal to the authority of the scientist Kant derives his strength.

But the ground on which Kant built was not so firm as he believed it to be. He regarded the physics of Newton as the ultimate stage of knowledge of nature and idealized it into a philosophical system. In deriving from pure reason the principles of Newtonian physics, he believed he had achieved the complete rationalization of knowledge, had attained the goal which his predecessors had been unable to reach. The title of his major work, *Critique of Pure Reason*, indicates his program of making reason the source of a synthetic a-priori knowledge and thus to establish as a necessary truth, on a philosophical ground, the mathematics and physics of his day.

It is a strange matter of fact that those who watch and admire scientific research from the outside frequently have more confidence in its results than the men who coöperate in its progress. The scientist knows about the difficulties which he had to eliminate before he could establish his theories. He is aware of the good luck which helped him discover theories that fit the given observations and which made later observations fit his theories. He realizes that discrepancies and new difficulties may arise at any moment, and he will never claim to have found the ultimate truth. Like the disciple who is more fanatical than the prophet, the philosopher of science is in danger of investing more confidence in scientific results than is warranted by their origin in observation and generalization.

The overestimation of the reliability of scientific results is not restricted to the philosopher; it has become a general feature of modern times, that is, of the period dating from the time of Galileo to our day, in which period falls the creation of modern science. The belief that science has the answer to all questions—that if somebody is in need of technical information, or is ill, or is troubled by some psychological problem, he merely has to ask the scientist in order to obtain an answer—is so widespread that science has taken over a social function which originally was satisfied by religion: the function of offering ultimate security. The belief in science has replaced, in large measure, the belief in God. Even where religion was regarded as compatible with science, it was modified by the mentality of the believer in scientific truth. The period of Enlightenment, into which Kant's lifework falls, did not abandon religion; but it transformed religion into a creed of reason, it made God a mathematical scientist who knew everything because he had a perfect insight into the laws of reason. No wonder the mathematical scientist appeared as a sort of little god, whose teachings had to be accepted as exempt from doubt. All the dangers of theology, its dogmatism and its control of thought through the guaranty of certainty, reappear in a philosophy that regards science as infallible.

Had Kant lived to see the physics and mathematics of our day he might very well have abandoned the philosophy of the synthetic a priori. So let us regard his books as documents of their time, as the attempt to appease his hunger for certainty by his belief in the physics of Newton. In fact, Kant's philosophical system must be conceived as an ideological superstructure erected on the foundation of a physics modeled for an absolute space, an absolute time, and an absolute determinism of nature. This origin explains the system's success and its failure, explains why Kant has been regarded by so many as the greatest philosopher of all time, and why his philosophy has nothing to say to us who are witnesses of the physics of Einstein and Bohr.

This origin also accounts for the psychological fact that Kant did not see the weak spot in the logical construction by which he intended to justify the synthetic a priori. It is the preconceived aim that makes the philosopher blind to the tacit assumptions he has introduced. In order to make my criticism clear, I will now discuss the second part of Kant's theory of the synthetic a priori, in which he proceeds to answer the question "how is the synthetic a priori possible?"

Kant claimed he could explain the occurrence of a synthetic a priori through a theory which shows the a-priori principles to be necessary conditions of experience. He argues that mere observation does not supply experience, that observations must be ordered and organized before they can become knowledge. The organization of knowledge, according to him, is dependent on the use of certain principles, such as the axioms of geometry and the principles of causality and the conservation of mass, which are innate in the human mind and which we employ as regulative principles in the construction of science. They are, so he concludes, necessarily valid because without them science would be impossible. He calls this proof the transcendental deduction of the synthetic a priori.

It must be recognized that Kant's interpretation of the synthetic a priori is widely superior to Plato's analysis of this point. In order to explain how reason can have knowledge of nature, Plato assumes that there exists a world of ideal things which reason perceives and which somehow controls the real objects. No such mysticism is found in Kant. Reason has knowledge of the physical world because it shapes the picture we construct of the physical world; that is Kant's argument. The synthetic a priori is of a subjective origin; it is a condition superimposed on human knowledge by the human mind.

Let me clarify Kant's explanation by a simple illustration. A man who wears blue spectacles will observe that everything is blue. If he were born with those glasses, however, he would regard blueness as a necessary predicate of all things, and it would take some time until he would discover that it is he, or rather his glasses, that introduce blueness into the world. The synthetic a-priori

45

principles of physics and mathematics are the blue glasses through which we see the world. We should not be astonished that every experience will confirm them because we cannot acquire experience without them.*

This illustration does not stem from Kant; in fact, it appears alien to the author of prolix books filled with abstract considerations in an involved language, which makes the reader thirst for concrete illustrations. Had Kant been accustomed to explain his ideas in the plain and simple language of the scientist he would perhaps have discovered that his transcendental deduction is of questionable value. He would have seen that his argument, if further extended, leads to an analysis of the following kind.

Assume it is correct that no experience can ever disprove the a-priori principles. This means that whatever observations will be made, it will always be possible to interpret or order them in such a way that these principles are satisfied. For instance, if measurements on triangles were made which contradicted the theorem of the angular sum, we would assign the deviations to observational errors and introduce "corrections" for the measured values in such a way that the geometrical theorem would be satisfied. But if the philosopher could prove that such a procedure is always possible for all a-priori principles, these principles would be shown to be

---

* The objection might be raised that a man born with blue glasses would not know other colors than blue and would therefore not conceive blue as a color. In order to avoid this consequence, let us assume that the man is born with his natural eye lenses colored blue, while his retina and his nervous system are normal. So far as his optical sensations were produced by internal stimulation, they would then be normal. The man would therefore be able to see other colors than blue in his dreams and come to the conclusion that the physical world is subject to restrictions which do not apply to the world of his imagination. He might very well eventually find out that this restriction stems from the composition of his eye lenses.

empty and thus analytic; they would not restrict possible experiences and thus not inform us about properties of the physical world. An extension of Kant's theory in this direction was, in fact, attempted by H. Poincaré under the name of *conventionalism*. He regards the geometry of Euclid as a convention, that is, as an arbitrary rule which we impose upon our system of ordering experiences. The limitations of this conception will be studied in Chapter 8. To illustrate the meaning of conventionalism in a field other than geometry, consider the statement that all numbers larger than 99 must be written with at least three digits. This statement is true only for the decimal system, but would break down for another notation, such as the duodecimal system of the Babylonians, who used the number 12 as the basis of their number system. The decimal system is a convention which we use for our number notation, and we can prove that all numbers can be written in this notation. The statement that all numbers larger than 99 must be written with at least three digits is analytic when it refers to this system. In order to interpret Kant's philosophy as conventionalism, we would have to prove that Kant's principles can be carried through in the face of all possible experiences.

But such a proof cannot be given. In fact, if the a-priori principles are synthetic, as Kant believed, such a proof is impossible. The word "synthetic" means that we can imagine experiences which contradict the a-priori principles; and if we can imagine such experiences, we cannot exclude the possibility that some day we might have them. Kant would argue that this case cannot happen because the principles are necessary conditions of experience, or, in other words, because, in the case considered, experience as an ordered system of observations would not be possible. But how does he know that experience will always be possible? Kant had no proof that we would never arrive at a totality of observations which could not be ordered in the frame of his a-priori principles and which would make experience impossible, at least experience in the Kantian sense. In the language of our illustration this case would occur if the physical world contained no light rays of the wave length corresponding to blue; the man with the blue glasses would then see nothing. If the corresponding case were to occur in science, if experience of the Kantian kind should become impossible, Kant's principles would be shown to be invalid for the physical world. And because of the possibility of such a disproof, the principles cannot be called a priori. The postulate that experience in the frame of the a-priori principles must always be possible is the unwarranted assumption of Kant's system, is the undemonstrable premise on which his system hinges. That he does not explicitly state his premise shows that the search for certainty made him overlook the limitations of his argument.

I do not wish to be irreverent to the philosopher of the Enlightenment. We are able to raise this criticism because we have seen physics enter a stage in which the Kantian frame of knowledge does break down. The axioms of Euclidean geometry, the principles of causality and substance are no longer recognized by the physics of our day. We know that mathematics is analytic and that all applications of mathematics to physical reality, including physical geometry, are of an empirical validity and subject to correction by further experience; in other words, that there is no synthetic a priori. But it is only now, after the physics of Newton and the geometry of Euclid have been superseded, that such knowledge is ours. It is difficult to conceive of the possibility of a breakdown of a scientific system in its heyday; it is easy to refer to such a breakdown after it has become reality.

Such experience has made us wise enough to anticipate the breaking down of any system. It has not discouraged us, though. The new physics has shown that we can have knowledge outside the frame of the Kantian principles, that the human mind is not a rigid system of categories into which it packs all experiences, but that the principles of knowledge change with its content and can be adapted to a much more complicated world than that of Newtonian mechanics. We hope that in any future situation our minds will be flexible enough to supply methods of logical organization that can cope with the given observational material. That is a hope, not a belief for which we pretend to have a philosophical proof. We can do without certainty. But it was a long way to this more liberal attitude toward knowledge. The search for certainty had to burn itself out in the philosophical systems of the past before we were able to envisage a conception of knowledge which does away with all claims to eternal truth.

4.

The Search for Moral Directives and the Ethico-Cognitive Parallelism

Socrates: Then shall we inquire together what virtue is?
Meno: Certainly.
Socrates: Since we know not yet what or of what nature it is, let us consider the question of its teachableness, saying hypothetically thus: if it be science or knowledge or other than science or knowledge, it will be or not be teachable. For is it not at least clear that a man can only be taught that which is science or knowledge?
Meno: So it seems to me.
Socrates: If then virtue be a kind of science or knowledge, it may be taught?
Meno: Of course.
Socrates: We are then quickly at the end of this hypothetical inquiry; if virtue be of such a nature it is teachable, if not, not.

IN THIS passage of Plato's dialogue *Meno,* presented here in an abbreviated form, Socrates discusses the question whether virtue is knowledge. As in Plato's earlier dialogue *Protagoras,* where the same question is discussed, Socrates does not answer by a clear "yes" or "no". He cannot come to a definitive answer because of his ambiguous use of the words "knowledge" and "teaching". Socrates often insists that he never teaches, but only helps a man to see the truth through his own eyes. The method he uses consists in asking questions. The student learns because the question directs his attention to certain points; and the true answer thus becomes known through focussing the relevant factors and drawing conclusions. Of this kind is the learning of geometry; the realization of the truth of the geometrical relations needed for a proof is always left to the student, and the teacher can merely induce him to perform these acts of insight. But if the student "learns" as a consequence of this so-called dialectic method, the person who makes him learn may very well be said to "teach". In fact, if Socrates were to extend his queer terminology to the realm of geometry and deny that geometry can be taught (which he sometimes does), it would follow that geometry is not knowledge (a conclusion which he does not draw). It will therefore appear correct to interpret Socrates' view as being that virtue is a form of knowledge in the same sense that geometry can be called a form of knowledge.

This interpretation is justified by Socrates' own exposition of the problem. He wants to show Meno by what method ethical questions can be solved and refers for this purpose to the process of acquiring geometrical knowledge. It is at this point that the dialogue is enlivened by the aforementioned scene, in which Socrates makes a young slave understand a geometrical theorem. He wishes to illustrate his contention that in order to know what is virtue, and what is the good, one has to perform an act of insight of the same kind as is required for the understanding of geometrical proofs. Ethical judgments are thus presented as being found through a peculiar form of vision, comparable to the visualization of geometrical relations. By the use of this argument, ethical insight is presented as a parallel to geometrical insight. If there is such a thing as geometrical knowledge, there must also be an ethical knowledge—this conclusion appears inescapable, once the Socratic-Platonic doctrine is freed from the sophistical terminology in which it is formulated. In this sense, this doctrine may be expressed by the thesis that virtue is knowledge.

With this thesis, Plato and Socrates established the *ethico-cognitive parallelism,* the theory that ethical insight is a form of cognition, that is, of knowing. If a man commits immoral actions, he is ignorant in the same sense that a man who makes mistakes in geometry is ignorant; he is unable to perform the act of vision which shows him the good, a vision of the same kind as the one that shows him geometrical truth.

If we compare this conception with the form in which ethical principles are presented in the Bible, we notice a remarkable difference. The Bible offers ethical rules as the word of God, the Hebrew God who gives to Moses the Ten Commandments on Mount Sinai. "Thou shalt not kill!" "Thou shalt not steal!" The imperative form of the rules makes it evident that it is meant as a command, not as a statement about matters of fact. The transformation of ethical rules into a form of knowledge seems to be a later invention. The Hebrew would have regarded it as a disparagement of the word of God to put the Ten Commandments on a par with a law of nature, or a law of mathematics. At the time when the Pentateuch was written, knowledge had not yet assumed the form of an organized system; the geometry of the Egyptians was no more than a set of practical rules for surveying the land and building temples. It was a Greek discovery that geometry could be established in the form of a logical proof. The conception of virtue as knowledge is therefore an essentially Greek mode of thought. Knowledge had first to acquire the perfection and the dignity which the Greek spirit conferred upon it through the construction of mathematics as a logical system, before it could be regarded as supplying the foundation of ethical rules. The laws of nature and of mathematics had first to be recognized as laws, as relations that impose recognition upon us and do not tolerate any exceptions, before they could be conceived as parallels of ethical laws. The double meaning of the word "law", as moral command and as the rule of nature or of reason, bears witness to the construction of this parallelism.

The motive for the parallelism seems to be a desire to establish ethics on a better ground than religion. The trust in God's command may satisfy a naïve mind that is not troubled by doubts of the superiority of the father. The people that constructed the logical form of mathematics discovered a new form of command, the command of reason. The impersonal form of this command makes it appear to be of a higher type; it demands assent whether or not we believe in the existence of gods, it eliminates the question whether the rules of the gods are good, it emancipates us from the anthropomorphic conception that doing good consists in the subordination to a superior will. No wonder that the best way to establish ethical rules as obligatory for everybody appeared to be given in an ethico-cognitive parallelism, in the thesis that virtue is knowledge.

A philosophical system which presents the ethico-cognitive parallelism in its extreme form is the ethics of Spinoza (1632–1677). In this system, Spinoza goes so far as to imitate Euclid's axiomatic construction of geometry, hoping thus to establish ethics on as firm a ground as that of geometry. Like Euclid he begins with axioms and postulates and then derives theorem after theorem; his *Ethics* reads, in fact, like a textbook of geometry. In its first parts, the book is not ethical in our sense; it develops a general theory of knowledge. It then goes on to the treatment of emotions. Spinoza develops the theory that passions derive from inadequate ideas of the soul, corresponding to Socrates' theory that immorality is ignorance, and in a chapter entitled "of human bondage, or the strength of the emotions" he wishes to show that passions cause sadness and are therefore bad. We arrive at happiness when we overcome the power of the passions; the power to such liberation is contained in reason, as he explains in a chapter "of the power of the understanding, or of human freedom". His ethics is stoical, good is only the intellectual pleasure of knowledge; the happiness derived from emotional satisfaction and the joys of life, though not regarded by him as immoral, appears to him irrelevant with respect to morality and is only recommended, in a moderate dose, as a sort of food for the body, necessary to keep the body capable of doing everything that is in its nature.

Among philosophers Spinoza enjoys a high reputation; I think this reputation is more the merit of his personality than of his philosophy. He was a modest and courageous man, who stood up for his theories and realized his ethics in his own life. He earned his living by grinding lenses for eyeglasses and refused to accept an academic position because it would have restricted the liberty of his thought. From various sides he was attacked as an atheist, and he was expelled from the Jewish community of Amsterdam for his heresy. He remained indifferent to all criticism, was kind to everybody, and never showed any hatred.

When we separate his ethics from its logical form, it represents the creed of a dispassionate personality to whom self-control and intellectual work appear as the highest good. By projecting his ethics into logic, he reveals that his admiration for logic was greater than his abilities in it; in fact, the logic of his derivations is poor, and they cannot be understood without many tacit additions and psychological interpretations. By no means can his system be regarded as at least internally valid, that is, as correctly derived from his axioms. His conclusions go far beyond the content of his premises. For instance, he takes over the ontological demonstration of the existence of God. But invalid logical constructions can still have the psychological function of strengthening subjective beliefs, and fallacious reasoning can be the indispensable instrument of a creed. Spinoza needed the logical form as a backbone to support him in his suppression of emotions, in his uncommon indifference to the pleasures of passion. The Socratic intellectualization of ethics was thus used by him, as by many of his predecessors, for the construction of an ethics that disparages emotion. That is perhaps the most preposterous outcome of the ethico-cognitive parallelism. From the time of the Stoics the conception of the philosopher as a man without passion has dominated public opinion and has made other people feel inferior when they found themselves unable to achieve such wisdom. I do not see why philosophers should live up to such a glorification of the impassive type. Those who derive satisfaction from impassivity I will not dissuade from their pleasure; but I do not see why the rest of us, whose pleasures are of a more human variety, should feel inferior. What makes life worth living is passion; this rule applies to philosophers, too, and it looks as though Spinoza's unfortunate passion for logic was not so different from the more sensational forms in which passion manifests itself in other persons.

Spinoza's deductive construction of ethics, with its intention of showing that ethical rules can be given a deductive proof, is a more elaborate version of Socrates' conception that virtue is knowledge. And it establishes this conception on an even more solid basis because it shows that ethical knowledge is not only a product of rational insight, but is also accessible to the most powerful technique of rational thought, to logical derivation. As in geometry, the axioms of ethics are merely the starting point of deductive constructions, which lead through chains of reasoning to further and further results. Ethics is knowledge not only because its first principles appear as "true", but also because it is subject to the principles of logical reasoning and admits of the technique of logical proof for the establishment of relations between moral laws—this is an argument which expresses the conception of Spinoza as well as that of Socrates and Plato.

Examples of derivations, selected from both the cognitive and the ethical field, will make the parallelism clear. Like the process of acquiring knowledge, that of finding out what is good is of a gradual nature, and is run through by steps of better and better insights; and teaching the truth, or teaching virtue, consists in helping a person to climb up these steps. We ask, for instance, whether a circle can be so drawn inside a triangle that the three sides are made tangents of the circle. We imagine pictures which show us circles and triangles having this relation, but do not know yet whether it can be done for all sorts of triangles, or whether it can be done in more than one way. Finally the geometrical proof is found that it can be done for every triangle, and for every one in only one way. This discovery is achieved in steps, whether the proof is found by ourselves or demonstrated to us by a teacher. Similarly, we ask whether lying to another person is good. We may answer that it is sometimes good, sometimes bad; but in further analysis we see that although lying may sometimes be to our personal advantage, it is not good because such behavior on our side might induce other persons to a similar behavior, a result that would eliminate mutual confidence from relations between human beings. The step process of this consideration seems analogous to mathematical reflection and explains why the ethical rules can be taught.

But the study of derivational processes also presents the cognitive conception of ethics in a new light. Logical derivation is not a means to find ultimate truth, but merely an instrument of connecting different truths. The mathematical derivation, in the illustration referred to, consists in a proof that if certain axioms are assumed, the conclusion concerning the inscribed circle of the triangle follows; the ethical derivation discussed represents a proof that if we want certain aims we must conform to the moral rule not to lie. More explicitly speaking, what we proved was that if we want a social order in which relations between human beings are carried by mutual confidence, we must not lie.

It is the *if-then* relation which is demonstrable in both instances, and it is the deducibility of this relation in which the two instances correspond to each other. That virtue can be taught results from the fact that ethical considerations, like mathematical derivations, contain a logical component which is accessible to an analysis by logical steps, corresponding to the logical steps of mathematical proof.

It cannot be overemphasized that logical deduction cannot create independent results. It is merely an instrument of connection; it derives conclusions from given axioms, but cannot inform us about the truth of the axioms. The axioms of mathematics therefore require a separate treatment, and as has already been explained, the question whether they are true leads into such questions as whether they are synthetic a priori. The analysis of ethical deductions arrives at similar results. As in mathematics, the axioms of ethics must be distinguished from derivable ethical theorems; and only the relation between the two, the *if-then* statement "if you accept the axioms you must accept the theorem" is capable of a logical proof. Analysis shows, therefore, that the validity of ethics is reducible to the validity of the ethical axioms; as in mathematics, the method of deduction can only shift the question of reliability from the theorems to the axioms, but it cannot supply the answer to the question.

In order to prove that virtue is knowledge, that ethical judgments are of a cognitive type, we would have to prove that the axioms of ethics are of a cognitive nature. The applicability of logical deduction to ethical problems does not prove anything in this respect. The question of the nature of ethics is thus reduced to the question of the nature of the ethical axioms.

Once more we have to give the credit for having seen the problem of ethics as a problem of ethical axioms to Immanuel Kant. He recognized that, as in mathematics, the analytic nature of deduction makes it impossible to base the validity of ethical rules on deduction alone. He insisted that only after the question of the axioms of ethics is answered can the nature of ethics be understood. Once more, however, what Kant claims credit for is not the question, but his answer to it. It is worth while to study this answer, which like Kant's answer to the problem of the axioms of mathematics and physics represents the last great position that rationalism has constructed.

Kant's answer consists in the thesis that the axioms of ethics are synthetic a priori, like those of mathematics and physics. In his *Critique of Practical Reason*, he tries to give for the axioms of ethics a derivation similar to the one carried through in his *Critique of Pure Reason* for

58

the axioms of mathematics and physics. He explains in this book that the axioms of ethics are reducible to one axiom, which he calls the categorical imperative and formulates as follows: "Act in such a way that the maxim of your action can be made the principle of a general legislation". He illustrates the use of this axiom by such examples as our consideration about lying: lying may be of advantage for some individuals, but cannot be made the principle of a general legislation because it would lead to the absurd consequence that no one could trust any other person. Kant claims that the validity of the categorical imperative is admitted by all human beings if they only attempt to follow the insight of reason, that the imperative is seen as valid through an act of vision like the one that reveals to us the axioms of mathematics and physics as necessary truths. In Kant's system, the ethico-cognitive parallelism has reached its climax through its foundation on a synthetic a priori which includes both cognitive and ethical axioms and has its ultimate source in the nature of reason. "The starry heavens above me and the moral law within me"—in this famous phrase Kant symbolizes the duality of cognitive and moral laws, which demand recognition from every human mind.

Kant could not foresee that this very parallelism would ultimately spell the breakdown of his ethics. It was explained in the preceding chapter that there is no cognitive synthetic a priori, that mathematics is analytic, and that all mathematical formulations of physical principles are of an empirical nature. If the moral law within me is of the type of law that the starry heavens reveal to me, it is either an empirical statement about the behavior of human beings or an empty statement of an implication between ethical axioms and conclusions, like mathematical theorems; but it is not an unconditional imperative, or in the language of traditional logic employed by Kant, not a categorical imperative. The failure of Kant's ethics has therefore the same root as the failure of his theory of knowledge: it derives from the erroneous conception that reason can establish synthetic statements.

That is a negative answer: it states that ethical axioms are not synthetic a-priori statements. There remains the task of finding a positive answer; that is, to explicate the nature of ethical axioms. I shall not discuss this question in the historical part of my investigation but will analyze it in Chapter 17. However, I should like to add some words about the psychological origin of Kant's conception.

When we study the psychology of the philosopher more closely, we discover that the establishment of the moral synthetic a priori satisfies Kant emotionally even more deeply than that of the cognitive synthetic a priori. The dry and learned style of his presentation is interrupted in his moral writings by poetical exclamations and glorifications of ethical rules and concepts.

Duty! Thou great and sublime name, not containing in thyself any lovable, or ingratiating, quality, but demanding submission; yet neither threatening us with anything that might frighten or create a natural antipathy—which origin is worthy of thee, and where does one find the roots of thy noble descent? Thou refusest all relations to inclination, and it is the necessary condition of a supreme value given by man to proceed from thy roots.

It is the concept of duty which supplies the key to Kant's ethics. As far as our action is based on inclination, it is neither good nor bad, even if our inclination turns to a worthy aim, like the support of persons in need; what makes our action moral is the impulse of duty that makes us act. What a distortion of the natural urge to help other people! What a twisted morality manifests itself in this intellectualization of ethical decisions! Kant was the descendant of a middle-class family in poor living conditions, his father a carpenter, his mother an ardent follower of a pietistic sect. In a social milieu of this kind, self-reliance and free response to natural inclination is often regarded as sin; and it looks as though the famous son was happy and proud to derive in learned books the very morality he was imbued with in his nursery.

The success which his philosophy had in his native country and which made him the philosopher of protestantism and Prussianism is further testimony to the fact that it is the ethics of a certain middle class of the population which he codified in his philosophic system. The glorification of duty represents the ethics of a social class existing in conditions of scarcity and depending for its existence on hard work that leaves no time for leisure; or it is the ethics of a military caste that requires subordination to the command of a superior. Both conditions were satisfied in the Prussia of Kant. That Kant refused to admit the authority of certain groups or institutions shows him of an independent mind, which, indeed, brought him into conflict with the Prussian government. Had he preached nothing but the maxim of social coöperation, which his categorical imperative expresses, we would regard him as the exponent of a democratic society and classify him along with Locke and the leaders of the American revolution. But his adoration of duty smacks too much of the pleasure derived from subordination and the satisfaction derived from servitude, which are characteristic of a bourgeois middle class that has been too long a time under the authority of a strong ruling caste. It is the tragedy of the philosopher of the synthetic a priori that what he advances as the ultimate structure of reason resembles astoundingly the social milieu in which he was imbedded. His cognitive a priori coincides with the physics of his time, his moral a priori, with the ethics of his social class. Let this coincidence be a warning to all those who claim to have found the ultimate truth.

Kant seems to have regarded his foundation of ethics as an achievement superior to his theory of knowledge, in the way that an end is superior to the means. Such a conception seems to be characteristic for all adherents of an ethico-cognitive parallelism. It appears that the search for moral directives is the motive of their inquiry, that cognitive certainty is aspired to chiefly because it offers the means of finding moral certainty. This shift of interest from the cognitive to the moral field has an unfortunate effect: the resulting theory of cognition is seen in a distorted way, is constructed for the end of providing support for an ethical absolutism and therefore does not represent an unprejudiced account of knowledge. The search for moral directives thus becomes an extralogical motive interfering with the logical analysis of knowledge, and it must now be shown to what extent its product, the ethico-cognitive parallelism, has influenced cognitive philosophies and become a major source of erroneous theories of knowledge.

Since actual man, in general, does not behave morally, it seems quite clear that ethics does not deal with the actual behavior of man. The difference between how man should act and how he does act is obvious enough, and ethics, therefore, appears to refer to the behavior of the ideal man. To account for this distinction, the theorist of ethics points to the difference between the geometrical laws and the relations holding for actual physical objects; he distinguishes the ideal triangle from the actual triangle and argues that the mathematician uncovers normative laws of geometrical objects in the same sense as the moral philosopher establishes normative laws of human behavior. The theorems of mathematics thus are construed as statements about what *should be,* as distinguished from what *is,* in the same sense as ethical theorems are to be construed.

An unprejudiced study of mathematics reveals immediately that this analogy is inadmissible. It is true that the ideal geometrical figures are not found in physical reality, but the laws of geometry at least tell us relations which hold approximately for real objects. Mathematics is descriptive of physical reality in that it supplies approximate knowledge of reality. It does not tell us how reality should be, but how reality is. What sense would it make to demand that the circumference of a tree should be a perfect circle? The imperfect circle which it actually is satisfies geometrical laws as much as a perfect circle does, and the laws of the perfect circle are useful for us because they inform us approximately about the relations holding for such imperfect circles as the circumference of trees.

To maintain the analogy we may attempt to interpret ethics as of a similar nature, as informing us about the approximate behavior of human beings. It is true that a descriptive ethics, a sociological account of existent ethical rules, is usually not given in this way, but by a description of the actual behavior of men. But we could at least theoretically construct a descriptive ethics by dealing with the ideal man, as the geometer deals with the ideal triangle. That is possible because within a certain approximation the ideal ethical laws are realized. As a matter of fact, for instance, most people do not steal or kill. Ethical ideals are approximately realized because otherwise men as a social group could not exist. We thus would arrive at a descriptive ethics which would inform us about the approximate ethical behavior of humans by depicting their ideal behavior, as geometry informs us about the approximate relations between measurements of physical space by dealing with ideal spatial figures.

But that is not what the philosopher of ethics wants. He wants moral directives, rules telling us how we should behave, not reports on how we do behave. Since he claims that reason, or a vision of ideas, can reveal such rules, he is compelled to construe, conversely, the function of mathematics as normative, not as descriptive. He thus arrives at a conception for which mind appears as a law giver. In a more modest version, mind is conceived as an instrument of vision that perceives the normative laws by looking into a higher sphere of existence. We meet here with the psychological origin of the plurality of realms of existence, whose leading exponent is Plato. The imperfect geometrical forms of actual physical objects are regarded as deficiencies, as imperfections in the moral sense, like the shortcomings in the behavior of actual humans, and a sphere of higher reality is introduced which is free from these imperfections, both on the cognitive and on the moral plane.

The moral evaluation of cognitive relations is visible in the penetration of moral arguments into Greek science, such as astronomy. The celestial paths of the stars, for instance, are regarded as perfect circles for reasons of prestige, so to speak. That the circumferences of trees are imperfect circles shows their inferiority. As a consequence of such conceptions the real things are regarded inferior to the ideal things. Plato's theory of ideas expresses this shift of valuation from physical to ideal reality.

Kant develops a similar conception, although it is introduced by less naïve arguments. He distinguishes between *things of appearance (phenomena)* and *things in themselves (noumena)*. All our knowledge is restricted to

64

things of appearance, because knowledge presents the objects of the physical world in the frame of the a priori principles. Behind the objects of appearance, he argues, there must be the things in themselves, that is, the things as they are before their incorporation into the principles of geometry, causality, and so on. Like Plato, he arrives at a transcendental world, different from and superior to the world that observation and science unlock to us.

It is obvious why Kant needs the things in themselves: he wishes to construct a realm open to the application of his moral and religious principles. Science, through its causal determinism, had left no place for freedom of human action or for a government by God—so, to Kant, the foundations of morality and religion appeared threatened. A way out seemed possible by restricting science to a sort of inferior reality and thus exempting the things in themselves from the determinism of the things of appearance. The subjective trait of Kant's synthetic a priori lent itself to such an interpretation: if the laws of causality and geometry are merely superimposed upon an absolute reality by the human mind, this reality itself is free and unimpeded to follow the moral instead of the causal law. It is painful to see how the philosopher of Newtonian physics busies himself to abandon all his physics in order to save his religious morality. Kant admits quite openly that this is the intention of his philosophy. In the preface to the second edition of his *Critique of Pure Reason* he says: "I had to set limits to knowledge in order to make place for faith". The devastating consequences of this program are shown in the final turn he gives to his "critical philosophy". The very book which lays the foundations of his theory of knowledge ends in a chapter, called *Transcendental Dialectic*, which virtually cancels all his previous results. Kant pretends to show in this chapter that when reason is extended beyond the world of appearance, it leads unavoidably to contradictions, called *antinomies,* and that the only escape from this breakdown of reason consists in a belief in God, freedom, and immortality, as principles holding for a reality behind the visible world.

Kant's so-called antinomies, which essentially concern the infinity of space and time, have not stood up to the test of logic. They are easily solved by a logic that has learned to deal consistently with infinite numbers. His interpretation of causality and geometry as principles superimposed upon things by a human mind has turned out untenable, too. The causal law, if it holds at all, must hold for things in themselves, since otherwise it could not be used for predictions of future observations: the human mind does not create its observations, but is essentially passive in the act of perception. And geometry, as we know today, describes a property of the physical world (see chap. 8). So there is no argument left for his artificial restriction of the powers of reason and his introduction of a metaphysical reality of things in themselves. But ever since its publication in his books, this antiscientific part of his philosophy has been the source from which the enemies of science drew their water. They used it for the construction of philosophical systems which belittled scientific thought and pretended to establish a world of ideal existence, knowledge of which was accessible to the philosopher, and to him only.

It is thus that rationalism leads to the conception of idealism, introduced above as a specific version of rationalism, which maintains that ultimate reality is reserved to ideas, whereas physical objects are but poor copies of the ideal ones. The conception has found its most absurd formulation in the theory that reason is the substance of all things, expressed in the passage quoted at the beginning of this book. We asked why a philosopher must phrase his conceptions in this way. We can now give the answer: because his primary interest is not an understanding of knowledge but something else. He wishes to construe knowledge in such a way that it supplies a basis for moral directives; he wishes to construct for knowledge a certainty which sense perception can never attain, with the intention to construct a parallel to such certainty in an absolute ethical knowledge. He does not hesitate to develop his system in picture language because he misunderstands the language of scientific explanation.

The author of the passage quoted is G. W. Hegel (1770–1831), from whose introduction to the *Philosophy of History* the passage is taken. A few remarks about his philosophy will be in order because Hegel's system can be regarded as the extreme of the idealist position—or should I say, its caricature? Hegel differs from Plato and Kant in that he does not share their admiration of the mathematical sciences; and he differs from them, furthermore, in that he does not reach the profundity of their questions. But he repeats all their mistakes and displays them in such a naïve way that his system can be studied as a model of what philosophy should not be.

The starting point of Hegel's philosophy is history, not science. He attempts to account for the evolution of historical man, that is, of the period of human history for which we possess written records, by the construction of some simple schemata which, he thinks, explain historical developments. One such schema compares history with the growth of the individual. There is childhood, represented by the early oriental peoples; there is youth, which he identifies with the period of the Greeks; there is the age of mature man, realized by the Romans; and there is old age, represented by our time—which, for Hegel, is a period not of decay but of highest maturity.

The highest stage of highest maturity was reached with the Prussian state, which employed Hegel as a professor in Berlin. I do not know what Hegel would have said about the Prussia of Hitler; maybe he would have assigned to it a place on the continuation of his line of historical development, but maybe he would have preferred to postpone his judgment until he saw the end of Hitler's empire.

This primitive schematization, worthy of a freshman who sets out to construct his own philosophical system, is much less known than another one of his historical schemata. Hegel saw that very often historical developments move from one extreme to another, like a pendulum, and then reach a third stage which includes, to a certain degree, the results of both preceding stages. For instance, political absolutism is sometimes followed by a democratic revolution, which in turn develops into a centralized government combined with rights of the people. He called this schema the *dialectical law*. The first stage is called the *thesis;* the second, the *antithesis;* and the third, the *synthesis*.

There are many illustrations for the dialectical law in the history of human thought. The development of astronomical conceptions of the universe offers an example: Ptolemy's conception of a geocentric universe, that is, a universe the center of which is occupied by the earth, was followed by Copernicus' system of a heliocentric universe, in which the earth is moving and the sun is the immovable center. These two opposite conceptions have been superseded and at the same time "synthesized" by Einstein's relativistic conception, according to which both the geocentric and the heliocentric conceptions can be made admissible interpretations if they are freed from the claim of an absolute motion. Another illustration is afforded by the development of the physical theories of light, which went from a particle to a wave conception, until finally the two were united in a dualistic conception of matter as interpretable both as particles and as waves (see chap. 11). The general procedure of empirical method, the method of trial and error and a success which is but a new trial, can also be regarded as an unending iteration of the dialectical law. These illustrations show, furthermore, that the dialectical law has a pliable meaning; it is no more than a convenient frame in which certain historical developments can be incorporated after they have been run through, but it is neither precise nor general enough to allow for historical predictions. And it cannot be employed as an argument for the truth of a certain scientific theory: the thesis that Einstein's theory of motion is true cannot be derived from the dialectical pattern of the historical process that led to the construction of this theory, but must be based on independent grounds.

Had Hegel been content to establish the dialectical law and illustrate it by a copious collection of historical and philosophical material, he might have been a great historian, a scientist of history. As a scientist he would have seen, too, the limitations of his law of the triple step, the many instances in which it does not hold, and would have looked for the special conditions of its applicability. But he was a philosopher and thus became a victim of the search for generality and for certainty. He generalized his law of dialectics into a law of logic and developed a system according to which contradiction is immanent in logic and, so to speak, pushes thought from one extreme to the other, thus producing the dialectical movement. Hegel argues, for instance, that the statement "the rose is red" is a contradiction, because in it the same thing is said to be two different things, namely a rose and red. Logicians have often explained the primitive error in this conception which confuses class membership with identity: according to the statement, the same thing is a member of two different classes, namely, of the class of roses and of red things, which is no contradiction. A contradiction would arise if the two different classes were asserted to be identical; but the statement does not mean this. By logical manipulations of this kind, Hegel tries to establish his law of dialectics as a logical law holding without exceptions.

Combining his explanation of the dialectical law with his conception of a progressive evolution of mankind, Hegel arrives at such conceptions as presented in the passage with which this book was opened. The substance of reality is reason; it pushes reality from extreme to extreme, uniting the extremes on a higher plane, and then beginning the process anew. That is picture language; but what Hegel says cannot be said otherwise, else its absurdity would become too obvious. If we interpret his conception as meaning that the world becomes more and more reasonable, or that all happenings serve a reasonable purpose, the falsehood of such a statement is evident. Human history, although it includes lines of intellectual and moral progress, is too complex a phenomenon to be classified in so simple terms; and who would contend that the development of the physical world, say, of the stellar systems, follows outlines satisfying the desires of human reason or fulfilling what humans might regard as a purpose? Hegel's system depends for its appeal on its odd language.

In Hegel, the search for moral directives has assumed the form of a projection of moral ends into history; the good will finally become reality, and we must aspire to the good because we take part in the process of history. In a less sophisticated language this means that statements about what will happen are derived from statements about what should happen. The man in the street calls it wishful thinking; the philosopher speaks of the teleological interpretation of history. There is no point in attempting to give a logical analysis of such a philosophy; it is interesting only from a psychological point of view, as a documentation of what happens if rationalism is no longer controlled by logic. It represents an instance where the philosopher believes that if reason can *discover* laws of the universe, reason can also *give* laws to the universe.

I doubt whether Hegel would have acquired his present fame had he not found support outside philosophy, in the economic materialism of Karl Marx (1818–1883). The application of Hegel's dialectical law within the framework of a political movement made Hegel's doctrine the center of heated controversy; socialism was discussed, both by its exponents and by its adversaries, in the light of Hegel's philosophy. And yet, in his fundamentals, Marx is the greatest opponent of Hegel because he refuses to share Hegel's primitive belief in the power of reason. The man who explained ideological movements as results of economic conditions and preached class struggle as the step toward progress, was not an idealist. Marx's historical position is on the line of empiricism, not only because he was strongly influenced by British empiricists like Ricardo, but also because Hegel's dialectical law can be consistently incorporated into his sociology only if it is conceived as an empirical law. We would have a much clearer picture of the history of sociological empiricism had Marx himself recognized this fact.

We must look for psychological explanations when we wish to understand why Marx did not sever himself clearly from Hegel's metaphysics. He extended his economic interpretation of history to economic determinism, and perhaps he needed the ties to an idealistic philosophy as a support for this doctrine, according to which historical developments are strictly determined by economic laws, in the same way that the course of the planets is determined by physical laws. But economic conditions are merely a contributing factor to historical developments; human psychology is another factor, and even both together cannot supply more than statistical laws for the evolution of human society. In regarding a contributing factor as the exclusive cause, Marx has abandoned the principles of empiricism. Only the rationalist and apriorist can overlook the merely statistical nature of sociological laws; the empiricist knows that the chance element can never be completely eliminated from historical occurrences and that it excludes a strict predictability even of major historical trends. The fanatical belief of the Marxists in the economic predictions of their master, which reminds one of a creed rather than of a scientific approach, is a revival of Hegelianism, of a philosophy which sets a priori intuitions above empirical evidence.

Hegel has been called the successor of Kant; that is a serious misunderstanding of Kant and an unjustified elevation of Hegel. Kant's system, though proved untenable by later developments, was the attempt of a great mind to establish rationalism on a scientific basis. Hegel's system is the poor construction of a fanatic who has seen one empirical truth and attempts to make it a logical law within the most unscientific of all logics. Whereas Kant's system marks the peak of the historical line of rationalism, Hegel's system belongs in the period of decay of speculative philosophy which characterizes the nineteenth century. I shall speak later about this period. One remark only may be made in advance: more than any other philosophy, Hegel's system has contributed to the division between scientists and philosophers. It has made philosophy an object of derision from which the scientist wishes to keep his course clear.

The gap between science and philosophy will now appear understandable. The rationalist philosopher is antiscientific from the very roots of his mind. The path of his thought is determined by extralogical motives which employ scientific results and methods as instruments for the attainment of nonscientific aims. We should not be deceived by the admiration and glorification of mathematics often exhibited by the prophets of the idealistic philosophy. Mathematics is for them but an illustration of their doctrines, a mirror of their own ideas; they do not know what knowledge, including mathematical knowledge, means to a man who studies knowledge in its own right.

There is no compromise between science and speculative philosophy. Let us not attempt to reconcile the two in the hope for a higher synthesis. Not all historical developments follow the dialectical law; one line of thought may die out and leave its place to another that springs from different roots—like a biological species that survives only in fossil form, once another species, better equipped, has taken over. Speculative philosophy, after its climax in the system of Kant, has found only mediocre representatives and is decaying. A different philosophy is in the ascendant, which is akin to science and has answered a great many of the questions which were raised in the philosophy of earlier periods. I shall discuss the historical roots of this philosophy before presenting its answers.

5.

The Empiricist Approach
Success and Failure

THE DISCUSSION of philosophical systems in the preceding chapters is not meant to supply an exhaustive picture of philosophy. The philosophers thus far referred to, are selected from a certain point of view; they exhibit a specific type of philosophy and must not be considered as representing philosophy as a whole. Their philosophy is characterized by the conception that there exists a special domain of knowledge, philosophical knowledge, which the human mind acquires through the use of a particular capacity, called reason, or intuition, or vision of ideas. The systems of these philosophers are the alleged products of this capacity; they are believed to supply a sort of knowledge which the scientist cannot attain, a superscientific knowledge inaccessible to the methods of sense observation and generalization by which the sciences are constructed. This kind of philosophy was here denoted by the name of *rationalism*. For the rationalist, apart from a few exceptions like Hegel, mathematics represents the ideal form of knowledge; it supplies the pattern after which philosophical knowledge is modeled.

From the time of the Greeks, however, there has existed a second type of philosophy which is essentially different from the first. The philosophers of the second type regard empirical science, and not mathematics, as the ideal form of knowledge; they insist that sense observation is the primary source and the ultimate judge of knowledge, and that it is self-deception to believe the human mind to have a direct access to any kind of truth other than that of empty logical relations. This type of philosophy is called *empiricism.*

The empiricist method differs radically from that of rationalism. The empiricist philosopher does not claim to discover a new kind of knowledge inaccessible to the scientist; he merely studies and analyzes observational knowledge, be it scientific or commonplace, and tries to understand its meaning and its implications. He does not mind if the theory of knowledge thus constructed is called philosophical knowledge; but he regards it as constructed by the same methods as employed by the scientist and refuses to interpret it as the product of a specific philosophical capacity.

Not always has the empiricist thesis been so clearly stated as we can state it now; the elaboration of the thesis of empiricism is in itself the product of a long historical development. The older empiricists did not possess the clear conception of empirical science which we have today, and were frequently influenced by rationalist systems. Furthermore, their philosophy often included parts which we regard today as belonging in empirical science, such as theories of the origin of the universe or of the nature of matter. Of this kind were the systems of the Greek empiricists, whom we find both in the pre-Socratic and later periods of Greek philosophy. The most prominent among them is Democritus, a contemporary of Socrates, who is regarded as the first to conceive of the idea that nature consists of atoms and hence has a place in the history of science as well as in the history of philosophy. His cosmogony is outstanding because it assumes

75

an evolution through the combination of atoms into complicated structures. Originally, there were only individual atoms traveling in all directions through space; through chance collisions, vortices developed which eventually led to the formation of bodies of all kinds and shapes. These ideas were taken up, some one hundred years later, by Epicurus, whose system was transmitted, in Roman times, to later generations, through Lucretius' famous poem *De Rerum Natura*. Epicurus gave a somewhat different version of the movement of the atoms in assuming that the atoms were originally all falling down along parallel lines for an infinite time, until by chance some atoms deviated from their paths and collided with others. This chance event started evolution.

Among later Greek philosophers, the skeptics may be regarded as representatives of empiricism. If they questioned the possibility of knowledge, it was because the Greeks identified knowledge with absolutely certain knowledge. Carneades (second century B.C.) recognized that deduction cannot supply such knowledge because it merely derives conclusions from given premises and cannot establish the truth of the axioms. He saw, moreover, that for the purpose of an orientation in everyday life absolute knowledge is unnecessary and that well-established opinion suffices as a basis for actions. From this point of view he developed a theory of probability which distinguished three kinds of probability, or degrees of certainty. With his defense of opinion and probability Carneades laid the foundations of the empiricist position in an intellectual environment where mathematical certainty was regarded the only permissible form of knowledge. Developed in constant clash with the prevalent rationalist doctrines, the conceptions of these early empiricists were predominantly skeptical; they exhibit the healthy but albeit negative trait of an attack against rationalism and do not go far in the construction of a positive empiricist philosophy.

The school of the skeptics was continued through the centuries; some three hundred years after Carneades, Sextus Empiricus (about 150 A.D.) wrote a synopsis of the skeptical doctrines, which informs us about his early predecessors and leaves no doubt that the author does not want to question the possibility of purposive action based on information derived from sense perception. He is also a leading representative of the school of empirical physicians, who attempted to purify the science of medicine from speculative additions. The Arabic philosophers include empiricists such as Alhazen, famous for his work in physiological optics. During the Middle Ages, philosophy was carried on by clerics only, and scholastic philosophy thus has not much room for empiricism. Men like Roger Bacon, Peter Aureoli, and William of Occam, who courageously attempted to defend the empiricist position, are too deeply imbued with theological modes of thought to be comparable with the empiricists of an earlier or a later time. This remark is not intended to belittle the historical significance of these men; in fact, if merit is measured by the deviation of a man's views from environmental opinions, their stand for empiricism deserves the admiration of all those who have been empiricists in more empirically minded periods.

The close connection between rationalism and theology is understandable. Since religious doctrines are not based on sense perception, they demand an extrasensory source of knowledge. The philosopher who pretends to have found a knowledge of this type is the natural ally of the theologian. The systems of the great Greek rationalists Plato and Aristotle were utilized by Christian theologians for the construction of a philosophy of Christianity; Plato became the philosopher of more mystically minded groups, Aristotle that of scholasticism. The relation to theology has at all times made the rationalist feel himself superior to the empiricist in a moral sense. The antagonism between the two groups, though felt on one side as strongly as on the other, is not of a symmetrical form; whereas the rationalist regards the empiricist as morally inferior, the empiricist regards the rationalist as devoid of common sense.

It was with the rise of modern science, about the year 1600, that empiricism began to assume the form of a positive and well-founded philosophical theory which could enter into successful competition with rationalism. The modern period has given us the great empiricist systems of Francis Bacon (1561–1626), John Locke (1632–1704), and David Hume (1711–1776). The positions of these British empiricists must now be compared with rationalism.

The thesis of empiricism found its clear elaboration in the philosophies of these men. The conception that perception is the source and the ultimate test of knowledge is the eventual result of their work. The mind, says Locke, begins as a blank page; it is experience that writes on this paper. Nothing is in the mind that was not previously in the senses. There are, however, two kinds of sense perception: perception of external and of internal objects. The latter kind of object is given by psychological occurrences, like thinking, believing, the feeling of pain, or the sensation of color, which we observe through an internal sense. Hume divides the contents of the mind into impressions and ideas; the impressions are supplied by the senses, including the internal sense, and the ideas are recollections of previous impressions. Only in their combination can ideas differ from observed phenomena. For instance, the observed impressions of gold and of a mountain can be put together to form the unobserved, but imaginable, combination of a golden mountain. In contrast to rationalism, empiricism thus reduces the mind to the subordinate role of establishing an order between impressions and ideas; the ordered system is what we call knowledge.

The function of the mind in the construction of knowledge may be illustrated by some examples which could have been used by Bacon, Locke, or Hume. Among the various experiences of a day, the mind picks out the brightness of fire as seen by the eyes and associates it with the feeling of heat perceived when we are close to a fire, thus arriving at the physical law that fire is hot. Similarly, the mind discovers the laws of the motions of the stars by comparing the various pictures we observe in looking at the night sky at different hours and days; in connecting the various positions of a star by imaginary lines, the mind plots the star's path, which in itself is not an object of observation.

When I say that mind is allotted a subordinate role in this conception of knowledge, I mean to say that mind is not regarded as the judge of truth. To the mind, a circle may appear as the most worthy form for the motion of a star; but whether this motion is actually circular is judged by perception. Reason may induce me to say that matter consists of small particles, because otherwise I do not see how matter can be compressible; but whether atomism is true must be judged by perceptions. In this instance perception cannot directly answer the question, because atoms are too small to be observable; but it answers the question indirectly by supplying us with a set of observable facts that make the atomic interpretation unavoidable. The latter instance, however, makes it obvious that the function of mind in the construction of knowledge cannot be called subordinate in another sense: reason is an indispensable instrument for the organization of knowledge, without which facts of a more abstract kind could not be known. The senses do not show me that the planets move in ellipses around the sun, or that matter consists of atoms; it is sense observation in combination with reasoning that leads to such abstract truths.

Bacon saw very clearly the indispensability of reason for an empiricist conception of knowledge. In a discussion of philosophical systems he compares the rationalists with spiders that make cobwebs out of their own substance, the older empiricists with ants that collect material without being able to find an order in it; the new empiricists, he claims, are like the bees that gather material and digest it, adding to it from their own substance and thus creating a product of a higher quality. That is a great program stated in a witty form. Let us see how far the empiricism of the seventeenth and eighteenth century has lived up to it.

What is the addition that reason makes to observational knowledge? We said it is the introduction of abstract relations of order. However, abstract relations in themselves would not be so interesting if they did not include statements of new concreta. If the abstract relations are general truths, they hold not only for the observations made, but also for observations not yet made; they include not only an account of past experiences, but also predictions of future experiences. That is the addition which reason makes to knowledge. Observation informs us about the past and the present; reason foretells the future.

Let me illustrate the predictive nature of abstract laws by some examples. The law that fire is hot goes beyond the experiences on which this law was established and which belong to the past; it predicts that whenever we shall see a fire it will be hot. The laws of the motion of the stars permit us to predict future positions of the stars and include predictions of observations like eclipses of the sun and the moon. The atomic theory of matter has led to chemical predictions, verified in the construction of new chemical substances; in fact, all industrial applications of science are based on the predictive nature of scientific laws, since they employ scientific laws as blueprints for the construction of devices that function according to a preconceived plan. Bacon had a clear insight into the predictive nature of knowledge when he coined his famous maxim: knowledge is power.

How can reason predict the future? Bacon saw that reason alone does not have any predictive capacity; it gains it only in combination with observation. The predictive methods of reason are contained in the logical operations by means of which we construct an order into the observational material and derive conclusions. We arrive at predictions through the instrument of the logical derivation. Bacon recognized, furthermore, that if logical derivation is to serve predictive purposes, it cannot be restricted to *deductive logic;* it must include methods of an *inductive logic.*

This distinction, on which the development of modern empiricism hinges, may be made clearer by a consideration of the syllogism. Consider the classic example: "All men are mortal, Socrates is a man, therefore Socrates is mortal". As explained above, the conclusion is analytically implied by the premises and does not add anything to them. It merely makes some part of their content explicit. Such emptiness is the very essence of deductive inference and represents the price which we pay for the necessary truth of the conclusion. Consider, in contrast, the inference "all crows so far observed were black, therefore all crows in the world are black." The conclusion is not contained in the premise; it refers to crows not yet observed and extends to them a property of the observed crows. Consequently, the truth of the conclusion cannot be guaranteed; it is possible that some day we might discover in a remote wilderness a bird that possesses all properties of a crow except for the black color. In spite of this possibility we are willing to make this kind of inference, especially when more important things than crows are concerned. We need it if we want to establish a general truth, which includes a reference to unobserved things, and because we need it, we are willing to take the risk of an error. An inference of this kind is called *inductive inference,* or more specifically, an inference of *induction by enumeration.*

It is Bacon's historical merit to have emphasized the importance of inductive inference for empirical science. He recognized the limitations of deductive inference and insisted that deductive logic cannot supply the methods that lead from observed facts to general truths and thus to predictions of further observations. A deductive inference can be predictive only if the premises include a reference to the future. For instance, because the premise "all men are mortal" includes a reference to human beings who, like us, have not yet died, it permits of a deductive derivation of the conclusion that some day we shall die, too. But such a premise must have been constructed by means of some inductive inference. Deductive logic, therefore, cannot establish a theory of prediction and must be supplemented by an inductive logic. The deductive logic which Bacon knew, and which was to remain the only deductive logic for some further centuries, was that of Aristotle; it had been transmitted to the learned world of the Middle Ages in a collection of writings carrying the name of *Organon.* Opposing his inductive logic to Aristotle's *Organon,* Bacon published it in a book which he called *Novum Organum.* The book is historically the first attempt at an inductive logic and therefore occupies, in spite of many deficiencies, a leading place in world literature.

In his positive attitude to the inductive inference Bacon also goes beyond older forms of empiricism. For instance, Sextus Empiricus directed attacks against the logic of the syllogism from the viewpoint of its emptiness; but he did not admit the use of the inductive inference, which he regarded as unfit for the establishment of knowledge. It was the Greek ideal of an absolutely certain knowledge, modeled after the pattern of mathematics, which British empiricism had to overcome. That is its historical function, which makes it the pioneer of modern scientific philosophy.

For all his emphasis on the inductive inference, Bacon saw very clearly its weaknesses. To overcome the weaknesses, Bacon worked out a method which classifies the observed facts with respect to a common property; thus he studied the nature of heat by gathering in one table various phenomena in which heat occurs, in another table various similar phenomena where heat does not occur, and in a third table those phenomena where heat occurs in various degrees. His classification is a strange hodgepodge in which observations like the occurrence of heat in horse dung are compared with the absence of heat in the light of the moon. We should not forget, however, that classification is the first step toward scientific investigation and that Bacon was in no position to construct a theory of the inductive methods of mathematical physics because mathematical physics was only in its beginnings. It is true that Galileo was a contemporary of Bacon and that Galileo's mathematical method is superior to Bacon's inductive classification. But the method of the mathematical hypothesis (chap. 6) had first to be developed with all its implications before it could be made the object of a philosophical inquiry. It was not before Newton's theory of gravitation, published some sixty years after Bacon's death, that the use of deductive methods in combination with inductive inferences became apparent. The reproach of having studied scientific method in an oversimplified model that neglects the contribution of mathematics to physics should go, not to Bacon, but to the later empiricists—in particular to John Stuart Mill, who, two hundred and fifty years after Bacon, developed an inductive logic which scarcely mentioned mathematical method and was essentially a reformulation of Bacon's ideas.

Bacon's inductive logic is naïve, being founded on confidence in a rule which common sense is willing to apply. Yet it is one which the scientist cannot dispense with, either. A critique of scientific method can hardly be expected at a time when such method is in its beginning and is buoyed up by the optimism of its first successes. Historians of philosophy who criticize Bacon's inductive logic as unscientific should realize that their judgment reflects the standards of a later time.

In Bacon, empiricism has found its prophet; in Locke, its public leader; in Hume, its critic. Locke took over Bacon's theory of empirical knowledge as derived inductively through generalizations of experiences. He is none too clear, though, about the question whether all synthetic knowledge is empirical. It seems that he regarded mathematical knowledge as absolutely certain, though synthetic, and thus distinguished it from empirical knowledge. The necessary propositions, according to him, are either "trifling" or "instructive", a distinction in which he presumably anticipates Kant's distinction between analytic and synthetic propositions and which, if so interpreted, would make him an adherent of a synthetic a priori. It is true, there is no clear commitment

84

to a synthetic a priori in Locke's writings. But his treatment of moral judgments as having the same kind of truth as mathematical theorems makes him an adherent of the ethico-cognitive parallelism and leads him to results which are scarcely compatible with an analytic conception of mathematics.

Empiricism, in its early phases, is not always consistent. Locke's empiricism is restricted to the principle that all concepts, even those of mathematics and logic, enter into our mind through experience; and he is not ready to extend it to the thesis that all synthetic knowledge is validated only by experience. In correspondence to this uncritical attitude, the inductive inference was taken over by him without criticism and regarded as a useful instrument of all empirical knowledge. That the legitimacy of this instrument might be questioned and the foundation knocked from under empiricism, is an eventuality which did not occur to Bacon or Locke; it was Hume's part to deal this blow to the philosophy of experience.

When Hume wrote his *Inquiry Concerning Human Understanding,* the *Novum Organum* was more than one hundred years old; but the theory of induction which Hume found in contemporary expositions of logic was still Bacon's theory. Hume, therefore, took it for granted that scientific inference has the form of induction by enumeration, the inference that was explained in the example of the crows. Whoever has studied mathematical physics knows that this result is questionable, that there exist various forms of inductive inference. The physics of Newton, for instance, applies a complicated deductive theory as an instrument of inductive validation, and it is by no means obvious that this theory is ultimately reducible to inferences of the simple form called induction by enumeration. But this problem will be dealt with later. At this place it may suffice to remark that modern analysis has shown all forms of inductive inference to be reducible to induction by enumeration, a result which makes it permissible to restrict the discussion of inductive method to this simplest form, as Hume did.

Hume is superior to Locke in his clear conception of empiricism. He has overcome the ethico-cognitive parallelism and sees very clearly that ethical judgments do not express truth, but, as he puts it, express sentiments of approbation or disapprobation; that "the distinction of vice and virtue . . . is not perceived by reason". Being free from the error of those who have to introduce a synthetic a priori in order to find a basis for morality, he is thus able to study knowledge without the preoccupation of the moralist. He arrives at the result that all knowledge is either analytic or derived from experience: mathematics and logic are analytic, all synthetic knowledge is derived from experience. By "derived" he means not only that concepts have their origin in sense perception but also that sense perception is the source of the validity of all nonanalytic knowledge. The addition to knowledge supplied by the mind, therefore, is of an empty nature.

As far as mathematics is concerned, Hume's interpretation is none too well founded. As he could not know the answer which the nineteenth century gave to the problem through the construction of non-Euclidean geometries, he had no means to account for the double nature of geometry as both dictated by reason and predictive of observation. But it seems that he did not see this problem very clearly. We may regard it as fortunate that here, as in the problem of induction, all forms of which he considered reducible to induction by enumeration, he anticipated later results although he had no good argument for his conceptions. I am not inclined to take such coincidence as the token of genius, but would rather call it good luck. And I would see Hume's genius exhibited, instead, in those results for which he could give good grounds, such as his rejection of the ethico-cognitive parallelism, and would praise him for the consistency with which he carried out his views against opposing traditions.

This consistency is shown in his treatment of induction. If all contributions of the mind to knowledge are analytic, there arise serious difficulties for the use of the inductive inference; and it is Hume's significance in the history of philosophy to have drawn attention to this problem, which can be analyzed without commitment to an analytic or synthetic interpretation of mathematics. The inductive inference is not analytic. Hume makes this fact clear by pointing out that we can very well imagine the contrary of the inductive conclusion. For instance, although all crows so far observed were black, we can at least imagine that the next crow we shall see will be white. We would not believe that it will be white, since we adhere to the inductive inference. But belief is irrelevant if mere possibilities are considered: we can imagine that the conclusion is false without being compelled to abandon the premise. The possibility of a false conclusion in combination with a true premise proves that the inductive inference does not carry a logical necessity with it. The nonanalytic character of induction is Hume's first thesis.

How, then, can we justify the use of the inductive inference? Hume discusses the possibility that the inference be validated by experience. Presumably, a validation of this kind was assumed by Bacon and Locke, who, however, never entered into a discussion of the legitimacy of induction. We might argue that we have often employed inductive inferences and have had good success; therefore we feel entitled to further application of the inference. However, the very formulation of the argument, as Hume explains, makes it clear that this justification is fallacious. The inference by which we wish to justify induction is itself an inductive inference: we believe in induction because induction has so far been successful—that is an inference of the crow type, and we thus move in a circle. Induction can be proved to be reliable if we assume that it is reliable; such reasoning is circular, and the argument breaks down. That induction cannot be justified by reference to experience, is Hume's second thesis.

The inductive inference is unjustifiable; that is what Hume claims to be the result of his critique. The seriousness of this result must be fully realized. If Hume's thesis is true, our instrument of prediction breaks down; we have no way of anticipating the future. We have so far seen that the sun rose every morning and believe that it will rise tomorrow, but we have no ground for this belief. We have seen water run downhill and believe it will always run downhill, but we have no proof that it will do so tomorrow. What if the rivers start to run uphill tomorrow? You think: I shall not be so foolish as to believe that. But why is such belief foolish? Because, you answer, I have never seen water run uphill, and because I have always had success with such inferences from the past to the future. There you are, a prey to the fallacy discovered by Hume; you prove induction by the use of an inductive inference. Over and again we fall into the trap; we see that induction cannot be justified, then go on making inductions and argue that we should be fools if we doubted the inductive principle.

That is the dilemma of the empiricist: either he is a radical empiricist and admits no results other than analytic statements or statements derived from experience

—then he cannot make inductions and must renounce any statement about the future; or he admits the inductive inference—then he has admitted a nonanalytic principle not derivable from experience and has abandoned empiricism. A radical empiricism thus arrives at the conclusion that knowledge of the future is impossible; but what is knowledge if it does not include the future? A mere report of relations observed in the past cannot be called knowledge; if knowledge is to reveal objective relations of physical objects, it must include reliable predictions. A radical empiricism, therefore, denies the possibility of knowledge.

The classical period of empiricism, the period of Bacon, Locke, and Hume, ends with the breakdown of empiricism; for that is what Hume's analysis of induction amounts to. Hume's critique leads from empiricism to agnosticism; with respect to the future, it calls for a philosophy of ignorance which teaches that all I know is that I do not know anything about the future. We must admire the acuity of the intellect which, though imbued with the trust in empiricism, does not refrain from drawing this annihilating conclusion. And yet, although Hume states his result rather frankly and calls himself a skeptic, he is not willing to admit the tragedy of his conclusion. He attempts to palliate his result by calling the inductive belief a habit; and in reading Hume one gets the impression that this turn satisfied his doubts, that it sufficed him to have a psychological explanation of the inductive belief. Hume was not a radical, but a British Tory; the radicalism of his intellect was not balanced by a radicalism of his volitional attitudes, and we thus are shown the strange aspect of a philosopher who dismisses with a friendly smile the decisive charge he has advanced against the philosophy of empiricism.

We cannot share Hume's quietism. We shall not deny that induction is a habit; of course, it is. But we wish to know whether it is a good habit or a bad one. We admit it is difficult to overcome this habit; in fact, who would be able to behave, say, on the assumption that from tomorrow all the water will flow uphill? But even if our conditioning to the habit of induction is so strong that we cannot help being addicts of induction, like dope addicts, at least we want to know whether we should try to get away from it. The logical problem of induction is independent of the question whether induction is a habit, and whether we can overcome the habit. The philosopher of empiricism wants to know whether or in what sense experience can supply knowledge of the future; if he cannot answer this question, he should admit frankly that empiricism is a failure.

When we turn to a comparison of empiricism with rationalism, we arrive at a strange sort of balance. The rationalist cannot solve the problem of empirical knowledge because he construes such knowledge after the pattern of mathematics, and thus makes reason the legislator of the physical world. The empiricist cannot solve the problem either; his attempt to establish empirical knowledge in its own right as derived from sense perception alone breaks down because empirical knowledge presupposes a nonanalytic method, the method of induction, which cannot be regarded as a product of experience. The empiricist does not repeat the mistakes of the rationalist; he does not use picture language, he does not aspire to absolute certainty, he does not try to model cognitive knowledge so as to attain a basis of moral directives. But in restricting the power of reason to the establishment of analytic principles he runs into a new difficulty: he cannot account for the method by which empirical knowledge proceeds from the past to the future, that is, he cannot explain the predictive nature of knowledge.

5. THE EMPIRICIST APPROACH

The conclusion offers itself that there must be some fundamental mistake in empiricism. The rationalist committed the mistake of regarding mathematical knowledge as the prototype of all knowledge and thus wanted to make reason the source of knowledge of the world, at least in its fundamentals; the empiricist corrected this mistake in insisting that empirical knowledge is derived from sense perception, that reason supplies only analytic relations, and that all synthetic knowledge is of the observational type. Observational knowledge, however, is restricted to the past and the present; knowledge of the future is not of the observational type. The older empiricists did not see the difficulties arising from this distinction; because predictions of the future can be verified or falsified at a later time, they regarded knowledge of the future as being of the same type as observational knowledge. They forgot that we wish to know the truth of predictions before the predicted events occur, and that when knowledge has become observational knowledge it is no longer a knowledge of the future. Hume saw the difficulty; but since he could not give up a conception of knowledge which implicitly demands that knowledge of the future should be of the same type as knowledge of the past, he concluded that the predictive methods of science are unjustifiable and that we cannot have any knowledge of the future.

The modern conception of empiricism has recognized the mistake. Since statements about the future are unjustifiable if they are regarded as being of the same type as statements about the past or the present, we infer that statements about the future must be given a different interpretation; knowledge of the future must be construed as essentially different from knowledge of the past. With this turn the question is reversed; instead of assuming the nature of knowledge of the future as being given and then asking how we can have a knowledge of the future, we ask what must be the nature of knowledge of the future if statements about the future are to be justifiable.

To make this reversal of the question was beyond the possibilities of Hume. His criticism of induction is an achievement great enough to insure him a leading position in the history of philosophy. I said above that philosophical progress must be sought not in the answers but in the questions that were asked by the philosophers; this maxim applies to Hume, too. To Hume goes the credit of having raised the question of the justification of induction and of having pointed out the difficulties of its solution. His answer is of no use to us.

Strangely enough, this judgment on British empiricism arrives at a criticism which corresponds to an objection raised above against rationalism. In spite of its intrinsic difference from rationalism, British empiricism has repeated one of the fundamental rationalist mistakes: to examine knowledge not with the detachment of the disinterested observer, but with the intention of proving a preconceived aim; to study the nature of knowledge from a picture modeled for the purpose of finding in it the structure which the philosopher wishes to find. The rationalist construes empirical science as a system the fundamentals of which must have the reliability of mathematics; the empiricist replaces mathematical reliability by observational reliability, but demands that sentences about the future must possess the same kind of reliability as sentences about the past. The rationalist thus arrives at the problem why nature must follow reason; the empiricist is confronted by the question of how to transfer the reliability of observations to predictions.

The way out of the dilemma could not be found by the philosophy of the eighteenth century. The reversal of the question into a question of the nature of predictive knowledge could not be undertaken before the foundations of science had gone through some fundamental changes. The science of the eighteenth century was propelled by uncritical confidence in its success; it had to experience the limits of its methods before it could become self-critical and ask for the meaning of its results. This development began with the nineteenth century and is still going on in our day. It did not grow out of philosophy; the scientist has never cared very much for the philosopher's interpretation, and even David Hume's criticism left him unconcerned. Indifference to philosophy has turned out to be a wholesome attitude for the scientist, though perhaps only as a matter of good luck. Success is often with those who act rather than reflect about what they should do. The explanation of the nature of knowledge could not be given within the frame of the science of the eighteenth century; the conception of the nature of mathematics, the conception of the nature of causality, had to be revised before a theory of knowledge could be developed that accounts at the same time for the power of deductive methods in mathematical physics and for the use of the inductive inference. It was the good luck of the scientist, then, that he did not turn to the question of a justification of his methods before he had the means to answer it.

It will appear plausible that this answer was given in the frame of a theory of probability, though the form of this theory is very different from what might be expected. To say that observations of the past are certain, whereas predictions are merely probable, is not the ultimate answer to the question of induction; it is only a sort of intermediate answer, which is incomplete unless a theory of probability is developed that explains what we should mean by "probable" and on what ground we can assert probabilities. Empiricists, including Hume, have repeatedly studied the nature of probability; but they came to the result that probability is of a subjective nature and applies to opinion, or belief, which they distinguished from knowledge. The idea that there can be such a thing as probable knowledge would have appeared to them as a contradiction. In his contention that the inductive inference is no legitimate instrument of knowledge, Hume reveals himself as still being under the influence of rationalism; like the ancient skeptics, he can only prove the rationalist ideal of knowledge to be unattainable, but he cannot replace it by a better conception of knowledge. Hume might have been led to the discovery of an objective meaning of probability, had he studied the mathematics of probability, which at his time already included the work of Pascal, Fermat, and Jacob Bernoulli; that he never referred to this work shows that he was not mathematically minded and was not the man to exploit the mathematical theory of probability for philosophical purposes.

Though the logical analysis of probability is a necessary prerequisite for the clarification of predictive knowledge, a more radical change of philosophic interpretation is indispensable before the ultimate answer to the puzzles of empiricism can be given. We know today that predictive knowledge even cannot be proved to be probable, and that the idea of probable knowledge is subject to a criticism similar to the one raised by Hume for a knowledge that claims certainty. The problem of predictive knowledge, therefore, requires a reinterpretation of the nature of knowledge. It was not possible to develop this new conception of knowledge within Newtonian physics. The solution of the problem of induction had to wait for the new interpretation of knowledge which grew from the physics of the twentieth century.

6.

The Twofold Nature of Classical Physics: Its Empirical and Its Rational Aspect

S O FAR WE have spoken only about philosophy. Now let us examine the evolution of science during those twenty-five hundred years in which philosophers were developing the various forms of rationalism and empiricism.

The Greek contributions to science are practically all in the mathematical sciences. In particular, geometry was highly developed; the theorem which carries Pythagoras' name is one of the outstanding geometrical discoveries of the Greeks, matched only by their treatment of the *conic sections,* the curves known under the names of ellipse, hyperbola, and parabola. Their arithmetic did not possess the numerical technique which we apply so successfully today; the Greeks did not write their numbers in the decimal system, which notation is a later discovery of the Arabs, nor did they know logarithms, which were invented in the seventeenth century. In spite of these technical imperfections, the Greeks developed the foundations of the theory of numbers; they recognized the importance of the prime numbers and discovered the existence of irrational numbers, that is, numbers that cannot be written as the quotient of two integers. Their greatest contribution to mathematics is the axiomatic construction of geometry given by Euclid, one of the mathematicians of Greek descent who about 300 B.C. made Alexandria a center of Greek civilization. Euclid's system has always been regarded as an overwhelming demonstration of the power of deductive reasoning.

Greek success in the empirical sciences was limited to those sciences that admitted of the use of mathematical methods. Greek astronomy found its great synopsis in the system of Ptolemy, an Alexandrian of the second century of the Christian era. Making use of earlier results of astronomical observation and geometrical reasoning, Ptolemy proved that the earth is spherically shaped. However, he regarded it as certain that the earth did not move, but that the heavenly vault moved around it, carrying with it the stars and the sun and the moon. There were also movements along this vault; the sun and the moon were not fixed to a definite position among the stars but moved on circular paths of their own. The planets described curves of a strange shape, which Ptolemy recognized as being the result of two circular motions performed at the same time, like the path of a man sitting in a merry-go-round that is set up eccentrically on a larger merry-go-round. Ptolemy's astronomical system, also called the geocentric system, is still used today to answer all those astronomical questions which refer merely to the aspect of the stars as seen from the earth, in particular, questions of navigation. This practical applicability shows that there was a large measure of truth in Ptolemy's system.

The conception that the sun was at rest and the earth and the planets revolved around it was not unknown to the Greeks. Aristarchus of Samos proposed this heliocentric system about 200 B.C., but could not convince his contemporaries of its truth. The Greek astronomers could not follow Aristarchus because of the imperfect state of the science of mechanics in their time. For instance, Ptolemy argued against Aristarchus that the earth must be motionless because otherwise a stone falling down would not fall in a vertical line, and because birds in the air would remain behind the moving earth and come down on a different part of the earth's surface.

An experiment showing Ptolemy's argument to be fallacious was not made before the seventeenth century. The French abbé Gassendi, a contemporary and philosophic adversary of Descartes, made a test on a moving ship: he let a stone fall from the top of the mast and saw that it arrived exactly at the foot of the mast. If Ptolemy's mechanics had been true, the stone should have lagged behind the motion of the ship and should have reached the deck on a point farther toward the rear end of the ship. Gassendi thus confirmed Galileo's law, discovered shortly before, according to which the falling stone carries in itself the motion of the ship and retains it while falling.

Why did Ptolemy not make Gassendi's experiment? Because the idea of the scientific experiment, as distinguished from mere measurement and observation, was not familiar to the Greeks. An experiment is a question addressed to nature; by the use of suitable devices the scientist initiates a physical occurrence the outcome of which supplies the answer "yes" or "no" to the question. As long as we depend on the observation of occurrences not involving our assistance, the observable happenings are usually the product of so many factors that we cannot determine the contribution of each individual factor to the total result. The scientific experiment isolates the factors from each other; the interference of man creates conditions in which one factor is shown at work undisturbed by the others, thus revealing the mechanism of the complex occurrences that happen without man's interference. The falling of a leaf from a tree, for instance, is a complex occurrence in which the gravitational force competes with aerodynamic forces resulting from the flow of air under the sliding leaf, which moves down in a zigzag course. If, on the one hand, we exclude the air by letting the leaf fall in an evacuated space, we see that with respect to gravitation, its fall is the same as that of a stone. If, on the other hand, a current of air is blown through a wind tunnel against a fixed surface, it reveals the laws of the flow of air. By means of the artificial occurrences of planned experiments, the complex occurrence of nature is thus analyzed into its components. That is why the experiment has become the instrument of modern science. That Greek science did not use experiments in any significant way proves how difficult it was to turn from reasoning to empirical science.

We date modern science from the time of Copernicus (1472–1543) and Galileo (1564–1641). With the establishment of the heliocentric system, Copernicus laid the foundation of modern astronomy and, at the same time, gave the decisive turn to modern scientific thought, emancipating it from the anthropomorphisms of earlier periods. Galileo gave to modern science the quantitative experimental method. The experiments in which he established his law of falling bodies have determined the pattern of a method that combines the experiment with measurement and mathematical formulation. With Galileo, a generation of scientists went over to the use of experiments for scientific purposes. Yet this general turn toward experimental method can scarcely be regarded as the effect of one man's work. It is better explained as the result of a change in social conditions which freed the minds of the scientists from preoccupation with Greek science in the form of scholasticism and led naturally to an empirical science.

The birth of experimental science was attended by a wave of energy and interest that spread all over Europe. The telescope, invented by a Dutch lens grinder, was first directed at the heavens by Galileo in Italy. Another Italian, Toricelli, pupil of Galileo, invented the barometer and demonstrated that air exerts a pressure which diminishes as the altitude increases. In Germany, Guericke invented the air pump and exhibited to a startled public the power of atmospheric pressure by putting two hemispheres together which, after being exhausted of the air, could not be pulled apart by teams of horses. The English also were prominent in the new field. William Gilbert, physician to Queen Elizabeth, performed and published extensive studies of magnetism; Harvey discovered the circulation of the blood; and Boyle established the law of gas pressures and volumes that bears his name. Thus did observation and experiment create a whole new world of scientific facts and laws.

This brief selection of events introducing the development of modern science illustrates the reason why the modern age has produced empiricist systems comparable in influence to the great rationalist systems of the Greeks. The rationalism of the Greeks reflects the success of mathematical research in their civilization; British empiricism mirrors the triumph of the experimental method in modern science, the method that addresses questions to nature and leaves it to nature to answer "yes" or "no".

But there is another development that deserves explanation, and that is the revival of rationalist philosophy in continental Europe during the very period in which British philosophers were formulating the new doctrines of empiricism. It was during this time that Descartes, Leibniz, and Kant, though versed in science and themselves contributors to scientific fields, constructed new rationalistic systems superior in method and cogency to those of the ancients.

In order to understand this counterdevelopment it must be recalled that experimental method, however revolutionary its appearance on the scene turned out to be, is only one of the two major instruments of modern science. The other is the use of mathematical methods for the establishment of scientific explanation. In this respect, Greek science is continued in modern time; and it is more than a mere coincidence that the Copernican system, which we regard as the symbol of the modern scientific age, was anticipated in Aristarchus' heliocentric system. The power of mathematical method for the analysis of the physical world, which the Greeks had discovered in their astronomy, was confirmed in the development of modern science; but combined with the use of experiments as criteria of truth it was more than confirmed, it was multiplied so as to lead to successes of a higher order of magnitude. What made modern science powerful was the invention of the *hypothetico-deductive method,* the method that constructs an explanation in the form of a mathematical hypothesis from which the observed facts are deducible. Let us study this method, also called *explanatory induction,* in a prominent example.

Copernicus' discovery would never have found the universal assent of the learned world had it not been improved by the research of Johann Kepler (1571–1630) and finally been incorporated into a mathematical explanation through the work of Isaac Newton (1643–1727). Kepler, a mystically minded mathematician who set out with an elaborate mathematical plan to prove the supposed harmony of the universe, was clever enough to drop his original hypothesis about the motions of the planets when he saw that observations proved very different laws of planetary motion. As a result, he became the author of three famous laws of planetary motion, which reveal that the orbits of the planets are not circles, but ellipses. Kepler's discoveries were followed by a still greater achievement, the greatest of this entire period; namely, Newton's law of attraction between masses. This law, familiarly known as the *law of gravitation*, has the form of a rather simple mathematical equation. Logically speaking, it constitutes an hypothesis, which is not accessible to direct verification. It is established indirectly, since, as Newton showed, all the observational results summarized in Kepler's laws can be derived from it. And not only Kepler's results; from Newton's law, Galileo's law of falling bodies is likewise derivable, and so are many other observational facts, such as the phenomenon of the tides in their correlation to the positions of the moon.

Newton himself saw clearly that the truth of his law depended on confirmation through a verification of its implications. In order to derive these implications, he had invented a new mathematical method, the differential calculus; but all the brilliancy of this deductive achievement did not satisfy him. He wanted quantitative observational evidence and tested the implications through observations of the moon, whose monthly revolution constituted an instance of his law of gravitation. To his disappointment he found that the observational results disagreed with his calculations. Rather than set any theory, however beautiful, before the facts, Newton put the manuscript of his theory into his drawer. Some twenty years later, after new measurements of the circumference of the earth had been made by a French expedition, Newton saw that the figures on which he had based his test were false and that the improved figures agreed with his theoretical calculation. It was only after this test that he published his law.

The story of Newton is one of the most striking illustrations of the method of modern science. Observational data are the starting point of scientific method; but they do not exhaust it. They are supplemented by a mathematical explanation, which goes far beyond a statement of what has been observed; the explanation is then subjected to mathematical derivations which make explicit various implications contained in it, and these implications are tested by observations. It is these observations to which is left the "yes" or "no", and thus far the method is empirical. But what the observations confirm as true is much more than what is directly said by them. They vouch for an abstract mathematical explanation, that is, for a theory from which the observable facts are mathematically deducible. Newton had courage enough to venture the abstract explanation; but he had also prudence enough not to believe in it before an observational test had confirmed it.

In its further development, which extended through more than two centuries, Newton's theory received ever-renewed confirmations. It was possible through an ingenious experiment by Cavendish to test the gravitational attraction emanating from a ball of lead not more than a foot in diameter. The perturbations of planets in their orbits, caused by mutual gravitational attractions, were subsequently computed and verified by improved techniques of observation. Finally, the existence of a then unknown planet, Neptune, was predicted by the French mathematician Leverrier (and independently by the English astronomer Adams) on the basis of calculations that made the new planet responsible for certain observed disturbances of the other planets. When the German astronomer Galle directed his telescope to the spot of the night sky that had been figured out by Leverrier, he saw there a tiny speck that changed its position slightly from night to night, and the planet Neptune was discovered (1846).

The mathematical method has given modern physics its predictive power. Whoever speaks of empirical science should not forget that observation and experiment have been capable of building up modern science only because they were combined with mathematical deduction. Newton's physics differs greatly from the picture of inductive science that had been drafted two generations earlier by Francis Bacon. A mere collection of observational facts, such as presented in Bacon's tables, would never have led a scientist to the discovery of the law of attraction. Mathematical deduction in combination with observation is the instrument that accounts for the success of modern science.

The application of mathematical method has found its most conspicuous expression in the conception of causality that was developed as the result of classical physics, that is, of the physics of Newton. Since it was possible to express physical laws in the form of mathematical equations, it appeared as though physical necessity could be transformed into mathematical necessity. Consider, for instance, the law that the tides follow the position of the moon, so that one swell of the ocean is directed toward the moon, the other in the opposite direction, while the earth revolves below the swell and makes it slide over its surface. This is an observational fact. Through Newton's explanation this fact is shown to be the consequence of a mathematical law, the law of attraction, and the certainty of the mathematical law is thus transferred to physical phenomena. "The book of nature is written in mathematical language"—this utterance of Galileo has, in the following centuries, manifested its truth beyond any measure that Galileo could possibly have imagined. The laws of nature have the structure of mathematical laws, their necessity and universality; that was the result of a physics which predicted the existence of a new planet with such precision that an astronomer had only to look through his telescope to see it.

The mathematical law thus appeared as the instrument not only of order, but also of prediction; it endowed the physicist with the power to foresee the future. The simple generalization performed in the inductive inference by enumeration appeared a poor instrument if compared with the power of the hypothetico-deductive method. How could this power be explained? The answer seemed obvious: there must exist a strict order among all physical happenings which is portrayed by means of mathematical relations, an order expressed through the name of causality.

The idea of a strict causal determination of all occurrences of nature is the product of modern time. The Greeks found a mathematical order in the motions of the stars; but other physical occurrences were regarded by them as at most partly determined by causal laws. True, some Greek philosophers adhered to a general determinism; but we do not know to what extent their conception of causal determination corresponds to the modern one. None of them left us a clear formulation of what he understood by determinism, and it is unlikely that anyone thought of causality as a law without exceptions, controlling insignificant occurrences as well as the most important ones and making every event the necessary product of the preceding event, regardless of what these mean to human pursuit. The complete detachment of causality from human valuation could not be conceived in a time which did not know mathematical physics.

For the Greek mind, predetermination has a religious tinge and is expressed through the concept of fate rather than through that of cause. The origin of fatalism is anthropomorphic and explainable only through a naïve projection of human valuations and human forms of action into the course of nature. As men control physical happenings in the pursuit of their purposes, the gods control human affairs; and the god of fate has made his plan for every human being—that is the doctrine of Greek fatalism. We may try to escape our fate by many means; we shall then only fulfill our fate in other ways. It was Oedipus' fate to kill his father and to marry his mother, a fate unknown to him, but known through an oracle to his father, the king of Thebes. The attempt of the father to elude fate by abandoning the newborn son in the mountains was doomed to failure; the baby was brought up by foster parents. When as a young man Oedipus travels to Thebes he has an encounter with an unknown man whom he slays; and when he is successful in freeing the town from the terror of the sphinx whose riddle he solves, his reward is the marriage with the queen. Later, it is revealed to him that the man he slew was his father, and that the queen, his wife, is his mother. That is a myth which the psychoanalysis of Freud interprets as the reflection of a general subconscious desire, the son's hatred of his father and his sexual love for his mother. The idea of fate may then be psychologically explained as the reflection of the helplessness which we feel in the face of subconscious urges. That is a modern explanation, unknown to the Greeks; whatever we may think of it, we shall be ready to admit that predetermination through fate is a conception to be explained by psychology but not by logical analysis.

The determinism of modern science is of a very different nature. It developed from the success of mathematical method in physics. If it was possible to construe physical laws as mathematical relations, if deductive methods turned out to be the instruments of precise predictions, there must be a mathematical order behind the apparent irregularity of experiences; there must be a causal order. If we do not always know the order, if it seems impossible ever to know it completely, such failure is due to human imperfection. The French mathematician Laplace has summarized this view in his famous simile of a superhuman intelligence that could observe position and momentum of every atom and could solve all the mathematical equations; to this superman, "the future like the past would be present", and he would be able to state precisely the minute details of every occurrence, be it thousands of years ahead of us or behind us. This physical determinism was the most general outcome of Newtonian physics. It is intrinsically different from fate; it is blind, not planning; it does not favor or hate men; it is a determinism not in terms of future aims but of past facts, a determinism not in terms of a supernatural command but of a physical law. But it is as strict and exceptionless as the determinism of fate. It makes the physical world comparable to a wound clock that goes automatically through its stages.

If that is the picture of the world developed by classical physics, it is small wonder that the age of Newton presents us with a wave of rationalism as well as of empiricism. The empiricists analyzed only one side of science, its observational side; the rationalists emphasized its mathematical side. Empiricism finally broke down in Hume's criticism because it could not account for the predictive nature of science; it could not explain how we could ever know the strictly causal order of the world, of whose existence the scientist felt certain and which he claimed to know at least in its outlines. Rationalists believed themselves to be justified when they attacked the empiricist position and developed systems that were intended to explain the part mathematics plays in the construction of the physical world.

It is of particular interest that two of the great rationalists of the modern age, Leibniz and Kant, developed their systems, at least in part, as a defense against the criticism of the British empiricists. Leibniz answered Locke's *Essay Concerning Human Understanding* with his *New Essay on Human Understanding;* Kant reports that Hume "awakened him from his dogmatical slumber", and he wrote his *Critique of Pure Reason* with the intention of saving scientific knowledge from the annihilating consequences of Hume's criticism.

G. W. Leibniz (1646–1716) was a contemporary of Newton and his equal in intellectual rank. Independently of Newton he discovered the differential calculus and applied it to the solution of many mathematical problems. However, he was no adherent of Newton's theory of gravitation, of which he disapproved in spite of its empirical success because it led to an absolutism of motion. Leibniz developed a theory of space based on the idea of the relativity of motion, in which he anticipated the logical principles of Einstein's theory of relativity; he saw clearly that the Copernican system differs from Ptolemy's system only in that it is another mode of speech. That he did not arrive at a fair evaluation of Newton's physics proves that the rationalist in him did not submit to the empiricist criterion of truth; that he could not develop Einstein's physics cannot be held against him.

In Leibniz' philosophy the rational side of modern science has found its most radical representation. The successful use of mathematical methods for the description of nature made Leibniz believe that all science can be ultimately transformed into mathematics. The idea of determinism, of a universe that passes through its stages like a wound clock, appealed to him because it meant that physical laws are mathematical laws. He applied this idea in one of the strangest creations of rationalism, in his doctrine of preëstablished harmony. According to him, the minds of different persons do not interact with each other; the semblance of such interaction is produced because the different minds, in their predetermined courses, go continuously through stages strictly corresponding to each other, like different clocks that keep the same time without being causally connected. I mention this doctrine in order to show that the mathematical mysticism of Pythagoras has found counterparts in the philosophies of other great mathematicians.

The rationalism of Leibniz, though inspired by mathematical science, is speculation in the cloak of logical reasoning and abandons the solid ground from which modern science has grown—its basis in empirical observation. His disregard of the empirical component of knowledge led Leibniz to the belief that all knowledge is logic. Although he saw the analytic nature of deductive logic, he believed that logic cannot only supply but even replace empirical knowledge. There are truths of the factual kind, that is, empirical truths, and truths of reason, that is, analytic truths; this distinction, however, is only a consequence of human ignorance, and if we could have a perfect knowledge, as God has it, we would see that all that happens is logically necessary. For instance, God could deduce from the concept of Alexander that he was a king and conquered the Orient. This analytic interpretation of empirical knowledge is a rationalist blunder which has been repeatedly committed in the hope thus to explain mathematical physics. It may be that we can define a concept Alexander in such a way that all the history of the man follows analytically from it; but then we could never know from pure logic whether the observable individual Alexander is correctly identified by that concept. In other words, the statement that the observable individual has the properties expressed in the concept would be synthetic and subject to all the quandaries of empirical knowledge. There is no way of evading the problems of empiricism by taking refuge in analytic logic.

Leibniz had never seen a system of radical empiricism; when he died, Hume was five years old. We know his criticism of Locke, in which he refuses to recognize Locke's principle that all concepts are derived from sense perception; the concepts that involve necessity, he argues, are innate in us. This argument is of little interest today, since the central problem of empiricism is now seen to be, not Locke's principle of the empirical origin of concepts, but Hume's principle that experience is the only judge of the truth of synthetic statements, which leads to the consequence that predictions are not justifiable. It would be more interesting, therefore, if we knew what Leibniz would have answered to Hume. Presumably Leibniz would have admitted Hume's principle of induction but would have regarded it as limited to the use of humans; the problem of induction, he would have said, does not exist for God. That is no answer, not even if the word "God" is used as a synonym for "the perfect logician", since Leibniz' thesis of a reduction of empirical knowledge to analytic knowledge cannot be accepted. The rationalism of an analytic a priori cannot solve Hume's problem. There is not much likelihood, however, that David Hume's incisive critique would have changed the opinions of Leibniz, who was too deeply affected by the search for certainty to overcome the illusions of rationalism.

The answer of rationalism to Hume was given by Kant, who was only thirteen years younger than Hume but whose major publications did not appear before Hume's death. I have explained Kant's philosophy of the synthetic a priori in Chapter 3; it is the merit of this philosophy that it steers clear of Leibniz' incomprehensible claim of having reduced knowledge about the world to analytic knowledge. Let us see, then, how the rationalism of a synthetic a priori attempts to answer Hume.

According to Kant, the principle of causality is synthetic a priori. He contends we know for certain that every occurrence has a cause; only the finding of the individual cause is left to observation. Let me use an illustration which Kant could have used: when we see the tides of the ocean in their periodic rhythm, we know from pure reason that this occurrence has a cause. What observation in combination with inductive inferences teaches us is merely the fact that in this case the cause is given by the position of the moon. The inductive inference, therefore, is restricted to finding the individual physical laws, but is not employed for the establishment of the general truths of physics, such as the principle of causality, which are imposed upon us by reason. Since we know for certain that there is a cause, induction is justified as the instrument of finding it—with this argument Kant believes he has overcome Hume's criticism of induction. The certainty of the synthetic a priori takes over where the empiricist resigns in skepticism: that is the essence of Kant's philosophy.

It is hard to see how Kant could regard this theory as an awakening from dogmatical slumber. Kant's argument does not answer Hume's question. Had Hume

6. TWOFOLD NATURE OF PHYSICS

lived to read the *Critique of Pure Reason,* he might have answered Kant: "How does it help us to know there is a cause if we wish to know what the cause is? It is true, if we knew there were no cause it would be nonsensical to search for one; but that is not our situation. We do not know whether there is a cause; in this situation we make inductive inferences, based on observation, and conclude, say, that the moon is the cause of the tides. This inductive inference is what I question; and it would remain just as questionable if you could prove the general statement that there is a cause. Incidentally, your proof of the general principle is inacceptable to me".

Let me amplify this imaginary defense of Hume by an illustration. Assume someone is looking for gold in Peru, but does not know at what place he should dig. You tell him: Yes, there is gold in Peru. Would that help him? He is no better off than before; what he wants to know is whether the spot he is digging on will provide the gold. He cannot dig on every spot in Peru. If he knew that there is gold within a certain small area of the land, he could proceed by trying square foot by square foot and would find the gold after a certain number of trials. But Peru is too large to admit of exhaustive trials, and therefore knowledge of mere existence of gold is useless. If you told him that there is no gold in Peru, this information would be valuable for him and induce him to stop digging; but telling him that there is gold in Peru helps him just as much as telling him that you do not know whether there is gold in Peru.

I should like to make this criticism of Kant more precise. Kant always emphasized that he was looking for the logical presuppositions of knowledge, distinguishing them from psychological presuppositions. "There can be no doubt that all our knowledge begins with experience . . . but it does not follow that all of it is derived from experience"—with these words he introduces the *Critique of Pure Reason*. Applied to the problem of causality, his argument would mean that we develop the notion of cause by finding particular causes, but that the knowledge of the general principle of causality is not logically derived from experiences. This principle, Kant argues, is the logical presupposition of every particular causal law; therefore it must be assumed true if we want to find such particular causal laws.

The term "logical presupposition" means a logical relationship; it means: if the particular causal law is true, then the general causal law is true. Now this statement requires a qualification. In order for causality to hold for one kind of occurrence, it need not hold for other kinds of occurrence. All that can be said is: if the particular causal law is true, then there exists a cause in this case. Only in this restricted form can an implication be set up. Therefore, the logical presupposition of any particular causal law is not the general principle of causality, but a corresponding principle stated merely for the occurrence under investigation.

It must be asked what can be derived from this restricted implication. If you have found the particular cause, then there is a cause for this occurrence—from this implication, Kant believes, one can derive the conclusion: if you search for the particular cause, say, the cause of the tides, you have to assume that there is a cause. Otherwise, Kant maintains, it would be unreasonable even to look for a cause.

This argument is fallacious. If we seek for a particular cause, we need not assume that there is one. We can leave this question open, like the question of what is the cause. Only if we knew that there is no cause would it be unreasonable to seek for a particular cause. But if nothing is known about there being a cause, we can search at the same time for the particular cause and for the answer to the question whether there is one. We know, if we succeed in finding a particular cause, we have proved that there is a cause for the case considered. This trivialism is all that remains of Kant's argument. The truth of the statement about the particular cause presupposes the truth of the statement about there being a cause—but the *search* for the truth of the first does not presuppose the truth of the second.

This analysis settles at the same time the question of the general principle of causality, according to which all occurrences have causes. A statement of this sweeping generality is certainly not the logical presupposition of the particular causal law under investigation. It would come in only when causal laws for all occurrences were investigated. Extending the previous results to this general case, the following statement can be made: if causal laws had been found for all occurrences, then all occurrences would have causes; but the *search* for all these causal laws does not presuppose the assumption that all occurrences have causal laws. The latter question may be left open and will be answered when the search has been successful in all cases.

Kant's program of finding a synthetic a priori by uncovering the logical presuppositions of knowledge thus breaks down. The fact that they are the presuppositions of scientific knowledge does not validate them. If we want to know whether they are true, we would first have to prove that scientific knowledge is true. The truth of the presuppositions is therefore no better established than that of scientific knowledge. This simple logical analysis shows that Kant's philosophy of the synthetic a priori is untenable.

The rationalist interpretation of classical physics did not solve the problems raised by the empiricist interpretation; that is the result of all this discussion. The mathematical precision of physics must not make us believe that deductive methods could account for all the thought operations involved in the construction of this science. In addition to deduction, the physicist depends on the use of induction, since he starts with observations and foretells further observations. The prediction of future observations is both his goal and the test of the truth of his hypotheses. Constructing an intricate network of deductive and inductive inferences, classical physics had developed predictive methods to a high degree of efficiency; but neither the physicist nor the philosopher could supply the answer to the question why we should trust these methods in the application to further predictions.

With the end of the eighteenth century, the philosophy of physics had arrived at a deadlock. The overwhelming system of knowledge which the human mind had created remained incomprehensible. This frank admission of the empiricist Hume appears superior to the claim of the rationalist Kant that the foundations of physics are a product of reason.

The physicists themselves did not notice this philosophical deadlock. They went on making observations and constructing theories, and marched from success to success, until they, too, arrived at a deadlock. From this physical deadlock sprang a new physics in the course of which eventually the philosophical deadlock was also overcome. These developments may be presented in a report on the nineteenth and twentieth century.

PART TWO

The Results of Scientific Philosophy

7.

The Origin of the New Philosophy

I N THE face of error we can ask only for a psychological explanation; truth calls for logical analysis. The history of speculative philosophy is the story of the errors of men who asked questions they were unable to answer; the answers which they nonetheless gave can be explained only from psychological motives. The history of scientific philosophy is the story of the development of problems. Problems are solved not through vague generalities, or picturesque descriptions of the relation between man and the world, but through technical work. Such work is done in the sciences, and in fact, the development of problems must be traced through the history of the individual sciences. Philosophical systems, at best, have reflected the stage of scientific knowledge of their day; but they have not contributed to the development of science. The logical development of problems is the work of the scientist; his technical analysis, though often directed toward minor details and seldom conducted for philosophical purposes, has furthered the understanding of the problem until, eventually, the technical knowledge was complete enough to allow for the answer to philosophical questions.

Scientific work is group work; the contributions of

individual men to the solution of a problem may be smaller or larger, but will always be small compared to the amount of work invested in the problem by the group. There are great mathematicians, physicists, and biologists; but even the greatest among them would have been unable to do their work without the preparation by preceding generations or the help of their contemporaries. The amount of technical work involved in the solution of a problem goes beyond the capacities of an individual scientist. That is true not only for the cumbersome work of observational and experimental research, but also for the logical and mathematical construction of a theory. The social character of scientific work is the source of its strength; the limited power of the individual is supplemented by the resources of the group, the slips of the individual are corrected by his fellow workers, and the resultant of the contributions of the many intelligent individuals is a sort of superpersonal group intelligence, which is able to discover answers that a single individual could never find.

These considerations may explain why the second part of my book follows a plan different from that of the first. The chapters of the first part were centered around the psychological sources of error; those of the second deal with problems. In order to be historically complete, I therefore would have to trace the lines of development back to antiquity. But it turns out that for the purposes of this book a short survey of ancient times suffices; the essential developments which concern the philosopher begin with the nineteenth century.

The history of nineteenth-century science offers the philosopher perspectives of an enormous reach. The abundance of technical discoveries is matched by a wealth of logical analysis; and on the ground of the new science there arose a new philosophy. This new philosophy began as a by-product of scientific research. The mathematician, the physicist, or the biologist, who wanted to solve the technical problems of his science, saw himself unable to find a solution unless he first could answer certain more general, philosophical questions. It was his advantage that he could look for these philosophical answers unburdened by preoccupation with a philosophical system. He could find, for every problem, an answer in its own right. He was not concerned with the task of combining answers into a neat philosophical system. He did not mind whether his results were derivable from some general doctrine sanctioned by a name recorded in the history of philosophy. And thus, carried along by the logic of the problems, he found answers unheard of in the history of philosophy.

It is the plan of this book to collect these results and to present them with all their interconnections. With the synopsis of scientific answers to philosophic questions, a new philosophy is outlined, a philosophic system not in the sense of a speculative creation of a fanciful mind, but in the meaning of an ordered totality attainable only as the product of group-work.

The nineteenth century has often been the target of the contempt of the historian. Writers for whom the great personality of an individual, the genius, constitutes the aim of historic developments, who measure the significance of a period by a scale gauged in numbers of masterminds, have spoken disparagingly of a century whose cultural aspect is not determined by its poets, or painters, or philosophers. Compared with the Renaissance, or the periods of the literary classics in England, France, and Germany, the century of science and industry offers the colorless picture of a civilization striving toward uniformity and mechanization. Mass production instead of creation by the artist or craftsman; mass satisfaction instead of the standards of taste of an intellectual nobility; mental group-work instead of the creative work of the individual thinker—those are the labels which the romantic interpretation of history has in stock for the nineteenth century.

But the history of the age of science and industry will never be understood by the romanticist. The intellectual achievements of the nineteenth century cannot be measured in terms of great personalities—although there are such personalities—because the contribution of an individual, outstanding as it may be, is small compared with the group product. The number of scientific discoveries through group-work during this period is overwhelming. The period that began with the steam engine and the discovery of the electric current, that went on by way of the railroad, the electric generator, the radio, the airplane, and that in our day has culminated in supersonic speed of transportation and the tapping of atomic energy—this period is not only a triumphal march of industrial discoveries. It represents, at the same time, a line of rapid progress of the powers of abstract thought. It has led to purely theoretical constructions of highest perfection, such as Darwin's theory of evolution or Einstein's theory of relativity; it has trained the human mind in the understanding of logical relationships which would have appeared incomprehensible to the educated man of earlier centuries.

The development of the power of abstraction is the necessary concomitant of an industrial civilization. The engineer who designs machines or airplanes is not identical with the man in the workshop who makes the machine, or the airplane; for him, his product exists completely in his imagination, materialized only in the form of a blueprint, before it can become concrete reality. The physicist who experiments in his laboratory has before him a maze of wires, glass tubes, and metal bars; but into this maze he sees an order of electric circuits, which makes him control his manual operations in such a way that observations result which reveal general laws of nature. The mathematician, equipped with writing paper and fountain pen, arrives at figures which determine the construction of bridges or airplanes or skyscrapers. Never in the history of mankind has a civilization demanded so intensive an intellectual training from those who work for it.

The philosophy of the nineteenth century is the product of such power of abstraction. It does not offer the persuasive solutions of systems that talk picture language and appeal to aesthetic desires. It presents answers understandable only to a mind trained in abstract thought; it requires that its disciples study every item with the precision of the engineer and the scrutiny of the mathematician. But to those who are willing to submit to these requirements it offers the reward of an intellectual insight of amazing proportions. It answers the questions which the founders of the great philosophical schools could not answer; often, though, it has first to rephrase the question in such a way as to render it capable of an answer. It shows the world in which we live to be of a much more complicated structure than that which the classical philosopher took for granted. And it has developed methods for dealing with such structures and for making the world comprehensible to human understanding.

The textbooks of philosophy usually include a chapter on the philosophy of the nineteenth century written in the same vein as those about the preceding centuries. This chapter mentions names like Fichte, Schelling, Hegel, Schopenhauer, Spencer, and Bergson, and records their systems as though they were philosophical creations in line with the systems of earlier periods. But the philosophy of the systems ends with Kant, and it is a misunderstanding of the history of philosophy to discuss the later systems on a level with those of Kant or Plato. Those older systems were expressive of the science of their time and gave pseudo answers when no better answers were available. The philosophical systems of the nineteenth century were constructed at a time when a better philosophy was in the making; they are the work of men who did not see the philosophic discoveries immanent in the science of their time and who developed, under the name of philosophy, systems of naïve generalizations and analogies. Sometimes it was the persuasive language of their presentations, sometimes the pseudoscientific dryness of their style, which impressed their readers and contributed to their fame. Yet considered historically, these systems would better be compared to the dead end of a river that after flowing through fertile lands finally dries out in the desert.

The history of philosophy, which up to the time of Kant manifested itself in the form of philosophical systems, should be regarded as continued after Kant not by the pseudosystems of the imitators of a great past, but by the new philosophy that grew out of the science of the nineteenth century and was continued in the twentieth century. Within the short period of its existence, this philosophy has undergone a rapid development, paced by the progress of science during the same period. In particular, the results evolving from Einstein's theory of relativity and Planck's quantum theory fall entirely into the twentieth century, which therefore offers a philosophical aspect differing greatly from that of the nineteenth century. The revolution of scientific thought, for which the science of the twentieth century is so often praised, is, however, a natural consequence of developments begun in the nineteenth century and should rather be called a rapid evolution.

Just as the new philosophy originated as a by-product of scientific research, the men who made it were hardly philosophers in the professional sense. They were mathematicians, physicists, biologists, or psychologists. Their philosophy resulted from the attempts to find solutions to problems encountered in scientific research, problems which defied the technical means thus far employed and called for a reëxamination of the foundations and the goals of knowledge. Rarely was such philosophy detailed or explicit, nor was it extended beyond the confines of the fields of their maker's particular interests. Instead, the philosophy of these men lurks in the prefaces and introductions of their books and in occasional remarks inserted in otherwise purely technical expositions.

It was not until our generation that a new class of philosophers arose, who were trained in the technique of the sciences, including mathematics, and who concentrated on philosophical analysis. These men saw that a new distribution of work was indispensable, that scientific research does not leave a man time enough to do the work of logical analysis, and that conversely logical analysis demands a concentration which does not leave time for scientific work—a concentration which because of its aiming at clarification rather than discovery may even impede scientific productivity. The professional philosopher of science is the product of this development.

The philosopher of the traditional school has often refused to recognize the analysis of science as a philosophy and continues to identify philosophy with the invention of philosophical systems. He does not realize that philosophical systems have lost their significance and that their function has been taken over by the philosophy of science. The scientific philosopher is not afraid of such antagonism. He leaves it to the old-style philosopher to invent philosophical systems, for which there still may be a place assignable in the philosophical museum called the history of philosophy—and goes to work.

8.

The Nature of Geometry

EVER SINCE the death of Kant in 1804 science has gone through a development, gradual at first and rapidly increasing in tempo, in which it abandoned all absolute truths and preconceived ideas. The principles which Kant had considered to be indispensable to science and nonanalytic in their nature have been recognized as holding only to a limited degree. Important laws of classical physics were found to apply only to phenomena occurring in our ordinary environment. For astronomical and for submicroscopic dimensions they had to be replaced by laws of the new physics, and this fact alone makes it obvious that they were empirical laws and not laws forced on us by reason itself. Let me illustrate this *disintegration of the synthetic a priori* by tracing the development of geometry.

The historical origin of geometry, which goes back to the Egyptians, supplies one of the many instances in which intellectual discoveries have grown from material needs. The annual floods of the Nile which fertilized the soil of Egypt brought trouble to landowners: the borderlines of their estates were destroyed every year and had to be reëstablished by means of geometrical measurements. The geographical and social conditions of their country, therefore, compelled the Egyptians to invent the art of surveying. Geometry thus arose as an empirical science, whose laws were the results of observations. For instance, the Egyptians knew from practical experience that if they made a triangle the sides of which were respectively 3, 4, and 5 units long it would be a right triangle. The deductive proof for this result was provided much later by Pythagoras, whose famous theorem explains the Egyptian findings by the fact that the sum of the squares of 3 and 4 is equal to the square of 5.

Pythagoras' theorem illustrates the contribution which the Greeks made to geometry: the discovery that geometry can be built up as a deductive system, in which every theorem is strictly derivable from the set of axioms (see p. 96). The construction of geometry in the form of an axiomatic system is forever connected with the name of Euclid. His logically ordered presentation of geometry has remained the program of every course in geometry and was used until recently as a text in our schools.

The axioms of Euclid's system appeared so natural and obvious that their truth seemed unquestionable. In this respect, Euclid's system confirmed earlier conceptions, developed before the principles of geometry acquired the form of an ordered system. Plato, who lived a generation before Euclid, was led by the apparent self-evidence of geometrical principles to his theory of ideas; and it was explained in Chapter 2 that the axioms of geometry were regarded by him as revealed to us through an act of vision, which showed geometrical relations as properties of ideal objects. The long line of development beginning with Plato, which did not essentially change this conception, terminated in the more precise though less poetical theory of Kant, according to which the axioms were synthetic a priori. Mathematicians more or less shared these views, but they were not so much interested in the philosophical discussion of the axioms as in the analysis of the mathematical relations holding between them. They tried to reduce the axioms to a minimum by showing some of them to be derivable from the others.

There was in particular one axiom, the axiom of parallels, which they disliked and attempted to eliminate. The axiom states that through a given point one and only one parallel can be drawn with respect to a given line; that is, there is one and only one line that does not ultimately intersect with a given line and yet lies in the same plane. We do not know why the mathematicians disliked this axiom, but we know of many attempts, dating back to antiquity, that were made with the intention of transforming this axiom into a theorem, that is, of deriving it from the other axioms. Mathematicians repeatedly believed that they had found a way of deriving the proposition about parallels from the other axioms. Invariably, however, these proofs have later been demonstrated to be fallacious. The mathematicians had unknowingly introduced some assumption which was not included in the other axioms but was of equal efficacy as the axiom of the parallels. The result of this development was, then, that there are equivalents of this axiom. But the mathematician had no more reason to accept these equivalents than to accept Euclid's axiom. For instance, an equivalent of the axiom of the parallels is the principle that the sum of the angles of a triangle is equal to two right angles. Euclid had derived this principle from his axiom, but it was shown that conversely the principle of the parallels is derivable when the principle of the angular sum is assumed as an axiom. What is an axiom in one system, thus becomes a theorem in another system, and vice versa.

The problem of parallels had occupied mathematicians for more than two thousand years before it found its solution. About twenty years after the death of Kant, a young Hungarian mathematician, John Bolyai (1802–

1860), discovered that the axiom of parallels is not a necessary constituent of a geometry. He constructed a geometry in which the axiom of parallels was abandoned and replaced by the novel assumption that there exists more than one parallel to a given line through a given point. The same discovery was made about the same time by the Russian mathematician N. I. Lobachevski (1793–1856) and by the German mathematician K. F. Gauss (1777–1855). The geometries so constructed were called *non-Euclidean geometries*. A more general form of a non-Euclidean geometry, which includes systems in which there exist no parallel lines at all, was later developed by the German mathematician B. Riemann (1826–1866).

A non-Euclidean geometry contradicts Euclidean geometry—for instance, in a non-Euclidean triangle the sum of the angles is different from 180 degrees. Still, each non-Euclidean geometry is free from internal contradictions; it is a consistent system in the same sense that Euclid's geometry is consistent. A plurality of geometries thus replaces the unique system of Euclid. It is true that the Euclidean geometry is distinguished from all others by the fact that it is easily accessible to a visual presentation, whereas it seems impossible to visualize a geometry in which there is more than one parallel to a given line through a given point. But the mathematicians were not very much concerned about questions of visualization and regarded various geometrical systems as being of equal mathematical validity. In keeping with this somewhat detached attitude of the mathematician, I shall postpone the discussion of visualization until I have discussed some other problems.

The existence of a plurality of geometries demanded a new approach to the problem of the geometry of the physical world. As long as there was only one geometry, the Euclidean geometry, there was no question of the geometry of physical space. In the absence of an alternative, Euclid's geometry was naturally assumed to apply to physical reality. It was Kant's merit to emphasize more than others that the coincidence of mathematical and physical geometry calls for an explanation, and his theory of the synthetic a priori must be regarded as the great attempt of a philosopher to account for this coincidence. With the discovery of a plurality of geometries the situation changed completely. If the mathematician was offered a choice between geometries, there arose the question which of them was the geometry of the physical world. It was obvious that reason could not answer this question, that its answer was left to empirical observation.

The first to draw this conclusion was Gauss. After his discovery of non-Euclidean geometry he attempted to carry through an empirical test by means of which the geometry of the physical world was to be ascertained. For this purpose, Gauss measured the angles of a triangle the corners of which were marked by three mountain tops. The result of his measurements was carefully worded: it said that within the errors of observation the Euclidean principle was true, or in other words, that if there was a deviation of the angular sum from 180 degrees, the inevitable errors of the observation made it impossible to prove its existence. If the world was non-Euclidean, it was controlled by a non-Euclidean geometry so slightly different from the Euclidean that discrimination between the two was impossible.

But Gauss' measurement requires some discussion. The problem of the geometry of physical space is more complicated than Gauss assumed and cannot be answered in so simple a way.

Assume for a moment that Gauss' result had been positive and that the angular sum of the triangle he measured had been different from 180 degrees. Would it follow that the geometry of the world is non-Euclidean?

There is a way to evade this consequence. Measuring angles between two distant objects is done by sighting the objects through lenses attached to a sextant or a similar instrument. Thus the light rays traveling from the objects to the sight device are used as defining the sides of the triangle. How do we know that the light rays move along straight lines? It would be possible to maintain that they do not, that their path is curved, and that Gauss' measurement did not refer to a triangle whose sides were straight lines. On this assumption the measurement was not conclusive.

Is there a way to test the new assumption? A straight line is the shortest distance between two points. If the path of the light ray is curved, it must be possible to connect the starting point with the end point by another line, which is shorter than the path of the light ray. Such a measurement could be made, in principle at least, with the help of measuring rods. The rods would have to be carried along the path of the light ray and then along several other lines of connection. If there is a shorter line of connection, it would thus be found by repeated trials.

Suppose that the test was carried through and it was negative, that is, we found the path of the light ray to be the shortest connection between the two points. Would this result, in combination with the previous measurement of the angular sum, prove the geometry to be Euclidean?

It is easily seen that the situation is as inconclusive as before. We questioned the behavior of light rays and checked it through measurements with solid rods. We now can question the behavior of the solid rods. The measurement of a distance is reliable only if the rod does not change its length while it is transported. We might assume that the rod transported along the path of the light ray was expanded by some unknown force; then the number of rods that can be deposited along the path is made smaller, and the numerical value found for the distance would be too small. We thus would believe the path of the light ray to be shorter than other paths, whereas in reality it is longer. Testing whether a line is the shortest distance thus depends on the behavior of measuring rods. How can we test whether a solid rod is really solid, that is, does not expand or contract?

We transport a solid rod from one place to a distant point. Is it still as long as before? In order to test its length we would have to employ a second rod. Assume that at the first place the two rods have equal length when one is put on top of the other; then one is transported to a different place. Do the two rods still have equal length? We cannot answer this question. In order to compare the rods, we should have either to transport the one rod back to the first place, or the other rod to the second place, since a comparison of length is possible only when one rod is on top of the other. In such a way we would find that they have equal length, too, when they are both at the second place. But there is no way of knowing whether two rods are equal when they are in different places.

The objection might be raised that there are other means of comparison. For instance, if a rod changes its length on transportation, we should discover the change if we compared the rod with the length of our arms. To eliminate this objection let us assume that the forces contracting or expanding transported bodies are universal, that is, that all physical objects, including human bodies, change their length in the same way. It is obvious that then no change would be observable.

The problem under consideration is the problem of congruence. It must be realized that there is no means of testing congruence. Suppose that during the night all physical objects, including our own bodies, became ten times as large. On awakening this morning we should be in no condition to test this assumption. In fact, we shall never be able to find it out. The consequences of such change are, in accordance with the conditions laid down, unobservable, and hence we can collect no evidence either for or against it. Perhaps we all are ten times as tall today as we were yesterday.

There is only one way to escape such ambiguities: to regard the question of congruence not as a matter of observation, but of definition. We must not say "the two rods located at different places *are* equal", but we must say that we *call* these two rods equal. The transportation of solid rods defines congruence. This interpretation eliminates the unreasonable problems mentioned. It no longer makes sense to ask whether today we are ten times as tall as we were yesterday; we *call* our height of today equal to that of yesterday, and it has no meaning to ask whether it really is the same height. Definitions of this kind are called *coördinative definitions*. They coördinate a physical object, a solid rod, to the concept "equal length" and thus specify its denotation; this peculiarity explains the name.

Statements about the geometry of the physical world, therefore, have a meaning only after a coördinative definition of congruence is set up. If we change the coördinative definition of congruence, a different geometry will result. This fact is called the *relativity of geometry*. To illustrate the meaning of this result, assume again that Gauss' measurement had proved a deviation of the angular sum from 180 degrees and that measurements with solid rods had confirmed light rays to be the shortest distance: still there would be nothing to prevent us from regarding the geometry of our space as Euclidean. We then would say that the light rays are curved and the rods expanded; and we could figure out the amount of these distortions in such a way that the "corrected" congruence leads to a Euclidean geometry. The distortions may be regarded as the effect of forces which vary from place to place, but are alike for all bodies and light rays and thus are *universal forces*. The assumption of such forces means merely a change in the coördinative definition of congruence. This consideration shows that there is not just one geometrical description of the physical world, but that there exists a class of *equivalent descriptions;* each of these descriptions is true, and apparent differences between them concern, not their content, but only the languages in which they are formulated.

On first sight this result looks like a confirmation of Kant's theory of space. If every geometry can be applied to the physical world, it seems as though geometry does not express a property of the physical world and is merely a subjective addition by the human observer, who in this way establishes an order among the objects of his perception. Neo-Kantians have used this argument in defense of their philosophy; and it was used in a philosophical conception called *conventionalism,* introduced by the French mathematician Henri Poincaré, according to whom geometry is a matter of convention and there is no meaning in a statement which purports to describe the geometry of the physical world.

Closer investigation shows the argument to be untenable. Although every geometrical system can be used to describe the structure of the physical world, the geometrical system taken alone does not describe the structure completely. The description will be complete only if it includes a statement about the behavior of solid bodies and light rays. When we call two descriptions equivalent, or equally true, we refer to complete descriptions, in this sense. Among the equivalent descriptions, there will be one, and only one, in which solid bodies and light rays are not called "deformed" through universal forces. For this description I shall employ the name *normal system*. The question can now be asked which geometry leads to the normal system; and this geometry may be called the *natural geometry*. Obviously, the question as to the natural geometry, that is, the geometry for which solid bodies and light rays are not deformed, can be answered only through empirical investigation. In this sense the question of the geometry of physical space is an empirical question.

The empirical meaning of geometry can be illustrated by reference to other relative concepts. If a New Yorker says "Fifth Avenue is to the left of Fourth Avenue", this statement is neither true nor false unless he specifies the direction from which he looks at these streets. Only the complete statement "Fifth Avenue is to the left of Fourth Avenue seen from the South" is verifiable; and it is equivalent to the statement "Fifth Avenue is to the right of Fourth Avenue seen from the North". Relative concepts like "to the left of" or "to the right of" thus can very well be used in the formulation of empirical knowledge but care must be taken that the formulation includes the point of reference. In the same sense, geometry is a relative concept. We can speak about the geometry of the physical world only after a coördinative definition of congruence has been given. But on that condition an empirical statement about the geometry of the physical world can be made. When we speak about physical geometry, it is therefore understood that some coördinative definition of congruence has been laid down.

Poincaré was right if he wanted to say that the choice of one from the class of equivalent descriptions is a matter of convention. But he was mistaken if he believed that the determination of natural geometry, in the sense defined, is a matter of convention. This geometry can only be ascertained empirically. It seems Poincaré believed erroneously that the "solid" rod and thus congruence can be defined only by the requirement that the resulting geometry must be Euclidean. Thus he argued that if measurements on triangles should lead to an angular sum different from 180 degrees, the physicist *must* introduce corrections for the paths of light rays and the lengths of solid rods because otherwise he could not say what he meant by equal length. But Poincaré overlooked the fact that such a requirement might compel the physicist to assume universal forces,* and that vice versa the definition of congruence can be given by the requirement that universal forces are to be excluded. By the use of this definition of congruence an empirical statement about geometry can be made.

I should like to explain my criticism of Poincaré more fully, because recently Professor Einstein has undertaken a witty defense of conventionalism by depicting an imaginary conversation between Poincaré and me.† Since I believe that there can be no differences of opinion between mathematical philosophers if only opinions are clearly stated, I wish to state my conception in such a way that it might convince, if not Poincaré, yet Professor Einstein, for whose scientific work I certainly have as much admiration as he has so charmingly expressed for the work of Poincaré.

---

* The rule always to use Euclidean geometry for the ordering of geometrical observations can even lead to further complications, namely, to certain violations of the principle of causality. This will be the case if the space of physics is topologically different from Euclid's space, for instance, if it is finite. In such cases, at least one of Kant's a priori principles, either Euclidean geometry or causality, has to be abandoned. See the author's *Philosophie der Raum-Zeit-Lehre* (Berlin, 1928), p. 82.

† In P. A. Schilpp, *Albert Einstein, Philosopher-Scientist,* Evanston, 1949, pp. 677–679.

Assume that empirical observations are compatible with the following two descriptions:

CLASS I

(a) The geometry is Euclidean, but there are universal forces distorting light rays and measuring rods.

(b) The geometry is non-Euclidean, and there are no universal forces.

Poincaré is right when he argues that each of these descriptions can be assumed as true, and that it would be erroneous to discriminate between them. They are merely different languages describing the same state of affairs.

Now assume that in a different world, or in a different part of our world, empirical observations were made which are compatible with the following two descriptions:

CLASS II

(a) The geometry is Euclidean, and there are no universal forces.

(b) The geometry is non-Euclidean, but there are universal forces distorting light rays and measuring rods.

Once more Poincaré is right when he argues that these two descriptions are both true; they are equivalent descriptions.

But Poincaré would be mistaken if he were to argue that the two worlds I and II were the same. They are objectively different. Although for each world there is a class of equivalent descriptions, the different *classes* are not of equal truth value. Only one class can be true for a given kind of world; which class it is, only empirical observation can tell. Conventionalism sees only the equivalence of the descriptions within one class, but stops short of recognizing the differences between the classes. The theory of equivalent descriptions, however, enables us

136

to describe the world objectively by assigning empirical truth to only one class of descriptions, although within each class all descriptions are of equal truth value.

Instead of using classes of descriptions, it is convenient to single out, in each class, one description as the *normal system* and use it as a representative of the whole class. In this sense, we can select the description for which universal forces vanish as the normal system, calling it *natural geometry*. Incidentally, we cannot even prove that there must be a normal system; that in our world there is one, and only one, must be regarded as an empirical fact. (For instance, it might happen that the geometry of light rays differs from that of solid bodies.)

The theory of equivalent descriptions thus does not rule out an empirical meaning of geometry; it merely demands that we state the geometrical structure of the physical world by the addition of certain qualifications, namely, in the form of a statement about the natural geometry. In this sense Gauss' experiment presents important empirical evidence. The natural geometry of the space of our environment, within the exactness accessible to us, is Euclidean; or in other words, the solid bodies and light rays of our environment behave according to the laws of Euclid. If Gauss' experiment had led to a different result, if it had revealed a measurable deviation from Euclidean relations, the natural geometry of our terrestrial environment would be different. In order to carry through a Euclidean geometry we then would have had to resort to the assumption of universal forces that distort light rays and transported bodies in a peculiar way. That the natural geometry of the world of our environment is Euclidean must be regarded as a fortunate empirical fact.

These formulations allow us to state the additions which Einstein made with respect to the problem of space. From his general theory of relativity he derived the conclusion that in astronomic dimensions the natural geometry of space is non-Euclidean. This result does not contradict Gauss' measurement according to which the geometry of terrestrial dimensions is Euclidean, because it is a general property of a non-Euclidean geometry that for small areas it is practically identical with the Euclidean geometry. Terrestrial dimensions are small as compared with astronomic dimensions. We are unable to observe the deviations from Euclidean geometry through terrestrial observations, because within these dimensions the deviations are too small. Gauss' measurement would have to be made with an exactness many thousands of times greater, in order to prove a deviation of the angular sum from 180 degrees. But such exactness is far beyond our reach and will presumably forever remain so. Only for larger triangles would the non-Euclidean character become measurable, since the angular deviation from 180 degrees grows with the size of the triangle. If we could measure the angles of a triangle whose corners were represented by three fixed stars, or better, by three galaxies, we would actually observe that the angular sum is more than 180 degrees. We shall have to wait for the establishment of cosmic travel before such a direct test can be made, since we would have to visit each of the three stars separately in order to be able to measure the three angles. So we have to be satisfied by the use of indirect methods of inference, which even in the present status of our knowledge indicate that stellar geometry is non-Euclidean.

There is a further addition made by Einstein. According to his conception the cause of the deviation from Euclidean geometry is to be found in the gravitational forces originating from the masses of the stars. In the neighborhood of a star the deviations are stronger than in interstellar space. Einstein has thus established a relation between geometry and gravitation. This amazing discovery, which was confirmed by measurements made during an eclipse of the sun and which had never before been anticipated, demonstrates anew the empirical character of physical space.

Space is not a form of order by means of which the human observer constructs his world—it is a system formulating the relations of order holding between transported solid bodies and light rays and thus expressing a very general feature of the physical world, which constitutes the basis for all other physical measurements. Space is not subjective, but real—that is the outcome of the development of modern mathematics and physics. Strangely enough, this long historical line leads ultimately back to the position held at its beginning: geometry began as an empirical science with the Egyptians, was made a deductive science by the Greeks, and finally was turned back into an empirical science after logical analysis of highest perfection had uncovered a plurality of geometries, one and only one of which is the geometry of the physical world.

This consideration shows that we have to distinguish between mathematical and physical geometry. Mathematically speaking, there exist many geometrical systems. Each of them is logically consistent, and that is all a mathematician can ask. He is interested not in the truth of the axioms, but in the implications between axioms and theorems: "if the axioms are true, then the theorem is true"—of this form are the geometrical statements made by the mathematician. But these implications are analytic; they are validated by deductive logic. The geometry of the mathematician is therefore of an analytic nature. Only when the implications are broken up, and axioms and theorems are asserted separately, does geom-

etry lead to synthetic statements. The axioms then require an interpretation through coördinative definitions
and thus become statements about physical objects; and
geometry is thus made a system which is descriptive of the
physical world. In that meaning, however, it is not a
priori, but of an empirical nature. There is no synthetic
a priori of geometry: either geometry is a priori, and then
it is mathematical geometry and analytic—or geometry
is synthetic, and then it is physical geometry and empirical. The evolution of geometry culminates in the disintegration of the synthetic a priori.

One question remains to be answered, the question of
visualization. How can we ever visualize non-Euclidean
relations in the way we can see the Euclidean relations?
It may be true that by means of mathematical formulas
we are able to deal with non-Euclidean geometries; but
will they ever be as presentative as the Euclidean geometry, that is, will we be able to see their rules in our imagination in the way we see the Euclidean rules?

The foregoing analysis enables us to answer this question satisfactorily. Euclidean geometry is the geometry
of our physical environment; no wonder that our visual
conceptions have become adjusted to this environment
and thus follow Euclidean rules. Should we ever live in
an environment whose geometrical structure is noticeably different from Euclidean geometry, we would get
adjusted to the new environment and learn to see non-
Euclidean triangles and laws in the same way that we
now see Euclidean structures. We would find it natural
that the angles in a triangle add up to more than 180 degrees and would learn to estimate distances in terms of
the congruence defined by the solid bodies of that world.
To imagine geometrical relations visually means to imagine the experiences which we would have if we lived
in a world where those relations hold. It was the physicist

Helmholtz who gave this explanation of visualization. The philosopher had committed the mistake of regarding as a vision of ideas, or as laws of reason, what is actually the product of habit. It took more than two thousand years to uncover this fact; without the work of the mathematician and all its technicalities we would never have been able to break away from established habits and free our minds from alleged laws of reason.

The historical development of the problem of geometry is a striking illustration of the philosophical potentialities contained in the development of science. The philosopher who claimed to have uncovered the laws of reason rendered a bad service to the theory of knowledge: what he regarded as laws of reason was actually a conditioning of human imagination by the physical structure of the environment in which human beings live. The power of reason must be sought not in rules that reason dictates to our imagination, but in the ability to free ourselves from any kind of rules to which we have been conditioned through experience and tradition. It would never have been possible to overcome the compulsion of established habits by philosophical reflection alone. The versatility of the human mind could not become manifest before the scientist had shown ways of handling structures different from those for which an age-old tradition had trained our minds. On the path to philosophical insight the scientist is the trail blazer.

The philosophical aspect of geometry has at all times reflected itself in the basic trend of philosophy, and thus philosophy has been strongly influenced in its historical development by that of geometry. Philosophic rationalism, from Plato to Kant, had insisted that all knowledge should be constructed after the pattern of geometry. The rationalist philosopher had built up his argument on an interpretation of geometry which, for more than two thousand years, had remained unquestioned: on the conception that geometry is both a product of reason and descriptive of the physical world. Empiricist philosophers had fought in vain against this argument; the rationalist had the mathematician on his side, and the battle against his logic appeared hopeless. With the discovery of non-Euclidean geometries the situation was reversed. The mathematician discovered that what he could prove was merely the system of mathematical implications, of *if-then* relations leading from the axioms of geometry to its theorems. He no longer felt entitled to assert the axioms as true, and he left this assertion to the physicist. Mathematical geometry was thus reduced to analytic truth, and the synthetic part of geometry was surrendered to empirical science. The rationalist philosopher had lost his most powerful ally, and the path was free for empiricism.

Had these mathematical developments begun some two thousand years earlier, the history of philosophy would present a different picture. In fact, one of Euclid's disciples might very well have been a Bolyai and might have discovered the non-Euclidean geometry; the elements of this geometry can be developed with rather simple means of the kind available in Euclid's era. After all, the heliocentric system was discovered in that time, and Greek-Roman civilization had developed forms of abstract thought that rank with those of modern times. Such a mathematical development would have greatly changed the systems of the philosophers. Plato's doctrine of ideas would have been abandoned as lacking its basis in geometrical knowledge. The skeptics would have had no inducement to be more skeptical toward empirical knowledge than toward geometry and might have found the courage to teach a positive empiricism. The Middle Ages would have found no consistent rationalism which could be incorporated into theology. Spinoza would not have written his *Ethics Presented after the Geometrical Method,* and Kant would not have written his *Critique of Pure Reason.*

Or am I too optimistic? Can error be weeded out by teaching the truth? The psychological motives which led to philosophic rationalism are so strong that one might well assume they would have found other forms of expression. They might have pounced upon other productions of the mathematician and turned them into alleged evidence for a rationalist interpretation of the world. In fact, since Bolyai's discovery, more than a hundred years have passed and rationalism has not died out. Truth is not a sufficient weapon to outlaw error—or rather, the intellectual recognition of truth does not always endow the human mind with the strength to resist the deep-rooted emotional appeal of the search for certainty.

But truth is a powerful weapon, and it has at all times collected followers among the best. There is good evidence that the circle of its followers is growing larger and larger. And perhaps that is all that can be hoped for.

9.

What Is Time?

TIME IS one of the most conspicuous characteristics of human experience. Our senses present
us their perceptions in the order of time;
through them we participate in the general
flow of time that passes through the universe, producing
event after event and leaving its products behind itself,
crystallizations of some fluid entity that was future and
now is unalterable past. We are placed in the center of
the flow, called the present; but what now is the present
slides into the past, while we move along to a new present,
forever remaining in the eternal now. We cannot stop the
flow, we cannot reverse it and make the past come back;
it carries us along relentlessly and does not grant us a
delay.

The mathematician who attempts to translate this
psychological description of time into the language of
mathematical equations finds himself confronted by no
easy task. No wonder that he begins by simplifying his
problem. He omits the emotional parts of the description, concentrates his attention on the objective structure
of the time relation, and hopes thus to arrive at a logical
construction which can account for all we know about
time. What we feel about it should, then, be explainable
as the reaction of an emotional organism to a physical
structure of those characteristics.

Such a procedure might disappoint the poetically

minded reader. But philosophy is not poetry. It is the clarification of meanings through logical analysis; and picture language has no place in it.

The first thing to interest the mathematician is the *metric* of time. We conceive of time as proceeding by a *uniform* flow, independent of the subjective speed which we observe and which varies with the emotional attention we pay to the content of our experience. Uniformity means the existence of a metric, that is, of a measure of equality. We compare consecutive time intervals and have means to tell when they are of equal length. What are these means?

We control the watches we carry by comparison with standard clocks; these clocks, in turn, are controlled by the astronomer. The astronomer controls his clocks by reference to the stars. Since the motion of the stars is the mirror image of the rotation of the earth, it is the rotating earth which we employ as our standard clock. How do we know that the rotating earth is a reliable clock, that is, that it records a strictly uniform time?

When we ask the astronomer how he knows this fact, he tells us that we must be very careful in employing the earth-clock. If we measure the day from one upper transit (crossing of the meridian) of the sun to the next, that is, from one noon to the next noon, we do not arrive at a uniform time. This kind of time, solar time, is not quite uniform because the revolution of the earth around the sun follows an elliptical orbit. To avoid the resulting error, the astronomer measures the rotation of the earth in periods defined by the upper transit of some fixed star. This kind of time, called sidereal time, is free from the irregularities caused by the revolution of the earth, because the fixed stars are so very far away that the direction from the earth to a distant fixed star practically does not change.

How does the astronomer know that sidereal time is really uniform? When we ask him, he will answer that, strictly speaking, even sidereal time is not quite uniform, because the axis of the rotation of the earth does not remain oriented in one direction, but precesses, that is, pendulates slightly in a way reminiscent of the swaying motion of a spinning top. (The precession is a very slow motion, however, since it takes about 25,000 years to complete one turn.) What the astronomer calls uniform time is therefore something not directly observable; he has to figure it out by means of his mathematical equations, and his results will appear in the form of certain corrections he adds to the observed figures. Uniform time, then, is some time-flow which the astronomer projects into the observable data by reference to mathematical equations.

There is but one question left. How does the astronomer know that his equations determine a strictly uniform time? The astronomer may answer that his equations express laws of mechanics and that they are valid because they are derived from the observation of nature. But in order to test these laws of observation we must possess a reference time, that is, a uniform time in terms of which we find out whether a certain motion is uniform, else we have no means to tell whether the laws of mechanics are true. We arrive at a circular reasoning. In order to know the uniform time we have to know the laws of mechanics, and in order to know the laws of mechanics we have to know the uniform time.

There is only one way to escape a circularity of this kind, namely, to regard the question of uniform time not as a matter of cognition, but of definition. We must not ask whether it is *true* that the time of the astronomer is uniform; we must say that astronomic time *defines* uniform time. There is no really uniform time; we call a certain flow of time uniform in order to have a standard to which we can refer other kinds of time flow.

This analysis solves the problem of the metric of time in the same way that we solved above the problem of the measure of space. Spatial congruence, we said, is a matter of definition; similarly we say now that temporal congruence is a matter of definition. We cannot directly compare two consecutive time intervals; we can only *call* them equal. What the equations of mechanics supply is merely a coördinative definition of uniform time. This result entails a relativity of time; any definition of uniformity can be used, and the resulting descriptions of nature, though verbally different, will represent equivalent descriptions. They are merely different languages; their content is the same.

Instead of employing the apparent rotations of stars for the definition of the metric of time, we can also use other natural watches, such as rotating atoms or traveling light rays. It is a matter of fact that all these time metrics coincide. Here is the source of the practical significance of the astronomic definition of uniformity; it supplies a definition which is identical with the one supplied by all natural watches. For the metric of time the natural watch thus takes over a role similar to the role played by the solid body for the metric of space.

From the problem of the *metric* of time I turn to the consideration of a second problem that concerns the mathematician. It is the problem of the *order* of time. Even more fundamental than the question of the measure of time is the question of temporal sequence, of the *earlier* and *later,* or of time order. How can we tell that one event is earlier than another? If we possess a watch, its uniform time flow includes a statement of time order; but the relation of time order should be accessible to a definition independent of the metric of time. For the various possible metrics of time, time order should be the same, and it must therefore be possible to define temporal sequence otherwise than by reference to the figures on watches.

A short survey of the methods by which we judge time order shows that one fundamental criterion of temporal sequence is always required. The cause must precede the effect; therefore, if one event is known to be the cause of another event, the first must be earlier than the second. For instance, if a detective discovers at a hidden spot a golden treasure wrapped in a newspaper, he knows that the wrapping of the treasure was not done before the date printed on the paper, since the printing of the paper was the cause that produced this copy of the newspaper. The relation of time order, therefore, is reducible to the relation of cause and effect.

We need not study at this place the cause-effect relation, which will concern us in a later chapter. Suffice it to say that causal connection expresses an *if-then* relation, testable through repeated occurrence of events of the same type. What we have to explain, however, is how to distinguish the cause from the effect. It would not help us to say that the cause is the earlier one of the two connected events, since we wish to define time order in terms of causal order; we must therefore be in possession of an independent criterion distinguishing the cause from the effect.

A study of simple instances of the causal relation shows us that there exist natural processes which clearly differentiate between the cause and the effect. Of this kind are processes of mixture and similar processes that proceed from an ordered state to a state of disorder. The physicist speaks of *irreversible* processes. Imagine you have in your hands a film taken with a motion picture camera and want to know which way it should be reeled. You see on one frame a cup of coffee with cream and an empty pitcher beside it, on another one, not far away from the first, the same cup filled with black coffee and the pitcher filled with cream beside it. Then you know that the second frame was taken before the other one, and you know which way to reel the film. We can mix coffee and cream, but we cannot unmix it. Or if one observer tells you he saw the burnt-out ruins of a house and another observer informs you that he saw the house undestroyed, you know the second observation was earlier than the first. The process of burning is irreversible, and the possibility that the house was rebuilt in the same shape may be excluded by the fact that we know the time interval between the two observations to be not longer than a few days. The relation between irreversibility and time order is well illustrated by the series of pictures which we see when a motion picture is run in reverse. The strange aspect of cigarettes becoming longer and longer while they burn, or of pieces of broken pottery that rise from the floor to the table and assemble into neat dishes and cups, is evidence of the fact that we judge about time order in terms of irreversible physical processes. (A closer study of irreversibility will be given in Chapter 10.)

The fact that the relation of causality establishes a serial order of physical events constitutes one of the fundamental features of the world in which we live. We must not believe that the existence of this serial order is logically necessary; we could imagine a world in which causality does not lead to a consistent order of *earlier* and *later*. In such a world the past and the future would not be irrevocably separated, but could come together in the same present, and we could meet our former selves of several years ago and talk to them. It is an empirical fact that our world is not of this type but admits of a consistent order in terms of a serial relation based on causal relationship and called time. Time order reflects the causal order of the universe.

The definition of time sequence has a counterpart in the definition of *simultaneity*. We call two events simultaneous if neither of them is earlier or later than the other. The problem of simultaneity leads into peculiar consequences, when events at distant places are compared, a problem that has acquired fame through Einstein's analysis.

When we wish to know the time of a distant event, we use a signal that transmits to us the message of the occurrence of the event. But since the signal takes time for traveling along its path, the moment of the arrival of the signal at our place is not identical with the time of the event we wish to ascertain. This fact is familiar from the use of sound signals. When we hear the thunder, several seconds have passed since it originated in a distant cloud. The light ray produced by the flash of lightning travels much faster, so that the moment of the aspect of the flash can be identified, for all practical purposes, with the time when the flash occurred in the cloud. For a more precise measurement, however, the time determination of the flash of lightning is of the same type as the time determination of the thunder stroke, and we would have to include in our consideration the time which it takes the light ray to travel from the cloud to our eyes.

The time of the transmission of the light could be easily figured out, if we knew the speed of light and the distance traveled. The problem is how to measure the speed of light. In order to measure a speed we have to send a light ray from one point to a distant point, observe the time of the departure and the time of the arrival, and thus ascertain the time of the transmission. Dividing this time into the length of the traveled path, we obtain the speed. But for the measurements of the time of the departure and the time of the arrival we need two watches, since these measurements occur at different space points. These watches must be set to each other, or synchronized, that is, they must show equal readings at equal times. That means we must be able to determine simultaneity at distant points. Our considerations have led us in a circle: we wanted to measure simultaneity and found that we have to know the speed of light for this measurement, and we saw that in order to measure the speed of light we have to know simultaneity.

It would be a way out if we could measure the speed of light by the use of one watch alone. For instance, instead of measuring the time of arrival of the light signal at the distant point, we might reflect the light ray by a mirror, so that it goes back to the first point. The time interval used for the round trip then might be measured by one watch alone. In order to determine the speed of light we would have to divide the time of the round trip into the double amount of the distance. Promising as this method appears at first sight, it reveals its inadequacy at closer inspection. How do we know that the light ray travels on the way back at the same speed that it traveled on the way forth? Unless we know this equality, the figure obtained for the speed makes no sense. But in order to compare the speeds on the two ways we would have to measure the speed for each way separately. Such a measurement requires two watches, and we thus arrive at the same difficulty as before.

The attempt might be made to ascertain simultaneity by the transport of watches. Two watches are set to each other and show the same reading as long as they both remain at the same space point; then one watch is transported to the distant point. But how do we know that the transported watch remains synchronized during the transportation? In order to test the synchronism of the watches we would have to use light signals and thus arrive at the same problem as before. Transporting the second watch back to the first space point would not help us, because we thus would obtain a result only for the case that the two watches are close to each other. This problem resembles that of the comparison of measuring rods at different points, discussed above.

Incidentally, the problem of transported watches is even more complicated than that of transported measuring rods; according to Einstein the transported watch after its round trip would be slow, if compared with the watch that remained all the time at its place. This result has important logical consequences. It applies to all kinds of watches, including atoms, which indicate the period of their rotation in the color of the light radiation emitted by them; and experiments with rapidly moving atoms have confirmed the delay in rotation predicted by Einstein. As living organisms are built up of atoms, any delay in atomic occurrences must express itself in a delay of the process of aging to which the organism is subjected. It follows that living persons traveling at great speed would be delayed in their aging process and that, for instance, if one of two twins goes on a cosmic trip, he would be younger than the other after his return (though he, too, would be older than he was when he left). This conclusion follows with unquestionable logic from Einstein's well-confirmed theory.

Returning to the problem of simultaneity, we come to the result that transported watches cannot be used for the definition of the relation "taking place at the same time". We have to look for suitable signals to achieve this definition. As light signals, though very fast, have a limited speed, it would help us if we had faster signals than light at our disposal. When we wish to measure the speed of sound, we can use light signals for the comparison of time, because the speed of light is so much greater than that of sound; the error thus committed is numerically so small that it can be neglected. Similarly, if we had a signal a million times faster than light, we could measure the speed of light with sufficient exactness by disregarding the time of transmission for the faster signal. Now this is another point where Einstein's physics differs from classical physics. According to Einstein there can be no faster signal than light. This does not only mean that no faster signal is known to us; for Einstein, the statement that light is the fastest signal is a law of nature, which may be called the principle of *the limiting character of the speed of light.* Einstein has adduced conclusive evidence for the principle, and we have as little reason to question it as we have to question the principle of the conservation of energy.

In combination with the previous analysis of the meaning of temporal sequence, Einstein's principle leads to strange consequences concerning simultaneity. Suppose a light signal is sent at 12 o'clock to the planet Mars and reflected from there; it will return, say after twenty minutes. What time should we assign to the moment of the arrival of the signal at the planet Mars? Putting this time equal to 12:10 means assuming equality of the speed of light for both ways; but we saw that we have no reason to assume this equality. In fact, any time of the interval between 12:00 and 12:20 can be assigned to the moment of the arrival of the light signal at Mars. We could, for instance, say that the signal arrived at 12:05; it then makes the first way in five minutes and the way back in fifteen minutes. What our definition of time sequence excludes is to say that the light arrived at the Mars station at 11:55, because on this time assignment the signal would arrive before the time of its departure, and the effect would be earlier than the cause. But as long as we select for the time of arrival at Mars a figure of the interval from 12:00 to 12:20, the definition of time order remains satisfied. Any event of this time interval, happening at our own location, is excluded from causal interaction with the event at Mars specified by the arrival of the light signal. Because simultaneity means the exclusion of possible causal interaction, any event of this time interval at our place may be called simultaneous with the arrival of the light signal at Mars. This is what Einstein calls the relativity of simultaneity.

We see that the causal definition of time order leads to an indeterminacy with respect to the temporal comparison of events at distant points. It does so because of the limiting character of the speed of light. Absolute time, that is, unambiguous simultaneity, would exist in a world in which there were no upper limit for the speed of signals. But because in our world the speed of causal transmission is limited, there is no absolute simultaneity. The *causal theory of time* explains the meaning of temporal sequence and of simultaneity in such a way that the explanation is applicable to the world of classical physics as well as to our world, in which the speed of causal transmission is subject to an upper limit and simultaneity is not unambiguously defined.

With these results the problem of time finds a solution similar to that of space. Time, like space, is not an ideal entity of a Platonic existence perceived by an act of vision, or a subjective form of order imposed upon the world by the human observer, as Kant believed. The human mind is capable of conceiving of different systems of time order, among which classical time is one system and Einstein's time, with its limitation of the speed of causal transmission, is another. Among this plurality of possible systems, the selection of the time order that holds for our world is an empirical matter. Time order formulates a general property of the universe in which we live; time is real in the sense space is real, and our knowledge of time is not a priori, but the result of observation. The determination of the actual structure of time is a chapter of physics—this is the result of the philosophy of time.

Surprising as the relativity of simultaneity may appear, it is logical and accessible to visualization. The strangeness of Einstein's conceptions would disappear in a world in which the restrictions of causal transmission would become more evident. If some day a radio-telephone connection with Mars is established and we have to wait twenty minutes for a reply to any question asked over the telephone, we shall get accustomed to the relativity of simultaneity and regard it as quite natural—just as, today, we regard as quite in order the different standard times of the time zones into which the surface of this globe is divided. And if some day interplanetary travel is instituted, it will appear familiar to us that persons returning from long trips have been delayed in their process of aging and have remained behind the age of other persons, who originally were of the same age. Results which the scientist finds through abstract reasoning and which at first acquaintance require the abandonment of traditional beliefs often become familiar habits for later generations.

Scientific analysis has led to an interpretation of time very different from the experience of time in everyday life. What we feel as the flow of time has been revealed to be identical with the causal process that constitutes this world. The structure of this causal flux has been discovered as being of a much more complicated nature than is exhibited by the time presented in direct observation—until some day with the conquest of interplanetary distances the time of everyday life will have become as complicated as that of the theoretical science of today. It is true that science abstracts from emotional content in order to proceed to logical analysis. But it is also true that science opens up new possibilities, which some day might acquaint us with emotions never experienced before.

10.

The Laws of Nature

THE IDEA OF causality has stood in the foreground of every theory of knowledge of modern times. The fact that nature lends itself to a description in terms of causal laws suggests the conception that reason controls the happenings of nature; and the foregoing presentation of the influence which Newton's mechanics had on philosophical systems (chap. 6) makes it evident that the concept of a synthetic a priori has its roots in a deterministic interpretation of the physical world. Since the physics of an era deeply influences its theory of knowledge, it will be necessary to study the development which the concept of causality underwent in the physics of the nineteenth and twentieth centuries—a development which led to a revision of the idea of laws of nature and terminated in a new philosophy of causality.

The exposition of this historical process will be greatly facilitated if it is preceded by an analysis of the meaning of causality. These considerations may be attached to the inquiry into the meaning of explanation (given above in chap. 2), according to which explanation is generalization. Since explanation is reduction to causes, the causal relation is to be given the same interpretation. In fact, by a causal law the scientist understands a relation of the form *if-then,* with the addition that the same relation holds at all times. To say that the electric current causes a deflection of the magnetic needle means that whenever there is an electric current there is always a deflection of the magnetic needle. The addition in terms of *always* distinguishes the causal law from a chance coincidence. It once happened that while the screen of a motion picture theater showed the blasting of lumber, a slight earthquake shook the theater. The spectators had a momentary feeling that the explosion on the screen caused the shaking of the theater. When we refuse to accept this interpretation, we refer to the fact that the observed coincidence was not repeatable.

Since repetition is all that distinguishes the causal law from a mere coincidence, the meaning of causal relation consists in the statement of an exceptionless repetition—it is unnecessary to assume that it means more. The idea that a cause is connected with its effect by a sort of hidden string, that the effect is forced to follow the cause, is anthropomorphic in its origin and is dispensable; *if-then always* is all that is meant by a causal relation. If the theater would always shake when an explosion is visible on the screen, then there would be a causal relationship. We do not mean anything else when we speak of causality.

True, we sometimes do not stop with the assertion of an exceptionless coincidence, but look for further explanation. Pressing a certain button always is accompanied by a ringing of a bell—this regular coincidence is explained by the laws of electricity, which reveal the ringing of the bell to be a consequence of the relations between electric current and magnetism. But if we proceed to a formulation of these laws, we find that they, in turn, consist in the statement of an *if-then always* relation. The superiority of the laws of nature over simple regularities of the push-button type consists merely in their greater generality. They formulate relations which are manifested in various individual applications of very different kinds. The laws of electricity, for instance, state relations of permanent coincidences observable in push-button bells, electric motors, radios, and cyclotrons.

The interpretation of causality in terms of generality, clearly formulated in the writings of David Hume, is now generally accepted by the scientist. Laws of nature are for him statements of an exceptionless repetition—not more. This analysis not only clarifies the meaning of causality; it also opens the path for an extension of causality which has turned out to be indispensable for the understanding of modern science.

The laws of statistics, originally observed for the results of games of chance, were soon discovered also to apply to many other domains. The first social statistics were compiled in the seventeenth century; the nineteenth century brought the introduction of statistical considerations into physics. The kinetic theory of gases, according to which a gas consists of a great many little particles, called molecules, which swarm in all directions, collide with each other, and describe zigzag paths at an enormous speed, was constructed by the help of statistical computations. The statistical method arrived at its greatest triumph when it succeeded in explaining the phenomena of *irreversibility,* which characterize all thermic processes and which are so closely connected with the direction of time.

Everybody knows that heat flows from the hotter body to the colder one, and not vice versa. When we throw an ice cube into a glass of water, the water becomes colder, its heat wandering into the ice and dissolving it. This fact cannot be derived from the law of the conservation of energy. The ice cube is not so very cold and it still contains a great amount of heat; so it might very well give off part of its heat to the surrounding water and make it warmer, the ice itself becoming colder. Such a process would be in agreement with the law of the conservation of energy, if the amount of heat given off by the ice equals the amount received by the water. The fact that a process of this kind does not happen, that heat energy moves only in one direction, must be formulated as an independent law; it is this law which we call the law of irreversibility. The physicist often calls it the second principle of thermodynamics, reserving the name of the first principle to the law of the conservation of energy.

The wording of the principle of irreversibility must be very carefully given. It is not true that heat always flows from the higher temperature to the lower one. Every refrigerator is an example to the contrary. The machine pumps heat from the interior of the ice box to the outside, thus making the interior cooler and the surroundings warmer. But it can do so only because it uses up a certain amount of mechanical energy supplied by the electric motor; this energy is transformed into heat of the average temperature of the room. The physicist has shown that the amount of mechanical energy transformed into heat is greater than the amount of heat energy withdrawn from the interior of the refrigerator. If we regard heat of a higher temperature, or mechanical or electric energy, as an energy of a higher level, there is more energy going down than going up in the refrigerator. The principle of irreversibility is to be formulated as a statement that if all processes involved are included in the consideration, the total energy goes down, so that on the whole there is a tendency to compensation.

It was the discovery of the Vienna physicist Boltzmann that the principle of irreversibility is explainable through statistical considerations. The amount of heat in a body is given by the motion of its molecules; the greater the average speed of the molecule, the higher the temperature. It must be realized that this statement refers only to the average speed of the molecule; the individual molecules may have very different speeds. If a hot body comes into contact with a cold body, their molecules will collide. It may occasionally happen that a slow molecule hitting a fast one loses all its speed and makes the fast molecule even faster. But that is the exception; on the average there will be an equalization of the speeds through the collisions. The irreversibility of heat processes is thus explained as a phenomenon of mixture, comparable to the shuffling of cards, or the mixing of gases and liquids.

Though this explanation makes the law of irreversibility appear plausible, it also leads to an unexpected and serious consequence. It deprives the law of its strictness and makes it a law of probability. When we shuffle cards, we cannot call it impossible that our shuffling will eventually lead to an arrangement in which the first half of the deck contains all the red cards and the second half all the black ones; to arrive at such an arrangement must merely be called very improbable. All statistical laws are of this type. They supply a high probability for unordered arrangements, and leave only a low probability for ordered arrangements. The larger the number involved, the smaller the probability of the ordered arrangements; but this probability will never become zero. The phenomena of thermodynamics refer to very large numbers of individual occurrences, since the number of molecules is very large, and therefore involve extremely high probabilities for processes going in the direction of a compensation. But a process going in the opposite direction cannot strictly be called impossible. For instance, we cannot exclude the possibility that some day the molecules of the air in our room, by pure chance, arrive at an ordered state such that the molecules of oxygen are assembled on one side of the room and those of nitrogen on the other.

161

Unpleasant as the prospect of sitting on the nitrogen side of the room may be, the possibility of such an occurrence cannot be absolutely excluded. Similarly, the physicist cannot exclude the possibility that, when you put an ice cube into a glass of water, the water starts boiling and the ice cube gets as cold as the interior of a deep-freezing cabinet. It may be a consolation to know that this probability is much lower than the probability of a fire breaking out at the same time in each house of a city by independent causes.

Whereas the practical consequences of the statistical interpretation of the law of irreversibility are insignificant because of the low probabilities for processes in the contrary direction, the theoretical consequences are of greatest significance. What was before a strict law of nature has been revealed as being merely a statistical law; the certainty of the law of nature has been replaced by a high probability. With this result the theory of causality entered into a new stage. The question arose whether the same fate might befall other laws of nature, and whether there would remain any strict causal laws.

The discussion of the problem led to two opposite conceptions. According to the first conception the use of statistical laws merely represents an expression of ignorance: if the physicist were able to observe and calculate the individual motion of every molecule, he would not have to resort to statistical laws and would give a strictly causal account of thermodynamic processes. Laplace's superman could do so; for him the path of every molecule would be foreseeable like the path of the stars, and he would not need any statistical laws. This conception does not abandon the idea of a strict causality; it merely regards causality as inaccessible to human knowledge, which by reason of its imperfection has to resort to probability laws.

10. THE LAWS OF NATURE

The second conception represents the opposite point of view. It does not adhere to the belief in a strict causality of the motion of the individual molecule. It advances the opinion that what we observe as a causal law of nature is always the product of a great number of atomic occurrences; the idea of a strict causality may therefore be conceived as an idealization of the regularities of the macroscopic environment in which we live, as a simplification into which we are led because the great number of elementary processes involved makes us regard as a strict law what actually is a statistical law. According to this conception we are not entitled to transfer the idea of strict causality to the microscopic domain. We have no reason to assume that molecules are controlled by strict laws; equal initial situations of a molecule might be followed by different future situations, and even Laplace's superman could not predict the path of a molecule.

The issue is whether causality is an ultimate principle or merely a substitute for statistical regularity, applicable to the macroscopic domain but inadmissible for the realm of the atoms. On the basis of the physics of the nineteenth century the question could not be answered. It was the physics of the twentieth century, with its analysis of atomic occurrences in terms of Planck's concept of the quantum, that gave the answer. From the investigations of modern quantum mechanics we know that the individual atomic occurrences do not lend themselves to a causal interpretation and are merely controlled by probability laws. This result, formulated in Heisenberg's famous principle of indeterminacy, constitutes the proof that the second conception is the correct one, that the idea of a strict causality is to be abandoned, and that the laws of probability take over the place once occupied by the law of causality.

If the logical analysis of causality, as set forth at the beginning of this chapter, is kept in mind, this result will appear as a natural extension of the older views. Causality was to be formulated as a law of exceptionless generality, as an *if-then always* relation. Probability laws are laws that have exceptions, but exceptions that occur in a regular percentage of instances. The probability law is an *if-then in a certain percentage* relation. Modern logic offers the means of dealing with such a relation, which in contradistinction to the *implication* of usual logic is called a *probability implication*. The causal structure of the physical world is replaced by a probability structure, and the understanding of the physical world presupposes the elaboration of a theory of probability.

It should be realized that even without the results of quantum mechanics, the analysis of causality shows that probability notions are indispensable. In classical physics the causal law is an idealization, and the actual occurrences are more complex than is assumed for the causal description. When a physicist calculates the trajectory of a bullet fired by a gun, he figures it out in terms of some major factors, such as the powder charge and the inclination of the barrel; but because he cannot take into account all the minor factors, like the direction of the wind and the moisture of the air, his calculation is limited in its exactness. That means he can predict the point where the bullet will hit only with a certain probability. Or if an engineer constructs a bridge, he can predict its capacity only with a certain probability; circumstances may occur which he did not anticipate and which make the bridge break down under a smaller load. The law of causality, even if true, holds only for ideal objects; the actual objects we deal with are controllable only within the limits of a certain high probability because we cannot exhaustively describe their causal structure. The significance of the probability concept was seen for such reasons before the discoveries of quantum mechanics. After these discoveries it is even more obvious that no philosopher can evade the concept of probability, if he wants to understand the structure of knowledge.

The philosophy of rationalism has at all times referred to causality for a demonstration of the rational character of this world. Spinoza's conception of a predetermined universe is unthinkable without a belief in causality. Leibniz' idea of a logical necessity, acting behind physical occurrences, is dependent on the assumption of a causal connection of all phenomena. Kant's theory of a synthetic a priori knowledge of nature quotes, in addition to the laws of space and time, the principle of causality as the foremost instance of such knowledge. Like the development of the problems of space and time, that of the principle of causality has led, ever since the death of Kant, to a disintegration of the synthetic a priori. The foundations of rationalism were shaken by the very discipline that had supplied—with its mathematical interpretation of nature—the rationalist's major support. The empiricist of modern times derives his most conclusive arguments from mathematical physics.

11.

Are There Atoms?

THAT MATTER consists of small particles, called atoms, is regarded as an established fact by the educated man of our day. If he has not learned it in school the newspapers have told him so. It seems evident that because there exist atom bombs there must also exist atoms.

The historian of science would display a more critical attitude. He knows that the existence of the atom has been contended since ancient times, but that it has always been controversial and that strong arguments have been adduced both in favor of the atom and against it. If his history of science includes the last twenty-five years, he knows, too, that although during the nineteenth century the theory of the atom had reached a stage at which the existence of the atom appeared unquestionable, recent developments have renewed the controversy and have made the existence of the atom more questionable than ever.

We date the theory of the atom from the philosophy of Democritus (420 B.C.), one of the prominent figures of Greek philosophy. Democritus saw that the physical properties of matter, its compressibility and divisibility, can be well explained when we assume that matter consists of little particles. Compressing a substance then consists in pushing the atoms closer together, while the atoms themselves are perfectly solid and remain unchanged in size. Democritus' theory is a good illustration of what reasoning can achieve and what it cannot do. It can offer possible explanations; whether the explanation is true, however, cannot be found out by reasoning, but must be left to observation. The Greeks were not able to verify the theory of atoms by an empirical test. They attempted to supplement the theory by further theory rather than by observation. They believed that atoms were held together by little hooks; that a finer substance, like the soul or the fire, was composed of very small and smooth atoms; and that larger bodies were formed by the gathering of atoms of equal size, a natural process exemplified in the sorting of pebbles by the surf. But imagination uninhibited by some test through experiment opens the door to empty speculation. For instance, one of the philosophic controversies concerning atomism was the question whether the empty space between the atoms was a logically permissible concept; an empty space is nothing, and if there is nothing between the atoms, they must touch each other and form a solid mass—in which case there would be no atoms.

The theory of the atom was transplanted from the ground of philosophical speculation to the soil of scientific research when, at the eve of the nineteenth century, it was given a foundation by quantitative experiments. J. Dalton measured the ratios of weights by which chemical elements enter into compounds, and discovered that these ratios are fixed and given by simple whole numbers. For instance, the two components of water, hydrogen and oxygen, always combine in the ratio one to eight; if originally more of one substance is present, it is not included in the compound. Dalton saw that these quantitative ratios call for an atomic explanation. The smallest parts of matter, the atoms, combine in fixed ratios; two atoms of hydrogen combine with one atom of oxygen, and the ratio of weights of the atoms is portrayed by the ratio observed in Dalton's measurements.

From the time of Dalton's law the history of the atom has been a march of triumph. Wherever the concept of the atom was employed for the interpretation of observational measurements, it supplied lucid explanation; conversely, such success became overwhelming evidence for the existence of the atom. In the kinetic theory of gases it was possible not only to explain the thermic behavior of gases from atomic conceptions, but also to compute the number of atoms or molecules in one cubic inch. This enormous number, which is written with twenty-one digits, presents a proof of the extreme smallness of the individual atom. The complicated structures of organic bodies could be explained as being built up by molecules composed of hundreds of atoms. The industrial achievements of chemistry would have been impossible without the theory of the atom.

The physicist, furthermore, saw that atomism is not restricted to matter; electricity, too, must be regarded as consisting of atoms. The atoms of electricity were discovered around the end of the nineteenth century and were called electrons; strangely enough they all carried a negative electric charge, and for some decades the physicists believed that the positive atoms of electricity could not be separated from matter. Recent discoveries have shown that there are also positive electrons, usually called positrons. Other recent investigations have revealed the existence of further elementary particles of matter, among which the neutrons play an important part.

While the triumphal march of the atom went on through so many domains of science, it was stopped short in one important domain: in the theory of light. Isaac Newton, known for his theory of gravitation, was also one of the greatest explorers of optics. He saw that the straight-line character of light rays is explainable on the assumption that light consists of small particles ejected at great speed from the light source. Following the laws of motion, such particles will travel along straight paths. Newton thus was the author of the corpuscular theory of light, which remained dominant until the beginning of the nineteenth century. The wave theory of light, the invention of his contemporary C. Huyghens, met with little success at its inception. A full century elapsed before certain decisive experiments were made, which proved the undulatory character of light and thus put an end to the atomistic interpretation of light rays. These experiments were centered around the phenomenon of interference, in which two light rays, superimposed on one another, annihilate each other, a result inconceivable under a corpuscular theory. Two particles moving in the same direction can produce only a stronger impact and provide an increase in light intensity; but two waves moving in the same direction will cancel each other if the crests of the one coincide with the troughs of the other. The phenomenon of interference is known from water waves and accounts for the strange patterns produced by intersecting trains of waves. The medium of propagation of light waves, however, was recognized not to be of the nature of ordinary matter like water or air, but was supposed to be a substance of a peculiar, almost immaterial structure, called ether.

The development of the mathematical means of analyzing waves followed immediately the experimental discoveries. Finally the theory of light waves was connected with that of electricity through the work of James Maxwell; the experimental demonstration of electric waves by Heinrich Hertz removed the last doubts of the possibility of ether waves, and the wave theory of light became "a certainty, humanly speaking", as Heinrich

Hertz put it in an address given on a meeting of the German association of scientists in the year 1888.

At about the end of the nineteenth century physics had reached an apparently final stage: light and matter, the two great manifestations of physical reality, seemed to be known in their ultimate structure. Light consisted of waves and matter of atoms. Anyone who dared to question these foundations of the science of physics would have been regarded as a dilettante, or an eccentric, and no serious scientist would have taken the trouble to argue with him.

Physical theories give an account of the observational knowledge of their time; they cannot claim to be eternal truths. Heinrich Hertz had been careful enough to coin the phrase "certainty, humanly speaking". No deeper insight has perhaps ever been documented by a physicist's utterance than is expressed in this modest phrase. The turn which the theory took a decade after Hertz's words is proof of the limits drawn to the certainty of scientific theories.

The year 1900 brought M. Planck's discovery of the quantum; the radical change in our understanding of physical reality which the twentieth century effected, could not be better illustrated than by this coincidence. In order to explain the laws found experimentally for the emission of radiation by hot bodies, Planck introduced the conception that all radiation, including light, is subject to a control by whole numbers, that is, proceeds by whole numbers of an elementary unit of energy, which he called the *quantum*. According to his conception, energy consists of elementary units, the quanta, and whenever energy is emitted or absorbed there will be one or two or one hundred quanta transported, but never will there be a fraction of a quantum. The quantum is the atom of energy, with the qualification, however, that the size of this atom, that is, the amount of the energy unit, depends on the wave length of the radiation through which it is transported; the shorter the wave length, the greater the quantum. Planck's discovery therefore appeared as a new victory of atomism; and when Albert Einstein extended Planck's theory to the idea that light consists of needlelike bunches of waves carrying one quantum of energy, it seemed that the idea of the atom had finally conquered the very domain of physics which so long had been inaccessible to atomistic conceptions. Einstein's equivalence of matter and energy, which in recent years has become so dramatically manifest in the fission of uranium, was another indication that atomism was to include radiation.

The quantum found its most important application in Niels Bohr's theory of the atom. It was in this theory that the two lines of development, of the theory of the atom and of the theory of radiation, were finally united. The study of the atom had made it clear that the atom itself must be regarded as an aggregate of smaller particles, which, however, are so tightly held together that for all chemical reactions the atom behaves as a relatively stable unit. That the atom has an inner structure was first indicated by a discovery of the Russian D. Mendelejeff, who in the middle of the nineteenth century saw that if the atoms of the chemical elements are arranged according to weight, their chemical properties assume a cyclical order. The English physicist E. Rutherford connected these chemical discoveries with the discovery of the electron and constructed the planetary model of the atom, according to which the atom consists of a nucleus around which there revolve, like planets on their orbits, a certain number of electrons. Niels Bohr, at that time a young assistant of Rutherford, discovered in 1913 that Rutherford's model of the atom must be connected with Planck's concept of the quantum of energy. The electrons can only revolve on orbits situated at certain definite distances from the center, so determined that the mechanical energy represented by each orbit is either one, or two, or three quanta, and so forth. Strange as this conception appeared to the physicist in the beginning, it led to an amazing success as far as the presentation of observational data is concerned, since Bohr's theory supplied an interpretation of the highest precision for the data of spectroscopy, that is, for the series of spectral lines that characterize each element. The years from 1913 to 1925 became a period of extensive application and confirmation of Bohr's theory, which was deepened to supply an account of the atomic structure of each individual element.

And yet, in spite of all these successes, the discovery of the quantum turned out to be a gift with strings attached. In exchange for its explanatory power for spectroscopy, inexplicable complications arose on other grounds. The very foundations of the quantum conception appeared incompatible with the classical theory of the generation of electric waves and the phenomenon of interference, known from optics. Thus the new theory imperiled the consistency of physics: some phenomena required a corpuscular conception of light, others required a wave conception, and no way was apparent by which the two contradictory theories could be reconciled.

The strangest phenomenon for the philosophical observer, however, was the fact that physical research was not paralyzed by these contradictions, that the physicist managed somehow to go on with two contradictory conceptions and learned to apply sometimes the one, sometimes the other, with an amazing success as far as observational discoveries are concerned. I do not think this fact proves that contradiction is irrelevant for physical theories and that only the observational success matters;

or that, as Hegelians believe, contradiction is immanent in human thought and acts as its propelling force. I rather think it proves that the discovery of new ideas follows other laws than laws of logical order; that knowledge of half the truth can be a sufficient directive for the creative mind on its path to the full truth, and that contradictory theories can be helpful only because there exists, though unknown at that time, a better theory which comprehends all observational data and is free from contradictions. While humans search, truth slumbers; it will be awakened by those who do not stop their search even when their path is obstructed by the brushwood of contradictions.

The decisive turn in the development of the theories of light and matter was a conception put forward by the French physicist Louis de Broglie. While physicists were struggling with the problem of whether light consists *either* of particles *or* of waves, de Broglie ventured the idea that it consists *both* of particles *and* of waves. He even had the boldness to transfer his idea to the atoms of matter, which so far had never required a wave interpretation; he developed a mathematical theory according to which each little particle of matter, too, is accompanied by a wave. The *either–or* was thus replaced by an *and*, and from de Broglie's discovery, therefore, dates the duality of interpretations, which ever since has been confirmed as an inescapable consequence of the structural nature of matter. In an experiment conducted by Davisson and Germer, who used an interference arrangement, de Broglie's waves could be shown to exist for a beam of electrons, so that the existence of waves of matter was insured beyond doubt.

De Broglie's ideas were taken up by E. Schrödinger, who devised a differential equation which has become the mathematical foundation of the modern theory of the quantum, usually called quantum mechanics. His mathematical theory coincided with some other theories, which at first glance looked very different and which were developed independently by W. Heisenberg, M. Born, and P. Jordan on the one hand and P. Dirac on the other. All these discoveries were made in the years 1925–1926; and in a rather short time a new physics of the elements of matter was developed, which placed in the hands of the physicist a powerful mathematical instrument that he had yet to learn to handle. The difficulties in the manipulations of this instrument derived from the duality of waves and corpuscles. What does it mean to say that matter consists both of waves and of particles? Although the mathematical theory was at hand, its interpretation presented great difficulties. We meet here with a development which manifests the relative independence of a mathematical formalism; the mathematical symbols have a life of their own, so to speak, and lead to the correct result even before the symbol-user understands their ultimate meaning.

De Broglie had interpreted the *and* in its simplest sense; he believed that there were particles accompanied by waves which travel along with the particle and control its motion. Schrödinger, in contrast, believed that he could dispense with the particles, that there were only waves which, however, were accumulated in certain small regions of the space so that something resembling a particle resulted. He spoke of wave packets behaving like particles. After both conceptions had been shown to be untenable, Born suggested the idea that the waves do not constitute anything material at all but represent probabilities. His interpretation gave the problem of the atom an unexpected turn: the elementary entities were assumed to be particles, whose behavior was controlled not by causal laws, but by probability laws of a form resem-

174

bling waves as far as their mathematical structure was concerned. In this interpretation the waves do not have the reality of material objects, but only that of mathematical quantities.

Carrying on this conception, Heisenberg showed that for the prediction of the path of particles there exists a specific indeterminacy, which makes it impossible to predict that path strictly, a result formulated in his *principle of indeterminacy*. With Born's and Heisenberg's discoveries the step was made that led from a causal interpretation of the microcosm to a statistical interpretation; the individual atomic occurrence was recognized as not being determined by a causal law, but as following only a probability law, and the *if-then* of classical physics was replaced by an *if-then in a certain percentage*. Combining Born's and Heisenberg's results, Bohr finally developed a *principle of complementarity*, according to which Born's interpretation supplies only one aspect of the problem; it is also possible to regard the waves as physically real, a conception for which no particles exist. There is no way of discriminating between the two interpretations, because Heisenberg's indeterminacy makes any *crucial experiment* impossible; that is, it excludes experiments precise enough to tell whether one interpretation is true and the other false.

The duality of interpretations thus assumed its final form: the *and* of de Broglie's discovery does not have the direct meaning that both waves and corpuscles exist at the same time, but has the indirect meaning that the same physical reality admits of two possible interpretations, each of which is as true as the other, although the two cannot be combined into one picture. The logician would say: the *and* is not in the language of physics, but in the *metalanguage,* that is, in a language which speaks about the language of physics. Or, in another terminology, the *and* belongs, not in physics, but in the philosophy of physics; it does not refer to physical objects, but to possible descriptions of physical objects, and thus falls into the realm of the philosopher.

That is, in fact, the final outcome of the controversy between the adherents of waves and of corpuscles, which began with Huyghens and Newton and, after a development of centuries, climaxed in the quantum mechanics of de Broglie, Schrödinger, Born, Heisenberg, and Bohr: the question *what is matter* cannot be answered by physical experiments alone, but requires a philosophical analysis of physics. Its answer is seen to be dependent on the question *what is knowledge.* The philosophic thought which stood at the cradle of atomism was replaced in the course of the nineteenth century by experimental analysis; but research finally reached a stage of complication which called for a return to philosophical investigation. The philosophy of this investigation, however, could not be supplied by mere speculation; only a scientific philosophy was able to come to the assistance of the physicist. In order to understand this latest development we shall have to inquire into the meaning of statements about the physical world.

Knowledge begins with observation: our senses tell us what exists outside our bodies. But we are not satisfied with what we observe; we want to know more, to inquire into things that we do not observe directly. We reach this objective by means of thought operations, which connect the observational data and account for them in terms of unobserved things. This procedure is applied in everyday life as well as in science; it is at work when we infer from puddles on the road that it rained shortly before, or when the physicist infers from the deflection of a magnetic needle that there is an invisible entity, called electricity, in the wire, or when the physician infers from the symptoms of a disease that there are certain bacteria in the blood stream of the patient. We must study the nature of this inference if we wish to understand the meaning of physical theories.

The inference may look trivial as long as we do not reflect about it; but in deeper analysis it reveals itself as being of a very complicated structure. You say that while you are in your office your house stands unchanged in its place. How do you know? You do not see your house while you are in your office. You will answer that you can easily verify your statement by going home and looking at your house. It is true that you will then see your house; but does that observation verify your statement? What you said was that your house was there when you did not see it; what you verify is that your house is there when you see it. How can you tell whether it was there while you were absent?

I see you are getting indignant. Those philosophers, you say; they are trying to make fools out of everybody. If the house was there in the morning and in the afternoon, how can it have been nonexistent in the forenoon? Does the philosopher think that a contractor could pull down a house in a minute and build it up in another minute? What is such a nonsensical question good for?

The trouble is that unless you can find a better answer to that question than is supplied by the arguments of common sense, you will not be able to solve the problem of whether light and matter consist of particles or waves. That is the point made by the philosopher: common sense may be a good instrument as long as questions of everyday life are concerned; but it is an insufficient instrument when scientific inquiry has reached a certain stage of complication. Science requires a reinterpretation of the knowledge of everyday life, because knowledge is ultimately of the same nature whether it concerns concrete objects or the constructs of scientific thought. We must therefore find better answers to the simple questions of everyday life before we can answer scientific questions.

The Greek philosopher Protagoras, the chief of the Sophists, was known for his principle of subjectivity, which he formulated as follows: "Man is the measure of all things, of things that are that they are, and of things that are not that they are not". We do not know exactly what he meant by this truly sophisticated statement, but let us assume he would have said with respect to our problem: "the house exists only when I look at it, but when I don't look at it, it always vanishes". What can you hold against him? He does not say that it vanishes and reappears in the ordinary way by the hands of bricklayers and carpenters; he means it vanishes in a sort of magical way. He insists that it is the observation by a human observer which produces the house and that therefore unobserved houses do not exist. What arguments do we have against such magical disappearance and creation by a human observer?

You may say that you can call up the janitor from your office and ask whether the house still stands. But the janitor is a human being like you; maybe his observation creates the house like yours. Will the house be there when nobody observes it?

You may say that you can turn your back toward the house and observe its shadow; then the unobserved house must exist because it throws a shadow. But how do you know that unobserved things throw shadows? What you have seen so far is that observed houses throw shadows. You could explain the shadow, which you see while you do not see the house, by assuming that shadows remain when the object has vanished, and that there is a shadow without a house. Do not argue that such shadows of non-existent objects have never been observed. That is true only if you assume what you want to prove, namely, that the house continues to exist while you do not see it. If you assume the contrary, like Protagoras, you have lots of evidence for his statement, because you have seen house-shaped shadows without seeing houses at the same time.

You will defend yourself by resorting to a new appeal to common sense. "Why should I assume", you answer, "that the laws of optics are different for unobserved objects? It is true that these laws were established for observed objects; but do we not have overwhelming evidence that they must hold for unobserved objects, too?" On a little afterthought, however, you will discover that we do not have such evidence at all. We have none because unobserved objects have never been observed.

There remains only one way out of this difficulty. We must regard our statements about unobserved objects not as verifiable statements, but as conventions, which we introduce because of the great simplification of language. What we know is that *if* this convention is introduced it can be carried through without contradictions; that *if* we assume the unobserved objects to be identical with the observed ones, we arrive at a system of physical laws which hold both for observed and unobserved objects. The latter statement, which is an *if* statement, is a matter of fact and verified as true. It proves that our usual language about unobserved objects is an *admissible* language. But it is not the only admissible one. A Protagoras who says that houses vanish when they are unobserved also speaks an admissible language, if he is willing to comply with the consequence that he has to construct two different systems of physical laws, one for observed and one for unobserved objects.

The result of this long discussion is that nature does not dictate to us one specific description; that truth is not restricted to one language. We can measure houses in feet or in meters, temperatures in Fahrenheit or in centigrades; and we can describe the physical world in a Euclidean or a non-Euclidean geometry, as was shown in Chapter 8. We speak different languages when we use different systems of measurement or of geometry, but we say the same thing. The plurality of descriptions repeats itself in a more complicated form when we speak about unobserved objects. There are many ways of saying the truth; they are all equivalent in a logical sense. There are also many ways of saying a falsehood. For instance, it is false to say that ice melts at thirty-two degrees, if we use the centigrade scale. Our philosophy, therefore, does not wipe out the difference between truth and falsehood. But it would be shortsighted to disregard the plurality of true descriptions. Physical reality admits of a class of *equivalent descriptions;* we choose one for the sake of convenience, and this choice rests upon a convention only, that is, on an arbitrary decision. For instance, the decimal system supplies a more convenient description of measurements than other systems. When we speak about unobserved objects, the most convenient language is the one selected by common sense, according to which unobserved objects and their behavior do not differ from observed objects and their behavior. But this language is based upon a convention.

It is the merit of the theory of equivalent descriptions that it allows us to express certain truths which the language of common sense cannot formulate. I refer to the truth formulated by the *if* statement above: it is true that if we assume the unobserved objects to be identical with the observed ones, we arrive at no contradictions, or in other words, that among the admissible descriptions of the physical world there is one in which the unobserved objects are on equal footing with the observed ones. Let me call this description the *normal system*. That the physical world admits of a normal system for its description is one of the most important truths. We have always taken this truth for granted; we did not even formulate it and thus did not know that it was a truth. We saw no problem in it, like the man who sees no problem in the falling of bodies toward the ground because this observation is too general an experience. But scientific mechanics began with the formulation of the law of falling bodies. Similarly, a scientific understanding of the problem of unobserved objects begins with the statement that a description of unobserved objects through a normal system is possible.

How do we know it is possible? All we can say is that the experiences of generations of men have proved it. We should not believe, however, that this possibility could be proved by logical laws. It is a fortunate matter of fact that our world can be so simply described that no difference between observed and unobserved objects results. This is all we can maintain.

Thus far we have spoken of unobserved houses. The particles of matter are also unobserved objects. Let us see how our results can be transferred to them.

As in the world of our daily life, there are observables and unobservables in the world of the atom. What can be observed are collisions between two particles, or between a particle and a light ray; the physicist has devised ingenious instruments that indicate each individual collision. What cannot be observed is what happens during the interval between two collisions, or on the path from the source of radiation to a collision. These occurrences, then, are the unobservables of the quantum world.

But why can they not be observed? Why can we not use a supermicroscope and watch the particles on their path? The trouble is that in order to see a particle we have to illuminate it; and illumination of a particle is something very different from the illumination of a house. A light ray falling on a particle pushes it out of its way; what we observe, therefore, is a collision and not a particle traveling peacefully on its path. Imagine that you wish to watch a bowling ball rolling along its path in a dark hall; that you turn on the light and the moment the light hits the ball it pushes the ball out of its way. Where was the ball before you turned on the light? You would not be able to tell. Fortunately our illustration is not true for bowling balls; they are so large that the impact by a light ray does not disturb them noticeably. It is different with electrons and other particles of matter. When you observe them, you have to disturb them; and therefore you do not know what they did before the observation.

There is some disturbance by the observation even in the macroscopic world. When a police car moves through the traffic of a boulevard, its occupants see all the surrounding cars move slowly within the required speed limits. If the police officer did not sometimes put on civilian clothes and drive an ordinary car, he would infer that all the cars all the time move at such a reasonable speed. In our intercourse with electrons we cannot don civilian clothes; when we watch them we always disturb their traffic.

You will argue: maybe it is true that we cannot observe how an undisturbed particle moves on its path; but can we not figure out, by means of scientific inferences, what they do when we do not look at them? This question returns us to our preceding analysis of unobserved objects. We saw that we can speak about such objects in various ways; that there is a class of equivalent descriptions; and that we shall preferably select a normal system for our description, that is, a system in which the unobserved objects do not differ from the observed ones. Our discussion of the observation of particles, however, has made it clear that for particles we do not have a normal system. The observer of electrons is a Protagoras; he produces what he sees, because seeing electrons means producing collisions with light rays.

Speaking of particles means attributing to them a definite place and a definite velocity for each time point. For instance, a tennis ball occupies at every moment a certain place on its path and has, at this moment, a determinate velocity. Both place and velocity can be measured, at each moment, by suitable instruments. For small particles, however, the disturbance by the observer, as Heisenberg has shown, makes it impossible to measure both values simultaneously. We can measure either the position or the velocity of the particle, but not both. This is the result of Heisenberg's principle of indeterminacy. The question arises whether there do not exist other ways of determining the unmeasured quantity, methods through which the unmeasured quantity is related indirectly to the observed quantities. This would be possible if we could assume that the unobserved quantities follow the same laws as the observed ones. The analysis of quantum mechanics, however, has given a negative answer; the unobserved objects do not follow the same laws as the observed ones in so far as a specific difference arises with respect to causality. The relations controlling unobserved objects violate the postulates of causality; they lead to *causal anomalies.*

This difference results when interference experiments are made, that is, experiments in which a beam of electrons or a light ray passes through a narrow slit and produces an interference pattern on a screen, consisting of black and white stripes. Such experiments have always been explained by the wave nature of light as the result of a superposition of wave crests and troughs. We know, however, that when we use a radiation of a very small intensity, the resulting pattern, although of the same structure when the radiation goes on for a sufficiently long time, is the effect of a great many small impacts on the screen; the stripes are therefore produced by a bombardment resembling machine-gun fire. These individual impacts cannot be reasonably explained as waves. The wave arrives on a large front covering the screen; then there occurs a flash at only one point of the screen, and the whole wave disappears. It is swallowed by the flash, so to speak, an occurrence which is incompatible with the usual laws of causality. This is the point where the wave interpretation leads to unreasonable consequences, or causal anomalies. If we assume, in contrast, that the radiation consists of particles, the impacts on the screen are easily explained. Difficulties arise, however, if two slits are used. Each particle then must pass either through the one or the other slit. The interference pattern is then the result of an interaction of the two slits; but the contribution which each slit makes to the total pattern can be shown to differ from the pattern which the slit would produce if the other slit were closed. This means that the path beyond the slit selected by the particle will be influenced by the existence of the other slit; the particle knows, so to speak, whether or not the other slit is open. This is the point where the particle interpretation arrives at a causal anomaly, that is, a violation of the usual laws of causality. Similar violations occur for all other experimental arrangements and all possible interpretations. This result is formulated in a *principle of anomaly,* which can be derived from the foundations of quantum mechanics.

The violation of the principle of causality in the form of anomalies must be carefully distinguished from the extension expressed in the transition from causal laws to probability laws. That atomic occurrences are controlled by probability laws, and not by causal laws, appears as a relatively harmless result if compared with the causal anomalies just mentioned. These anomalies concern the principle of action by contact, formulating a well-established property of causal transmission: the cause has to spread continuously through space until it reaches the point where it produces a certain effect. If a locomotive starts moving, the individual cars of the train will not follow immediately, but by intervals; the pull of the locomotive has to be transferred from car to car until it finally reaches the last car. When a searchlight is turned on, it will not immediately illuminate the objects to which it is directed; the light has to travel through the space in between, and if it did not move at such a high speed we would notice the time required for the spreading of the illumination. The cause does not affect distant objects instantaneously, but spreads from point to point until it affects the object by contact—this simple fact is one of the most conspicuous features of all known causal transmissions; and the physicist would not easily give up the belief that he holds in this property an indispensable factor of causal interaction. Even the transition to probability laws does not necessarily imply the abandonment of this property. Probability laws can be so constructed that the probability is transferred from point to point, resulting in a probability chain, which is the analogue of a causal action by contact. The fact that the analysis of the unobservables of quantum physics compels us to give up the principle of action by contact, that it leads to a principle of anomaly, is a much heavier blow to the idea of causality than the transition to probability laws. This breakdown of causality makes it impossible to speak of unobserved objects of the microcosm in the same sense as of the macrocosm.

We thus arrive at a specific difference between the world of large things and the world of small things. Both worlds are constructed on the basis of observables by the addition of unobservables. In the world of large things such a supplementation of the observed phenomena involves no difficulties; the unobservables follow the pattern of the observables. In the world of small things, however, a reasonable supplementation of the observables cannot be constructed. The unobservables, whether introduced as particles or as waves, behave unreasonably, violating the established laws of causality. There exists no normal system for the interpretation of the unobservables, and we cannot speak of unobservables in the same sense as is implied for the world of everyday life. We can regard the elementary constituents of matter as particles or waves; both interpretations fit the observations equally well and equally badly.

This, then, is the end of the story. The controversy between the adherents of the wave and the corpuscle interpretation has been transformed into a duality of interpretations. Whether the constituents of matter are waves or particles is a question concerning unobservables; and the unobservables of atomic dimensions, unlike those of the world at large, cannot be uniquely determined by the postulate of a normal system—because there exists no such system.

We should call ourselves fortunate that this indeterminacy is restricted to small objects; for large objects it drops out because Heisenberg's indeterminacy, on account of the small size of Planck's quantum, is not noticeable for them. Even for the atoms as wholes the indeterminacy can be neglected, because they are rather large; and we can treat them as corpuscles, disregarding wave notions. Only the interior structure of the atom, in which lighter particles like electrons play a leading part, requires the quantum mechanical duality of interpretations.

To understand what the duality means, let us imagine a world in which a similar duality holds for large bodies. Assume there is machine-gun fire passing through the windows of a room and we later find the bullets stuck in the walls of the room, so that it seems beyond doubt that the fire consists of bullets. The passage of the fire through the windows, we further assume, follows the laws for waves passing through slits; the fire produces, in the distribution of the bullets in the walls, a pattern of stripes like those of an interference pattern. When we open another window, for instance, the number of bullets hitting a certain place of the wall becomes smaller instead of larger, because the waves interfere at this point. If it were impossible to observe directly a bullet on its path, we then could interpret the fire as consisting of waves or of corpuscles; both interpretations would be true, although each would involve certain unreasonable consequences.

The unreasonableness of such a world will always exist in consequences only, not in what is observed. The individual observations would not be different from what we see in our world; but their totality would determine implications that contradict the fundamentals of causality. It is our good luck that our world of stones and trees and houses and machine guns is not of this type. Indeed, it would be rather unpleasant to live in such an environment, in which things play tricks on us behind our backs, while they behave reasonably as long as we look at them. But we cannot infer that the world of the small things must be of the same simple structure as that of the large ones. The atomic dimensions do not lend themselves to a unique determination of unobservables. We have to learn that their unobservables can be described in various languages, and that there is no question of one being the true language.

It is this characteristic feature of quantum-mechanical occurrences which I would regard as the deeper meaning of Bohr's principle of complementarity. When he calls the wave and the particle description complementary, this means that for questions where one is an adequate interpretation the other is not, and vice versa. For instance, considering the interference pattern on a screen we shall refer to the wave interpretation; but in face of observations with Geiger counters, which show us individual and localized impacts, we shall use the particle interpretation. It should be noticed that the word "complementarity" does not explain, or eliminate, the logical difficulties of quantum-mechanical language; it merely gives them a name. It is a fundamental fact that there is no normal system for the interpretation of quantum-mechanical unobservables and that we have to resort to different languages when we wish to avoid causal anomalies for different occurrences—this is the empirical content of the principle of complementarity. And it should be emphasized that this logical situation has no analogues in our actual macrocosm. I therefore do not think that it clarifies the quantum-mechanical problem when reference is made to such "complementarities" as love and justice, freedom and determinism, and so forth. I would rather speak here of *polarities* and indicate by the change in the name that these macrocosmic relationships have a structure very different from the complementarity of quantum mechanics. They have nothing to do with the extension of language from observables to unobservables and therefore do not bear upon the problem of physical reality.

A different approach has been made by the help of a revision of logic. Instead of a duality or complementarity of languages, a language of a more comprehensive form has been constructed, wide enough in its logical structure to be adaptable to the peculiarities of the quantum-mechanical microcosm. Our usual language is based on a two-valued logic, that is, on the logic of the two truth values "truth" and "falsehood". It is possible to construct a three-valued logic, which possesses an intermediate truth value of indeterminacy; in this logic, statements are either true or false or indeterminate. By the help of such a logic, quantum mechanics can be written in a sort of neutral language, which does not speak of waves or corpuscles, but speaks of coincidences, that is, of collisions, and leaves it indeterminate what happens on the path between two collisions. This logic appears to be the ultimate form of the physics of the quanta—humanly speaking.

It was a long way from Democritus' atoms to the duality of waves and corpuscles. The substance of the universe—in the physicist's sense and not in the metaphoric connotation of the philosopher who identified it with reason—has turned out to be of a rather dubious nature, if compared with the solid particles in which both the philosopher and the scientist believed for some two thousand years. The conception of a corporeal substance, similar to the palpable substance shown by the bodies of our daily environment, has been recognized as an extrapolation from sensual experience. What appeared to the philosophy of rationalism as a requirement of reason—Kant called the concept of substance synthetic a priori—has been revealed as being the product of a conditioning through environment. The experiences offered by atomic phenomena make it necessary to abandon the idea of a corporeal substance and require a revision of the form of the description by means of which we portray physical reality. With the corporeal substance goes the two-valued character of language, and even the fundamentals of logic are shown to be the product of an adaptation to the simple environment into which human beings were born. Speculative philosophy has never exhibited a power of imagination equal to the ingenuity which scientific philosophy has displayed under the guidance of scientific experiments and mathematical analysis. The path of truth is paved with the errors of a philosophy too narrow to envisage the variety of possible experiences.

12.

Evolution

To the eye of the untrained observer there appears to be an intrinsic difference between living organisms and inorganic nature. Practically all forms of animal life display the ability of independent motion and indicate through their behavior a planned activity directed toward the benefit of the organism itself. Not only with human beings, but also with some species of animals the planned activities may exhibit a long-range anticipation of future needs: birds build their nests to have protection for the night and a place to breed, the hamster digs his shelter into the ground and fills it with provisions for the winter, and the bee lays in a store of honey. And a great deal of planned behavior is always directed toward reproduction, that amazing mechanism which makes the species survive where individuals die.

Plants do not show activities which we would like to call planning; but they certainly function in such a way that their reactions serve the purpose of feeding the individual and preserving the species. They grow roots into the ground as deep as necessary to reach water, they turn their green leaves toward the sun whose rays they need as a source of life energy; and their reproductive mechanism assures plentiful progeny.

The living organism is a system functioning toward the aim of self-preservation and preservation of the species; that is true not only for those visible manifestations of life which we call "behavior", but also for the chemical mechanism of the body, which is at the basis of all behavior. The chemical process of digestion and oxidation of food is so arranged that it supplies the organism with the calories necessary for its activities; and plants have even devised a process which enables them, by the help of chlorophyl particles, to utilize directly the radiant energy of the sun for the benefit of their existence.

Compared with the blind functioning of the inorganic world, the falling of stones, the flow of water, the blowing of the wind, the activities of living organisms appear to be controlled by a plan, to be directed toward a certain purpose. The inorganic world is controlled by the laws of cause and effect; the past determines the future by way of the present. For living organisms this relation seems to be reversed; what happens now is so arranged that it serves a future purpose, and the happenings of the present appear to be determined by the future rather than by the past.

Such a determination in terms of the future is called *teleology*. In his concept of a final cause Aristotle has assigned to teleology, or *finality,* a place parallel to that of *causality* in the description of the physical world. Ever since Aristotle's time the scientist has been confronted by the dual nature of the physical world: whereas inorganic nature was seen to be controlled by the laws of cause and effect, organic nature appeared to be governed by the law of purpose and means. Finality thus is assigned the function of a logical parallel of causality; the one appears as fundamental as the other, and the physicist, who thinks of nature in terms of cause and effect alone, is regarded as a victim of the fallacy of vocational preoccupation, which makes a man blind to the exigencies of research outside his own narrow field.

12. EVOLUTION

Although this conception of a parallelism between causality and finality sounds like the verdict of a neutral observer, we listen to its claims with reluctance and cannot suppress the feeling that there is something fundamentally wrong in its thesis. Physics is not a parallel of biology, but a more elementary science. Its laws do not stop short of living bodies but include both organic and inorganic bodies, whereas biology is restricted to the study of those specific laws which, in addition to physical laws, govern living organisms. There is no exception to physical laws known in biology. Living bodies fall down like stones if not supported; they cannot produce energy from nothing, they verify all the laws of chemistry in their digestive processes—there is no physical law which has to be qualified by the clause "unless the process occurs in a living organism".

If living organisms display properties which require the formulation of specific laws, to be added to those of physics, there is nothing strange in such addition. We know that hot bodies display properties not referred to in mechanics, that a wire through which an electric current is passed shows properties which neither mechanics nor thermodynamics can account for. There is no logical difficulty in according to matter of a more complex state of organization properties which matter of a simpler state does not reveal. But it appears inadmissible to assume that living matter possesses properties which contradict those of inorganic matter.

In fact, teleology contradicts causality. If the past determines the future, then the future does not determine the past, at least not in the sense in which the word "determine" is used in this phrase. There is a static sense of the word for which determination works both ways; for instance, the number x determines its square x^2, and the square x^2 determines its positive root x. But causality is a determination in the generic sense. The wind determines the bent shape of a tree, but not vice versa. It is true that from the bent shape of trees we can infer the direction of the prevalent wind; but if we say that in this sense the shape of the tree determines the direction of the wind, we use the word "determination" in the static sense of a mere correlation. The bent tree is indicative of the wind, but does not produce it, whereas the wind produces the bent shape of the tree. The word "produce" need not be understood as inaccessible to logical analysis; I have explained above (chap. 10) that the unidirectional character of causality is capable of a logical formulation. If our conception of the flow of time is to have any meaning, causality is opposed to teleology; determination in the generic sense can take place in one direction only. An interpretation for which life is essentially different from physical processes and controlled by purpose rather than by cause is incompatible with the idea of a direction of time. The biologist who appeals to common sense in his claims for the alleged duality should not forget that he contradicts common sense in another field: he abandons the conception of becoming.

Some further analysis shows that in this dilemma the teleologist has no good defense. Whenever purposeful action is involved, what determines the action is not the future occurrence, but a living organism's anticipation of the future occurrence. We plant the seed in order to grow the tree; what determines our action is not the future tree, but our present images of the future tree, by which we anticipate its future existence. That this is the correct logical interpretation is seen from the fact that the growing seedling can be destroyed so that there will be no future tree; the anticipated future event then never happens, whereas the present action, the planting of the seed, remains unchanged. And what never happens cannot possibly determine what happens now. Generic determination goes from the past to the future and not vice versa. Purposeful action as observable in human behavior is misinterpreted when it is regarded as a generic determination of the past by the future. Neither common sense nor science can admit a generic determination which contradicts causality. The parallelism between teleology and causality is the product of a logical misunderstanding.

What then remains of teleology? If a purpose is to be compatible with causality, the determination of the present cannot be the product of the future, but must be a determination in terms of a plan. A plan, however, can have effects only through the medium of some organism possessing the abilities of thinking. But the teleological organization goes far beyond the species *Homo sapiens*. We can scarcely say the hamster follows a plan while he stores his provisions, and nobody would be willing to say that a plant carries out the plan of reproducing its species when it sheds its seeds over the ground. A formulation avoiding anthropomorphisms must be carefully worded: the activities of living organisms present a pattern of the type the organisms would follow if they acted according to plan. To go from this fact to the existence of a plan, which in some mystical fashion controls organismic behavior, means interpreting the whole organic world by analogy with human behavior, means putting an analogy in the place of an explanation. Teleology is analogism, is pseudo explanation; it belongs in speculative philosophy, but has no place in scientific philosophy.

What then is the correct explanation? The fact remains that organismic activity represents a pattern as though it were controlled by a plan. Should we record this fact as a mere coincidence, as a product of chance? The conscience of the statistician revolts against this conception: the probability of such a coincidence would be so extremely small that we cannot accept this interpretation. The desire for causal explanation seems to have arrived at a deadlock. How can causality ever assume the appearance of purposeful behavior?

A man who sees for the first time the pebbles on a beach might very well conceive the idea that they were deposited according to a certain plan. Close to the ocean, partly covered by the water, there lie the larger pebbles, followed a little further up by the smaller ones, which in turn are followed by layers of sand, first consisting of coarse grains and eventually changing into the fine-grained sand of the upper parts of the beach. It looks as though someone has cleaned up the beach, neatly assorting pebbles and sand according to size. We know that it is unnecessary to assume such an anthropomorphic interpretation; the water transports the pebbles and casts the lighter ones farther up the beach, thus automatically assorting them as to size. It is true, the individual impacts by the waves follow the irregular pattern of chance; and nobody could predict the place where a certain pebble will finally be deposited. But there is a selection at work; whenever a larger and a smaller rock are transported by the same wave, the smaller one will be carried a little farther. Chance in combination with selection produces order.

It was the great discovery of Charles Darwin that the apparent teleology of living organisms can be explained in a similar way by a combination of chance and selection. Like most great ideas, Darwin's principle of selection had been anticipated at earlier times. The Greek philosopher Empedocles had developed a fantastic theory according to which living bodies grew from the ground as fragments; individual limbs, heads, and bodies moved around and united by chance into odd combinations, only the fittest of which survived. But a good idea stated within an insufficient theoretical frame loses its explanatory power and is forgotten until it is rediscovered and imbedded into a conclusive theory. Darwin's principle of natural selection and the survival of the fittest was developed with the means of scientific research and presented in the frame of an elaborate theory of evolution. This is the reason that the name "Darwinism" has come to denote the conception of an evolution through natural selection. And the extent of his scientific work justifies the preference given to Darwin over his younger contemporary A. R. Wallace, who developed the idea of natural selection independently of Darwin, but whose scientific work does not compare with Darwin's comprehensive achievements.

When we classify the existing species with respect to the degree of their differentiation, always going from one species to the one which resembles it most closely in anatomical structure and organismic build, we arrive at a *systematic* order, that is to say, at a series in which relationships of similarity allocate to each species its place on the scale. At the upper end of the line we have human beings; below them follow the apes, in turn to be followed by other mammals; and through birds, reptiles, and fishes, the line proceeds to the various forms of marine animals, until it reaches its lower end in the form of one-celled living organisms, the amoebae. Darwin made the inference that the *systematic order* of coexisting species represents the *historical order* of their genesis, that life began with the one-celled amoeba and in the course of millions of years proceeded to higher and higher forms.

The inference is good inductive logic. Everyone would be willing to apply it in simpler instances. Imagine what a May fly, which lives only one day, would observe of types of human beings: it would see babies, children, teen-agers, adults, and aged persons, but would not notice any growth or change in the individual persons. If among the May flies there turned up a Darwin, such an outstanding fly might very well infer that the coexisting stages of human beings which it observes represent a historical succession. As far as time ratios are concerned, the May fly is much better off than we are: compared with the time length of evolution, the span of a human life is much shorter than the one-day life of a May fly compared with the longest lifetime of a human being. No wonder that we cannot actually observe evolutionary change, for which even the six thousand years of recorded human history form a period of merely infinitesimal length. So we shall always depend on an inference from systematic order to historical order, a cross-inference from the order of the simultaneous to the order of succession.

There is, of course, further evidence to be adduced in favor of the inference. There are the findings of geology: the various geological layers contain fossils of different kinds, but so arranged that the more differentiated forms are included in the upper strata. It appears legitimate to identify the spatial order of the strata with the time order of their deposition. Geology thus keeps a record of the state of animal life reached at any time considered. Furthermore, excavations have provided us with specimens of many a species that is missing in the systematic order of the existing species, with the effect of closing the gaps. In particular the missing link between man and ape was discovered in some specimens of skulls that combine the bulging eye ridges of the apes with a cranial capacity larger than that of the apes, though smaller than that of man; the receding forehead left little space for the prefrontal area of the brain. The brain of this ape-man made possible certain mental activities, though the faculty of profiting by experience through recalling the consequences of previous responses to experience, located in the prefrontal area of the brain, was developed to a very limited degree. Incidentally, the ape-man is now regarded as the ancestor of both man and the living apes, so that the latter represent a side-line rather than the ancestor of man.

If we regard the evidence referred to as conclusive, we have to admit the fact of an evolution of life from the amoeba to man. But there remains the question of the *why* of this evolution. Why did life develop into higher forms? Evolution looks like a process according to plan; one might be tempted to say that evolution offers the strongest support to teleology that can be imagined.

It is here that Darwin's greatest contribution intervenes: Darwin saw that the progress of evolution can be explained in terms of causality alone and does not require any teleological conceptions. The random variations of reproduction produce differences in the individuals which imply different adaptation for survival; in the struggle for existence the fittest survive, and since they transfer their higher abilities to their offspring, there will result a progressive change to higher and higher forms. Like the pebbles on the beach, biological species are ordered through a selective cause; chance in combination with selection produces order.

Darwin's theory of selection has been much discussed and improved, but never has it been shaken in its fundamentals. Influenced by his great predecessor Lamarck, Darwin believed in the heredity of acquired characters; he thought that the functional adaptation, which an individual acquires through training, is transferred to its progeny. There has been much controversy about this point and the part which this view held in Darwin's own conception of his theory. Two precise statements, however, can be made today: first, that all experimental evidence available today speaks against a heredity of acquired characters, and second, that "Darwinism" does not need any assumption of this kind. Combining Darwin's idea of a natural selection with certain experimental discoveries, modern biology has supplied a satisfactory explanation for "directed" hereditary change and thus freed itself from "Lamarckism".

This explanation is based on the experimental demonstration of *mutations,* that is, changes in the hereditary substance of individuals. Such mutations can be artificially produced by X-rays or heat; in nature they occur through random causes and are not due to any adaptation of the individual to its living conditions. Many of these random mutations will be useless; but if there occur useful mutations, they will equip individuals with higher abilities of survival. Once the existence of hereditary mutations due to random causes is demonstrated, the rest is left to the laws of probability, which, slow working as they are, will eventually produce higher and higher forms of life.

No criticism could diminish the cogency of this proof. If it is objected that most of the mutations are so small that they do not entail a visible advantage of survival, the theorist of probability will answer that then random variations will occur in all directions, until by pure chance they have accumulated in one direction so as to produce a noticeable advantage of survival. The smallness of mutations can delay the process of evolution, but cannot stop it. If it is objected that many mutations are useless, the answer is that it is sufficient if *there are* useful mutations. Selection through struggle for existence is an irrefutable fact, and chance in combination with selection produces order—there is no escape from this principle. Darwin's theory of natural selection is the tool by which the apparent teleology of evolution is reduced to causality. The problems of mutation and heredity have been studied in all their ramifications by modern geneticists and will have to be still further explored; but the need for teleology is eliminated by Darwin's principle.

The theory of evolution is based throughout on indirect evidence. Will it ever be possible to construct a direct evidence for it, say, by producing human beings in the test tube?

To copy within the short time of a laboratory experiment a process which nature took millions of years to perform, might appear to be demanding very much— if nature had not supplied short-time copies of this process in the growth of the embryo of every human being. This growth begins with the one-cell stage and proceeds by more complicated stages, which, as was shown by Haeckel, recapitulate the entire history of evolution, though in an abridged form. There is, for instance, a stage in which the human embryo develops gill slits, and in which its exterior appearance is scarcely distinguishable from the embryo of a fish. It appears not so far fetched a possibility to put the fertilized ovum of a mammal into a test tube and develop it into a complete individual. But the experiment would not prove very much, because the initial material, the fertilized ovum, would be a natural product and not the work of a chemical synthesis. Whether it will ever be possible artificially to produce the ova and sperm cells of mammals is highly questionable. The modern biologist would be glad if he could produce an amoeba by synthetic processes.

But such an experiment would be in fact highly conclusive. The indirect evidence we have for the evolution from the amoeba to the human being is so good that it scarcely needs an amplification by direct experiments.

The production of just one living cell from inorganic matter is the most urgent problem which concerns the biologist who wants to make the theory of evolution complete. A successful experiment of this type may be not so far off. The study of chromosomes has shown that the genes, those short parts of the threadlike structure of the chromosomes which transfer individual properties, are no larger than large molecules of albumen. Presumably, biologists will some day construct synthetic albumen molecules of the gene type and of the protoplasm type, put them together, and thus produce an aggregate which possesses all the characteristics of a living cell. Should the experiment succeed, it would demonstrate conclusively that the origin of life can be traced back to inorganic matter.

The problem of life does not involve contradictions to the principles of an empiricist philosophy—such is the result of the biology of the nineteenth century. Life can be explained along with all other natural phenomena, and biology requires no principles that violate the laws of physics. The apparent teleology of living organisms is reducible to causality. Life does not call for the existence of an immaterial substance, a *vital force,* an *entelechy,* or whatever names have been proposed for such a supernatural entity. The philosophy of *vitalism,* which maintains the existence of a specific life substance of this kind, is historically to be classified as a descendant of philosophic rationalism. It springs from a philosophy which endows the mind with the power of controlling the universe and looks for a biology that explains the origin of mind in a substance not subject to the laws of the physical world. Empiricism manifests itself not only in the constructions of the philosopher, but also in the attitude with which the scientist pursues his experimental research. In this sense modern biology is empiricist, even though some of its experts still attempt to combine their scientific work with a vitalist philosophy.

The evolution of life is but the last chapter in a longer story, the story of the evolution of the universe. Ever since the fanciful cosmogonies of the ancients, the question of how this universe came into being has fascinated the human mind. Modern science, by the use of precision methods of observation and of inference, has given an answer more fanciful than anything ever dreamed of by the ancients. I should like to give a brief outline of these theories, which display the power of scientific method in one of its greatest achievements.

First there had to be a logical step: instead of asking how this universe came into being, the scientist asks how the universe came into being what it is now. He looks for an evolution from previous states to the present state and tries to push this history back as far as he can. Whether anything more remains to be asked is a question which I shall discuss presently.

The first answer is given by the results of geological research, which reveal that the crust of this earth was formed through the cooling down of a glowing gas ball. The interior of the earth is still glowing; the original crust is visible in the granite rocks, on top of which oceans have deposited the layers of sediment which form the greater part of the surface of our continents. Strangely enough, the duration of the process of crust formation is measured by a sort of geological clock, whose dial science has learned to read. The radioactive elements, uranium, thorium, and so forth, decay at well-known rates into more durable matter and finally wind up as lead. Measuring the amount of radioactive material in its ratio to the amount of lead, as found in the earth's surface at the present stage, the geologist can determine the time it took to develop all this material from pure radioactive substances. Assuming that in the gaseous state of the earth the radioactive elements were formed, while no decay products were yet existent, the geologist can identify the age of the earth's crust with this time. The age of the earth is thus found to be about two thousand million years.

The second answer concerns the stars. A fixed star, like our sun, obviously goes through an evolution; it gives off radiation at an enormous rate and must possess energy sources to make up for this continuous loss of energy. One such source is gravitation, as was recognized by Helmholtz; the star shrinks, and the matter moving toward its center exchanges its speed for heat. A more powerful source is the transformation of elements, such as occurs in the explosive processes of the atom bomb. At the high temperature in the interior of the star—the sun is estimated to have a temperature of twenty million degrees centigrade at its center—the processes of nuclear integration and disintegration go on permanently, and mass is transformed into energy. These processes were analyzed by Bethe, Gamow, and others in the light of recent discoveries concerning the formation of atomic nuclei. The major process of energy supply is the formation of helium from hydrogen, which liberates great amounts of energy, while the loss in the mass of the substance is relatively small. (This is the process which the projected hydrogen bomb is intended to copy.) Calculations made for the sun show that the "burning up" of its hydrogen supply allows for a life of about twelve thousand million years, of which two thousand million years have passed. During this process, the sun will slowly become hotter, until a maximum is reached after which stage it will cool off rapidly.

The theory of the evolution of a star is confirmed by inferences of a very different type, resembling the inferences used in Darwin's theory of evolution. For the totality of stars visible in the night sky, astronomers have discovered a systematic order, which can be regarded as representing the historical order of the stages run through by each individual. Once more the inference from the systematic order of the simultaneous to the order of temporal succession displays its power. It was more difficult to apply this inference to stars than to biological systems because the systematic order of the stars is not easily visible. The basis of these investigations is a statistical diagram compiled by the astronomers H. N. Russell and E. Hertzsprung. In this diagram, stars are classified as to spectral type, that is, with respect to certain lines which the spectroscope shows in the light of the star and which indicate its temperature. In combination with the brightness of the star, the spectral type leads to a certain arrangement of stars in a series. If the systematic order thus constructed is regarded as expressing the average historical succession of a star's life stages, this interpretation corresponds to the conclusions derived from conceptions about the heat generation in the interior of the stars. Young stars are gas balls of an enormous size and a very low density of matter; their light is reddish because their temperature is not very high. Old stars are of small extension, but of a high density of matter. As long as their temperature is still high, they show a white light, until they finally cool off to become invisible. Between the stages of the red giant and the white dwarf extends the life history of a star. The end is not very promising: our sun will get hotter for some time and make the oceans boil, so that mankind may have to emigrate to a more distant planet; but finally it will cool off and become a cold and dead piece of matter in whose environment no life is possible. Since the same fate is reserved to all other stars, the universe will eventually die the death of temperature equalization foretold by the second principle of thermodynamics (chap. 10).

The third answer concerns the history of the galaxies. A galaxy is an accumulation of hundreds of millions of stars. Our sun with its planetary system belongs to the galaxy whose periphery we see on the night sky as the Milky Way. Other galaxies are found in the spiral nebulae, which are millions of light years away from our own galaxy, separated by empty spaces from us and from each other. Spectroscopic observations, first made by Hubble, show that practically all galaxies run away from us at great speeds, the speed being the greater the farther away the spiral nebula is from our system. Assuming that each galaxy has always moved at the same speed on its path, we can figure out where it came from. The figures show that all galaxies, about two thousand million years ago, were close together at the same place and presumably constituted one huge gas ball of a very high temperature.

The appearance of the figure two thousand million years in all these computations is most striking. Some two thousand million years ago, there seems to have been the beginning of our universe, of our sun, and of our earth. The heavens reveal an evolution pointing to a common beginning at a remote date inscribed in the figures of spectroscopy and geology. Even pieces of meteorites, captured by our earth on their path through the universe, show the same date stamped into their material in terms of radioactive decay products. Once upon a time there was a huge glowing gas ball, the amoeba from which the universe sprang—that is how the story of evolution begins.

Is that all we can ask? Science has traced back the history of the universe to a date of two thousand million years ago. What was before that date? Are we allowed to ask how the primordial gas ball came into being?

Whoever asks this question has stepped on philosophical ground; and the scientist who tries to answer the question has turned philosopher. I should therefore like to explain what the modern philosopher would answer.

Philosophers of the speculative type answered the question by inventing a cosmogony which put fiction in the place of science, or stipulated an act of creation of matter from nothing—an answer which is but a badly veiled "we do not know". To go even further and base this answer on a "we shall never know" means arrogating to oneself, in the guise of humbleness, the ability of anticipating future scientific developments.

The modern philosopher reacts by a different attitude. He declines to give a definite answer, which would free the scientist from his responsibility. All he is able to do is to clarify what can be meaningfully asked and to outline several possible answers, leaving it to the scientist some day to say which answer is true. In fact, modern physics has contributed much material to this logical task and will find ways of further solutions, if the possible answers presently known were to turn out insufficient.

To ask how matter was generated from nothing, or to ask for a first cause, in the sense of a cause of the first event, or of the universe as a whole, is not a meaningful question. Explanation in terms of causes means pointing out a previous event that is connected with the later event in terms of general laws. If there were a first event, it could not have a cause, and it would not be meaningful to ask for an explanation. But there need not have been a first event; we can imagine that every event was preceded by an earlier event, and that time has no beginning. The infinity of time, in both directions, offers no difficulties to the understanding. We know that the series of numbers has no end, that for every number there is a larger number. If we include the negative numbers, the number series has no beginning either; for every number there is a smaller number. Infinite series without a beginning and an end have been successfully treated in mathematics; there is nothing paradoxical in them. To object that there must have been a first event, a beginning of time, is the attitude of an untrained mind. Logic does not tell us anything about the structure of time. Logic offers the means of dealing with infinite series without a beginning as well as with series that have a beginning. If scientific evidence is in favor of an infinite time, coming from infinity and going to infinity, logic has no objection.

It has become a favorite argument of antiscientific philosophies that explanation must stop somewhere, that there remain unanswerable questions. But the questions so referred to are constructed by a misuse of words. Words meaningful in one combination may be meaningless in another. Could there be a father who never had a child? Everyone would ridicule a philosopher who regarded this question as a serious problem. The question of the cause of the first event, or of the cause of the universe as a whole, is not of a better type. The word "cause" denotes a relation between two things and is inapplicable if only one thing is concerned. The universe as a whole has no cause, since, by definition, there is no thing outside it that could be its cause. Questions of this type are empty verbalisms rather than philosophic arguments.

Instead of asking for a cause of the universe, the scientist can ask only for the cause of the present state of the universe; and his task will consist in pushing farther and farther back the date from which he is able to account for the universe in terms of laws of nature. Today this date is two thousand million years ago—that is a good

208

long stretch of time, and to derive its chronicle from astronomical observations is a scientific achievement of the first order. Some day the date may be set back by another two thousand million years.

We wish to set the date back because a hot gas ball concentrated in a narrow spot surrounded by empty space is not a suitable state for a beginning—it calls for an explanation in terms of an earlier history. It is not a state that can have existed for any long time, because it is not a state of equilibrium. Perhaps the gas ball will some day be interpreted as a nebula in a superuniverse, which went through an evolution similar to ours. We do not know what the telescopes of the future will tell us—perhaps they will bring us a message from more distant spiral nebulae that do not belong to our expanding system. (See the footnote on p. 214.)

Einstein's theory of relativity supplies a more satisfactory interpretation of the initial gas ball. According to Einstein the universe is not infinite, but a closed Riemannian space of a spherical type. This is not to mean that the universe is enclosed in a sort of spherical shell, which in turn is imbedded in an infinite space. It means that the total space is finite, without having a border. Wherever we are, there is always some space around us in all directions, and no end is visible; but if we move along on a straight line, we shall some day come back to our starting point from the other direction. We may compare these properties of three-dimensional space to the observable properties of the two-dimensional surface of our earth, which everywhere exhibits the aspect of a practically plane surface, while the totality of all these areas is closed, so that someone always proceeding in a straight line will finally return to his starting point. Like all other conceptions of non-Euclidean geometry, a closed space is accessible to visual pictures, although such visualization requires some training to overcome a conditioning by a simpler geometrical environment.

These conceptions of Einstein were amended by the mathematicians Friedmann and Lemaître to the assumption that the total finite space does not have a constant size, but expands. We may compare this expansion to the stretching of the surface of a rubber balloon which is being inflated. Some two thousand million years ago, the universal space was rather small and all filled by the primordial gas; but ever since that time it has been expanding at the rate indicated by the speed of the receding galaxies. It is an important fact that the mathematics of relativity opens the possibility of such an expanding universe, although it does not lead to an unambiguous answer. Einstein's equations are what the mathematician calls differential equations, and such equations are compatible with various different solutions. The physicist tries to single out the solution that fits best the observational results. At present the astronomical data are still too meager for a definite answer.

It would be a very satisfactory solution of the problem of the beginning of the universe, if instead of leaving it always to a new phase of science to push the date of the initial stage farther back, we could devise a formula which determines for every state a preceding state and thus controls the whole evolution for an infinite past. This possibility is offered by the expanding universe, because there exist solutions of the relativistic equations of such a kind that it took an infinity of time for the universe to grow from the size zero to the small size of two thousand million years ago. The solution could also be somewhat varied, so that the initial stage in the infinite past has a small finite volume. To this mathematical schema we could add the following interpretation: as long as the universe was small, the gas filling it was in a stable condition; only from a certain size on did the gas break up into individual fragments, which by gravitational attraction developed into stars. Associated with this interpretation, the mathematical formula of the expanding universe would answer all questions that could be reasonably asked; it would not say that the universe ever had the size zero, or the small limiting size, since it would maintain only an asymptotic convergence, but would answer at one stroke all questions of the type: "what was the cause of this state", by assigning a predecessor to every given state. The question of the origin of the universe would then be answered in the same way as the question of the smallest number: the formula of the expansion would say that there is no origin of the universe, but that there is an infinite series of calculable states ordered in time. It remains to be seen whether this interpretation is compatible with astronomical data.

A somewhat different conception along similar lines was developed by Eddington. A small closed universe filled by a glowing gas can persist for a long time and is thus in an equilibrium, unlike a ball of gas suspended in an infinite universe. But it is not in a stable equilibrium inasmuch as the slightest disturbance starts an expansion, which leads to the evolution of twelve thousand million years accounted for by the laws of astrophysics. The instability to which this conception refers can be shown to be a consequence of the relativistic equations. After the period of evolution, the universe reaches equilibrium again, but it is dead because of thermodynamic degradation, which means that the equilibrium is stable and that small disturbances cannot start any major change. This world picture resembles astonishingly Democritus' and Epicurus' theory of atoms that moved in good order through space for an infinite time until a slight disturbance occurred, which by chain reaction turned the orderly motion into a chaos, from which the complicated structures of our world evolved. Epicurus' assumption of a slight disturbance without cause, often attacked by adherents of a strict determinism, appears admissible for an indeterministic physics. Quantum mechanics would regard the primordial gas as subject to fluctuations controlled by the laws of chance, and there is no difficulty in assuming that it took a long time until chance produced a fluctuation large enough to start the expansion of the universe. The abandonment of determinism makes it possible to conceive of a beginning of evolution which is not a creation but a product of chance. And it is a gradual beginning, because the transition from chance fluctuations to the disturbance is continuous and cannot be assigned to one definite time point.

There is also the possibility of a very different solution. The study of time order has led to the result that the direction of time derives from the irreversibility of thermodynamic processes and is thus a matter of statistics (chap. 10). It is very probable, but not absolutely certain, that energy "runs down" from higher forms to a state of uniform temperature. The "running down" of the universe is therefore a matter of statistics, and it is not impossible that reverse processes occur, that even the whole universe "runs up" for some time. The phrase "for some time" in this sentence has a questionable meaning, because if the universe "runs up", what we call the direction of time would be the opposite direction, and human beings living in such a period would regard this opposite direction as the direction of "becoming". In fact, the possibility referred to, which was envisaged by Boltzmann, means nothing less than that there is no such thing as a linear time sequence for the universe as a whole, but that time disintegrates into separate threads each of which has a serial order, whereas there is no supertime in terms of which the threads themselves could be ordered. Toward both ends the time of each thread would run out without terminating in a sharp point of demarcation, like a river in the desert. The stretch of time which the astronomers accord to our universe, from two thousand million years ago to ten thousand million years hence, might be one of those time threads. The nature of such a broken-up time has not yet been much investigated; but there is no doubt that it offers one of the possible forms for a solution of the time problem.

Incidentally, Eddington's conception of the beginning of the world must also be related to such an analysis of time. As Eddington indicates, only the period of evolution can be regarded, in this conception, as possessing a time; the two long periods of equilibrium before and after this time thread cannot be said to possess a time order because they do not represent irreversible processes. It therefore does not make much difference whether they are regarded as finite or infinite. To regard them as finite and to ask what was before the first stationary period, or after the second, would mean to employ a supertime, which we saw cannot be meaningfully defined. It seems there is no reason to describe the universe in an infinite time scale, which is anyway a mathematical schema rather than a warranted conclusion from physical reality. Observable phenomena can always be accounted for in terms of a finite time thread extending from one timeless state to another without a sharply demarcated beginning or end.

These are some possible answers to the question of the origin of the universe. What will be the true answer science will some day decide. The problem of the closed but expanding universe is still controversial; the astronomical evidence which, at present, is available for it is not conclusive. The solution will have to wait for much more observational material.* Difficult as it is to find the answer, there is no reason to end a discussion of evolution with a dogmatic "we shall never know". Those who believe that such is the last word should reëxamine their questions; they will find that what they were asking had no meaning. It has no meaning to ask what is the cause of the universe. All explanation must start with some matter of fact. Science can only push the matter of fact back to some logical place where it supplies a maximum of explanation.

The elimination of meaningless questions from philosophy is difficult because there exists a certain type of mentality that aspires to find unanswerable questions. The desire to prove that science is of a limited power, that its ultimate foundations depend on faith rather than on knowledge, is explainable in terms of psychology and education, but finds no support in logic. There are scientists who are proud when their lectures on evolution conclude with a so-called proof that there remain questions unanswerable for the scientist. The testimony of such men is often invoked as evidence for the insufficiency of a scientific philosophy. Yet it proves merely that scientific training does not always equip the scientist with a backbone to withstand the appeal of a philosophy that calls for submission to faith. He who searches for truth must not appease his urge by giving himself up to the narcotic of belief. Science is its own master and recognizes no authority beyond its confines.

---

* The new telescope on Mount Palomar in California is capable of doubling the range of observable stars and nebulae. A much wider range would be opened if it were possible to set up a telescope on the moon. The absence of an atmosphere would enable us to look a hundred or a thousand times farther into the universe than is possible at the present time.

13.

Modern Logic

THE CONSTRUCTION of symbolic logic has become one of the outstanding characteristics of scientific philosophy. Originally the secret code of a small group of mathematicians, this logic has more and more attracted the attention of the student of philosophy and has become the stage of important developments of philosophical thought. A short presentation of the evolution that led to symbolic logic, of its problems and its solutions, may appear welcome to all those who have no time for a technical study of the new branch of philosophy.

The science of logic is a discovery of the Greeks. That does not mean that there was no logical thinking before the Greeks. Logical thought is as old as thought; every successful act of thinking is controlled by the rules of logic. But it is one thing to apply these rules unknowingly in practical thought operations, and another to formulate them explicitly, so as to collect them in the form of a theory. It is this planned inquiry into logical rules which began with Aristotle.

Aristotle concentrated his investigations on what we know today to be a very special chapter of logic. He formulated the rules of class inference, that is, an inference referring to membership in classes. By "class" we understand all kinds of groups, or totalities, like the class of human beings, or of cats. That Socrates is a man is, for the logician, an instance of class membership: Socrates is a member of the class of men. An inference concerning class membership is called a syllogism. For instance, from the two premises "all men are mortal" and "Socrates is a man" we infer the conclusion "Socrates is mortal".

At first sight, inferences of this type appear trivial; but such judgment would be unfair to Aristotle. What Aristotle discovered was that there is such a thing as the *form* of an inference, to be distinguished from its *content*. The relation between premises and conclusion, illustrated by the inference concerning Socrates, is independent of the particular classes referred to; it would hold as well for other suitable classes and individuals. With the study of logical forms Aristotle made the decisive step that led to the science of logic. And he explicitly formulated some of the fundamental principles of logic, such as the principle of identity and that of contradiction.

But it is only the first step that was made by Aristotle. His logic covers merely some particular forms of thought operations. In addition to classes, there are relations. A relation does not have individual members, but refers to pairs of members (or triplets of members, or even groups of more members); that Abraham is the father of Isaac is a fact which concerns both Abraham and Isaac and therefore requires the relation "father of" for its expression. Similarly, if Peter is taller than Paul, the relation "taller than" holds between the two persons. Inferences concerning relations cannot be expressed in a class logic. For instance, Aristotle's logic cannot prove that if Abraham is the father of Isaac, Isaac is the son of Abraham; his logic does not have the means of expressing the form of this inference.

One would like to believe that it should not have been too difficult for the discoverer of class logic to extend his work to a logic of relations, since the language he spoke was as sophisticated as ours and had all the grammatical forms necessary for the treatment of relations. Moreover, Aristotle knew the existence of relations; in his book on categories he explains very clearly that a relation like "greater than" requires two things between which it holds. But he does not extend his theory of inference so as to include relations. It may be that the author of class logic was too much interested in more metaphysical questions to have the time for making his logical work complete. But then one of his disciples could have undertaken a logic of relations. Strangely enough, no such thing happened. Aristotle seems never to have realized the limitations of his logic. His disciples added a few details, but did not go essentially beyond the work of their master. And there was no change for the better in the following centuries. The history of logic shows the peculiar picture of a science that for more than two thousand years remained in the rudimentary stage in which its founder had left it.

What is the explanation of this historical fact? Compared with the enormous progress which mathematics and science made within those two thousand years, the history of logic looks like a barren spot in the garden of knowledge. What cause can account for this stagnation?

More than any other chapter of philosophy, logic requires a technical treatment of its problems. Logical problems are not solved through picture language, but require the precision of the mathematical formulation; even the statement of the problem is often impossible without the help of a language as technical as that of mathematics. It was the merit of Aristotle and his school to have created the beginnings of a technical language of logic, to which the Middle Ages made a few insignificant additions. But that is all that was done in this direction during those two thousand years. While great mathematicians provided their science with a highly efficient technique, the technique of logic was neglected; in fact, traditional logic offers the poor aspect of a science that never became the workshop of a great man. It appears that the born masters of abstract thought, instead of being attracted by logic, were absorbed by the science of mathematics, which offered to them greater possibilities of success. This applies even to the time of Aristotle; the logical analysis invested in the construction of mathematics by men like Pythagoras and Euclid surpasses by far the analytic achievements arrived at in Aristotle's logic. Without the help of the mathematical mind, logic was doomed to remain in an infantile stage. Kant, although unable to create a better logic, judged the situation correctly when he expressed his astonishment at the fact that logic was the only science that had not made any progress since its beginnings.

The first great mathematician whose interest turned toward logic was Leibniz. His results were revolutionary, and he started out with the program of a symbolic notation which, had he pursued it with the same energy and genius that he bestowed upon his invention of the differential calculus, would have speeded up the growth of symbolic logic by 150 years. But his work remained fragmentary and unknown at his time; writers of the nineteenth century had to collect it from letters and unpublished manuscripts. The turning point in the history of logic was the middle of the nineteenth century, when mathematicians like Boole and de Morgan undertook to set forth the principles of logic in a symbolic language of the kind of the mathematical notation. The construction of symbolic logic was carried on by men like G. Peano, C. S. Peirce, E. Schröder, G. Frege, B. Russell, with whom a new type of philosopher, the mathematical logician, entered upon the scene of history.

Like the philosophy of space and time, the new logic grew not from traditional philosophy, but from the soil of mathematics. A domain that so long had been neglected by mathematical thought was discovered to offer possibilities for a technical treatment similar to the technique of mathematics. With the construction of symbolic logic the nineteenth century made another contribution to philosophy. If the position of the nineteenth century in the history of thought is seen as described above, such a development will appear natural. The attempt to create a practicable technique, so successful within all sciences, was transferred to the domain of logic. The technique of logic, at the same time, offered itself as a tool for the investigation of the foundations of knowledge, which inquiry, in turn, appeared a natural consequence of the complication and the refinement of scientific thought. And the barren spot in the garden of knowledge began to be tilled with the highly developed technique of mathematics.

Why is the introduction of a symbolic notation of so much import to the science of logic? It has about the same significance as a good mathematical notation. Suppose you are given the problem: "If Peter were 5 years younger, he would be twice as old as Paul was when he was 6 years younger, and if Peter were 9 years older, he would be thrice as old as Paul, if Paul were 4 years younger". Try to solve it in the head by adding and subtracting and considering all the "if's", and you will soon arrive at a sort of dizziness as though you were riding on a merry-go-round. Then take a pen and paper, call Peter's age x and Paul's age y, write down the resulting equations and solve them the way you learned it in high school—and you will know what a notational technique is good for. There are similar problems in logic. "It is certainly not the case that Cleopatra was alive in

1938 and was not married to Hitler and not to Mussolini". What does that sentence combination mean? The mathematical logician shows you how to write it in symbols, then transforms the expression by operations similar to those you learned for the use of x and y, and finally tells you that the sentence means "if Cleopatra had been alive in 1938, she would have been married to Hitler or to Mussolini". I do not wish to say that the unraveled utterance is of great political significance; but the example illustrates the use of a symbolic technique. The application of the notation to problems of greater significance cannot be explained here, but it will appear obvious that the symbolic notation will also be useful if it is applied to formulations of technical issues in the sciences.

The symbolic notation is not only a tool to solve problems, but also clarifies meanings and enhances the functioning of logical thought. One of my students, whose brain was slightly injured through an automobile accident, complained that he had difficulties in understanding the meaning of involved sentences. I gave him exercises of the above-mentioned type which he did by the help of the symbolic notation, and after a week or two he told me that his thinking had greatly improved.

Symbolic logic, furthermore, has found an important application in the grammatical analysis of language. The grammar which we learned in school has grown out of Aristotelian logic and is by no means appropriate for delineating the structure of language. Aristotle's unfortunate failure to proceed to a logic of relations has led grammarians to the conception that every sentence must have one subject and a predicate, an interpretation inadequate for a great number of sentences. It is true that the sentence "Peter is tall" has the subject "Peter" and the predicate "tall". But the sentence "Peter is taller than

Paul" has two subjects, namely, "Peter" and "Paul", since the predicate "taller than" is a relation. The misunderstanding of linguistic structures, originating from adherence to Aristotelian logic, has seriously impaired the science of linguistics.

New prospects are offered by a coöperation of the logician and the linguist. For instance, the nature of the adjective, of the adverb, of the moods, voices, and tenses of verbs and of many other features of language appears in a new light when seen through the eyes of the logician. The comparative study of different languages is offered new possibilities when it is based on a neutral system of reference, the symbolic language of logic, which allows us to judge the various means of expression of the individual languages.

I have spoken so far of the practical use of the symbolic notation. But a good notation has also a theoretical use; it enables the logician to discover and to solve problems which could not be seen before.

The construction of symbolic logic made it possible to investigate from a new angle the relations between logic and mathematics. Why do we have two abstract sciences dealing with the products of thought? The question was taken up by Bertrand Russell and Alfred N. Whitehead, who arrived at the answer that mathematics and logic are ultimately identical, that mathematics is but a branch of logic developed with special reference to quantitative applications. This result was set forth in a lengthy book, written almost completely in the symbolic notation of logic. The decisive step in the proof was made by Russell's definition of number. Russell showed that the integers, the numbers 1, 2, 3, and so forth, can be defined in terms of the fundamental concepts of logic alone. It is obvious that such a proof could never have been given without the help of a symbolic notation; word language is too involved to express logical relations of this degree of complexity.

With his reduction of mathematics to logic, Russell completed an evolution which began with the development of geometry and which I described above as a disintegration of the synthetic a priori. Kant believed not only geometry but also arithmetic to be of a synthetic a-priori nature. With his proof that the fundamentals of arithmetic are derivable from pure logic, Russell has shown that mathematical necessity is of an analytic nature. There is no synthetic a priori in mathematics.

But if logic is analytic, it is empty; that is, it does not express properties of physical objects. Rationalist philosophers have repeatedly tried to regard logic as a science descriptive of some general properties of the world, as a science of being, or *ontology*. They believe that such principles as "everything in the world is identical with itself" inform us about properties of things. They overlook the fact that all the information supplied by this sentence consists in a definition laying down the use of the word "identical" and that what we learn from the sentence is not a property of things, but a linguistic rule. Logic formulates rules of language—that is why logic is analytic and empty.

I should like to explain more precisely the analytic nature of logic, the reason logic is said to be empty. Logic connects sentences in such a way that the resulting combination is true independently of the truth of the individual sentences. For instance, the sentence combination "if neither Napoleon nor Caesar reached an age of sixty years, then Napoleon did not reach the age of sixty years" is true whether or not Napoleon, or Caesar, died before the age of sixty years; this combination therefore does not inform us about the age reached by the persons referred to. That is what we mean by emptiness. On the

other hand, the example illustrates why logical relations
are necessarily true: they are so because no empirical
observation can ever falsify them. If one consults a reference book and finds that Napoleon died at the age of
fifty-four, this result will not falsify the sentence combination; but if one had found that Napoleon died at
the age of sixty-five, such result would not falsify it either.
Logical necessity and emptiness go together and make
up the analytic, or tautological nature of logic. All purely
logical statements are tautologies, like the given example; they say nothing and thus inform us just as much, or
as little, as the tautology "it will rain tomorrow or it will
not rain". It is not always so easy, however, to discover
the analytic character of a sentence combination. Consider the combination: "if any two men either love each
other or hate each other, then either there is a man who
loves all men or for every man there exists some man
whom he hates". Logic proves that this combination is
analytic; but the analytic character is by no means obvious.

Russell's conception of mathematics as analytic has
stirred up much attention, and some mathematicians
have resented an interpretation of their science according to which mathematical theorems are as empty as the
principles of logic. Such a judgment reveals a misunderstanding of the nature of logic. It is no disparagement
of mathematical thought if it is called analytic. The very
usefulness of mathematical thought derives from its analytic nature; just because mathematical theorems are
empty, they are absolutely reliable, and it is permissible
to employ them in the natural sciences. The use of mathematics can never falsify a scientific result, because mathematics cannot introduce any unapproved hidden content into a science. However, to say that mathematical
relations are empty does not mean that they are easy to

find. As explained, the discovery of empty relations can be an extremely difficult task, and the amount of labor and ingenuity involved in mathematics is evidence of the far-reaching significance of mathematical research.

Symbolic logic was widely used in the elaboration of a new mathematical discipline constructed in the nineteenth century: the theory of sets. The word "set" has the same meaning as the word "class" explained above with reference to Aristotelian logic. But how different is the theory of classes developed by the mathematicians of the nineteenth century from the class calculus of the Aristotelian logic! It is incomprehensible why the Aristotelian class logic still fills the usual textbooks on logic in an era which differs from that of Aristotle about as much as the railroad from the oxcart.

But symbolic logic has not always bestowed success on the logician. It has also led into difficulties, which were discovered by Russell and formulated in the antinomies of the theory of classes. An example may illustrate the problem.

When we regard a property, we can ask whether this property has itself the same property. In general, this will not be the case. Thus the property *red* is not red. It is different with other properties; for instance, the property *imaginable* is imaginable, the property *determined* is determined, and the property *old* is old, since it certainly existed even in prehistoric times. Let us use the name *predicable* for properties of the second kind; the others are then called *impredicable*. We have here an exhaustive classification; every property must be either predicable or impredicable. Where, then, must we classify the property *impredicable?*

Assume that *impredicable* is predicable; then it has the property which it represents, like *imaginable,* and therefore, *impredicable* is impredicable. Now assume that *impredicable* is impredicable. Our assumption states that *impredicable* has the property it represents; therefore, *impredicable* is predicable. Wherever we classify the property *impredicable,* we arrive at a contradiction.

Antinomies of this kind constitute a serious problem. If logic is to be absolutely reliable, we must have a guarantee that it will never lead to contradictions. It is an interesting fact that even the ancient logicians had constructed antinomies, among which the paradoxes of Zeno are familiar. Most of these paradoxes, however, are eliminated in the modern theory of classes by means of a more careful treatment of the concept "infinite". Russell's antinomy calls for a more radical cure. It shows that not every combination of words can be admitted as a meaningful statement, that some word combinations, although they have the form of a sentence, must be regarded as meaningless. For instance, the sentence "the property *determined* is determined", although reasonable at first sight, must be ruled out from the domain of meaningful sentences. These restrictions of language were formulated by Russell in his theory of types. A property of a property is of a higher type than a property of a thing. This distinction makes the formulation of the antinomy impossible and thus saves logic from contradictions.

Are we sure that logicians will never discover other kinds of antinomies? Do we possess a guarantee that logic is free from contradictions? This problem has concerned the German mathematician D. Hilbert, one of the greatest mathematicians of our time. He started a series of investigations which were aimed at the construction of a proof that logic and mathematics are free from contradictions. His work was continued by others; but the proof has been given so far only for rather simple logical systems. Difficulties have arisen for an extension of the proof to the complicated system of mathematics used by the modern mathematician, and it is still an open question whether Hilbert's program of a proof of consistency can be carried through. What the answer will be is one of the unsolved problems of modern logic. That such problems exist may demonstrate the fact that modern logic requires further research; a great deal of analysis of a kind never anticipated in traditional logic remains to be done.

The study of the antinomies and the theory of types have led to a distinction of great importance: the distinction between *language* and *metalanguage*. (The name is derived from the Greek word "meta", meaning "beyond".) Whereas the usual language speaks about things, the metalanguage speaks about language; it is the metalanguage, therefore, which we talk when we construct a theory of language. Such words as "word", "sentence", and so forth, are words of the metalanguage. A frequent means of expressing the transition to the metalanguage is the use of quotation marks; when we speak about the word "Peter", we include it in quotes and thus indicate that we do not speak about the man. For instance, "Peter" has five letters, whereas Peter plays baseball. If the two languages are mixed up, certain antinomies can be constructed, and the distinction of levels of language is therefore a necessary prerequisite of logic. The sentence "what I say right now is false" leads to contradictions, because if it is true, it is false, and if it is false, it is true. Such a sentence must be regarded as meaningless because it speaks about itself and violates the distinction of levels of language.

The study of the metalanguage has led into a general theory of signs, often called *semantics*, or *semiotics*, which investigates the properties of all forms of linguistic expression. This term includes such signs as traffic signs, or pictures, which are used like articulate language as instruments of communicating meanings to other persons. The highly emotional connotations of various forms of language, such as poetry or the language of the orator, are studied in the theory of signs with the help of modern psychology. Logic accounts only for the cognitive usage of language; the investigation of the instrumental usage of language requires another science, the science of semantics. Thus the rise of modern logic has brought to life another science, which deals with those properties of language that are, and must be, disregarded in logical analysis.

In addition to its use for mathematics, symbolic logic has acquired significance for other sciences. When physicists discovered that quantum mechanics leads to certain statements that cannot be verified as true or false (see chap. 11), it was possible to incorporate such statements in the frame of a three-valued logic, that is, a logic which assumes a category *indeterminate* between the two truth-values of truth and falsehood. The structure of such a logic had been developed by the methods of symbolic logic even before anyone thought of its application in physics. Similarly, other forms of *multivalued logic* have been developed. One of them, used for the interpretation of probability statements, replaces the two truth-values of truth and falsehood by a continuous scale of probabilities, varying from 0 to 1.

Symbolic logic has been applied, furthermore, to the analysis of biology, and it promises to be helpful in the study of the social sciences. It may even be used to transcribe logical problems in such a way that they can be "fed" into an electronic computer; and a modern robot of this kind might some day very well be able to solve logical problems which would defy the capacities of the human brain, in the same way that it already solves mathematical problems. Leibniz has voiced the opinion that if symbolic logic were sufficiently developed, all scientific controversies could be eliminated: instead of arguing against each other, scientists would say *calculemus,* meaning "let us figure it out". The modern logician is not that optimistic. Knowing that the operations of the machine would be restricted to deductive logic and its achievements would thus depend on the quality of the premises which the human operator feeds into it, the logician of our day would be content if, at least, *some* controversies could be settled in that way.

Logic is the technical part of philosophy; for that very reason, it is indispensable for the philosopher. The old-style philosopher, afraid of the precision of a technique, would like to exclude symbolic logic from the domain of philosophy and leave it to the mathematician. He does not have much success. The younger generation, as far as it has learned the symbolic notation in elementary logic classes, knows the value of the new form of logic and insists on its application. Like every notational technique, symbolic logic at first appears cumbersome and confusing to the student; it is only after some training that the new technique is recognized to be an instrument that facilitates logical understanding and makes ideas clear. In the teaching of symbolic logic I have had the experience that in the beginning the majority of the students are afraid of the notation and hate it; but after about two weeks of practice the picture changes and an amazing enthusiasm for the symbolism spreads through the class. There remain only a few students who never fully understand and always dislike the symbolism.

It seems to be the fate of symbolic logic that it is either hated or welcomed enthusiastically. Those who cannot attain the second stage might accomplish more in other fields than scientific philosophy and find success in less abstract applications of the powers of human thought.

14.

Predictive Knowledge

THE SYMBOLIC logic referred to in the preceding chapter is a deductive logic; it deals only with those thought operations that are characterized by logical necessity. Empirical science, though making wide use of deductive operations, in addition calls for a second form of logic, which because of its use of inductive operations is named inductive logic.

What distinguishes the inductive inference from a deductive one is the fact that it is not empty, that it leads to conclusions not contained in the premises. The conclusion that all crows are black is not logically contained in the premise that all crows so far observed were black; the conclusion may be false while the premise is true. Induction is the instrument of a scientific method that is intended to discover something new, something going beyond a summary of previous observations—the inductive inference is the instrument of predictive knowledge.

It was Bacon who clearly saw the indispensability of inductive inferences for scientific method, and his place in the history of philosophy is that of a prophet of induction (chap. 5). But Bacon also saw the weaknesses of inductive inference, the lack of necessity in its method, and the possibility of false conclusions. His endeavors to improve inductive inference were none too successful; inductive inferences of a more complicated structure, such as employed in the *hypothetico-deductive method* of the scientist (chap. 6), are far superior to Bacon's simple induction. But this method cannot supply logical necessity either; its conclusions may be false, and the reliability of deductive logic is unattainable for predictive knowledge.

The hypothetico-deductive method, or *explanatory induction,* has been much discussed by philosophers and scientists but its logical nature has often been misunderstood. Since the inference from the theory to the observational facts is usually performed by mathematical methods, some philosophers believe that the establishment of theories can be accounted for in terms of deductive logic. This conception is untenable, because it is not the inference from the theory to the facts, but conversely, the inference from the facts to the theory on which the acceptance of the theory is based; and this inference is not deductive, but inductive. What is given are the observational data, and they constitute the established knowledge in terms of which the theory is to be validated.

Moreover, the way this inductive inference is actually made has led some philosophers to a second form of misunderstanding. The scientist who discovers a theory is usually guided to his discovery by guesses; he cannot name a method by means of which he found the theory and can only say that it appeared plausible to him, that he had the right hunch, or that he saw intuitively which assumption would fit the facts. Some philosophers have misunderstood this psychological description of discovery as proving that there exists no logical relation leading from the facts to the theory; and they contend that no logical interpretation of the hypothetico-deductive method is possible. Inductive inference is for them guesswork inaccessible to logical analysis. These philosophers do not see that the same scientist who discovered his theory through guessing presents it to others only after he sees that his guess is justified by the facts. It is this claim of justification in which the scientist performs an inductive inference, since he wishes to say not only that the facts are derivable from his theory, but also that the facts make his theory probable and recommend it for the prediction of further observational facts. The inductive inference is employed not for finding a theory, but for justifying it in terms of observational data.

The mystical interpretation of the hypothetico-deductive method as an irrational guessing springs from a confusion of *context of discovery* and *context of justification*. The act of discovery escapes logical analysis; there are no logical rules in terms of which a "discovery machine" could be constructed that would take over the creative function of the genius. But it is not the logician's task to account for scientific discoveries; all he can do is to analyze the relation between given facts and a theory presented to him with the claim that it explains these facts. In other words, logic is concerned only with the context of justification. And the justification of a theory in terms of observational data is the subject of the theory of induction.

The study of inductive inference belongs in the theory of probability, since observational facts can make a theory only probable but will never make it absolutely certain. Even when this incorporation of induction in the theory of probability is recognized, new forms of misunderstanding arise. It is not easy to see the logical structure of the probability inference performed in the confirmation of theories through facts. Some logicians have believed that they have to construe confirmation as the reverse of a deductive inference; this is to say that if we can derive deductively the facts from the theory, we can derive inductively the theory from the facts. This interpretation, however, is oversimplified. In order to make the inductive inference, much more has to be known than the deductive relation from the theory to the facts.

A simple consideration makes it obvious that the inference by confirmation has a more complicated structure. A set of observational facts will always fit more than one theory; in other words, there are several theories from which these facts can be derived. The inductive inference is used to confer upon each of these theories a degree of probability, and the most probable theory is then accepted. In order to differentiate between these theories obviously more must be known than the deductive relation to the facts, which holds for each of them.

If we want to understand the nature of the inference by confirmation, we have to study the theory of probability. This mathematical discipline has developed methods which cover the general problem of *indirect evidence,* of which the inference that validates scientific theories is but a special case. For an illustration of the general problem I should like to mention the inferences made by a detective in his search for the perpetrator of a crime. Some data are given, such as a blood-stained handkerchief, a chisel, and the disappearance of a wealthy dowager, and several explanations offer themselves for what has happened. The detective tries to determine the most probable explanation. His considerations follow established rules of probability; using all the factual clues and all his knowledge of human psychology, he attempts to arrive at conclusions, which in turn are tested by new observations specifically planned for this purpose. Each test, based on new material, increases or decreases the probability of the explanation; but never can the explanation constructed be regarded as absolutely certain. The logician who tries to reconstruct the inferential schema of the detective finds all the necessary logical equipment in the calculus of probability. Even though he lacks the statistical material required for exact computations of probabilities, he can at least apply the formulas of the calculus in a qualitative sense. Numerically precise results are of course unattainable, if the given material admits only of rough estimates of probabilities.

The same considerations hold for the discussion of the probability of scientific theories, which are also to be selected among several possible explanations of observed data. The selection is achieved by the use of the general body of knowledge, in the face of which some explanations appear more probable than others. The final probability is therefore the product of a combination of several probabilities. The calculus of probability offers a suitable formula of this kind in the *rule of Bayes,* a formula which applies to statistical problems as well as to the inferences of the detective or the inference by confirmation.

The study of inductive logic, for these reasons, leads into the theory of probability. The inductive conclusion is made probable, not certain, by its premises; the inductive inference must be conceived as an operation belonging in the framework of the calculus of probability. In combination with the development that transformed causal laws into probability laws, these considerations will make it obvious why the analysis of probability is of so primary an import for the understanding of modern science. The theory of probability supplies the instrument of predictive knowledge as well as the form of the laws of nature; its subject is the very nerve of scientific method.

One would like to believe that the theory of probability has always been a province of empiricism; but the history of probability proves that this is not the case.

Rationalists of modern times, seeing the indispensability of probability notions, have attempted to construct a rationalist theory of probability. Leibniz' program of a logic of probability in the form of a quantitative logic, to measure degrees of truth, was certainly not meant to represent an empiricist solution of the problem of probability. The challenge was taken up by logicians who had the resources of symbolic logic at their disposal. Boole's logic of probability is perhaps to be classified on the rationalist side; and certainly Keynes' symbolic theory of probability belongs on this side, with its attempt to interpret probability as a measure of rational belief. These ideas have been taken up by some contemporary logicians who would not like to be classified as rationalists, but whose work actually puts them in this group, at least as far as their interpretation of probability is concerned.

For the rationalist, a degree of probability is the product of *reason* in the absence of *reasons*. If I toss a coin, will heads or tails turn up? I do not know anything about it, and I have no reason to believe in one alternative rather than in the other; therefore I regard the two possibilities as equally probable and accord to each the probability of one-half. The absence of reasons is construed as a reason to assume equality of probabilities; such is the principle of a rationalist interpretation of probability. This principle, known under the name of the principle of *indifference*, or of *no reason to the contrary*, is considered by the rationalist as a postulate of logic. It appears to him self-evident, like logical principles.

The difficulty with this interpretation of probability is that it abandons the analytic character of logic and introduces a synthetic a priori. A probability statement is not empty; when we toss a coin and say that the probability of heads turning up is one-half, we say something about future events. What we say is perhaps not easy to formulate; but there must be some reference to the future contained in the statement, since we employ it as a guide for action. For instance, we regard it as advisable to lay a fifty-fifty bet on heads, but would advise no one to offer higher odds for it. In fact, we employ probability statements because they bear upon future events; every act of planning requires some knowledge of the future, and if we have no perfectly certain knowledge, we are willing to use probable knowledge in its place.

The principle of indifference leads rationalism into all the familiar difficulties known from the history of philosophy. Why must nature follow reason? Why must events be equally probable, if we know equally much, or equally little about them? Does nature conform to human ignorance? Questions of this type cannot be given a positive answer—or the philosopher has to believe in a harmony between reason and nature, that is, in a synthetic a priori.

Some philosophers have attempted to construct an analytic interpretation of the principle of indifference. According to this interpretation the statement that a probability is one-half does not mean anything about the future, but simply expresses the fact that we have no more knowledge about the happening of the event than about that of the opposite event. In this interpretation the probability statement is, of course, easily justified, but it loses its character as a guide for action. In other words: it is true that the transition from equal ignorance to equal probability is then analytic, but a synthetic transition remains to be explained. If equal probabilities mean equal ignorance, why should we regard equal probabilities as justifying a fifty-fifty bet? In this question the very problem returns which the analytic interpretation of the principle of indifference was intended to evade.

The rationalist interpretation of probability must be regarded as a remnant of speculative philosophy and has no place in a scientific philosophy. The philosopher of science insists that the theory of probability be incorporated in a philosophy which does not have to resort to a synthetic a priori.

The empiricist philosophy of probability is based on the *frequency interpretation*. Probability statements express relative frequencies of repeated events, that is, frequencies counted as a percentage of the total. They are derived from frequencies observed in the past and include the assumption that the same frequencies will hold approximately for the future. They are constructed by means of an inductive inference. If we regard the probability of heads for the tossing of a coin as being given by one-half, we mean that in repeated throws of the coin heads will turn up in 50 per cent of the cases. In this interpretation the rules of betting are easily explained; to say that fifty-fifty is a fair bet for tossing a coin means that the use of this rule will in the long run afford equal gains to both parties. The merits of this interpretation are obvious; what we have to study are its difficulties. In fact, there are two essential difficulties connected with the frequency interpretation.

The first is the use of the inductive inference. It is true that for the frequency interpretation the degree of probability is a matter of experience and not of reason. If we had not observed that in tossing a coin we eventually arrive at an equal frequency for both faces, we would not speak of equal probabilities; the principle of indifference is merely a rationalist misinterpretation of a knowledge acquired from experience. This misinterpretation recalls similar rationalist fallacies, like the apriorist interpretation of the laws of geometry and of the principle of causality, which modern science has likewise revealed to be a product of experience. But the assertion that frequent repetitions of similar events are subject to numerical regularities can only be established by the use of inductive inferences and seems to involve a principle not derivable from experience. Between an empiricist philosophy and a solution of the problem of induction stands Hume's criticism of the inductive inference, which shows that induction is neither a priori nor a posteriori (chap. 5).

The second difficulty of the frequency interpretation concerns the applicability of a probability statement to a single case. A close relative of mine is seriously ill and I ask the doctor about the probability that my relative will live. The doctor answers that in 75 per cent of cases of this disease the patient survives. How does this frequency statement help me? It may be of use to the doctor, who has many patients; it will tell him what percentage of them will not die from the disease. But I am interested only in this particular person and want to know with what probability *he* will live. It seems to make no sense when a probability of a single event is stated in terms of frequencies.

I shall answer the two objections one after the other, beginning with the second. It is true that we often assign a probability to a single event. But it does not follow that the meaning we usually associate with our words is a correct interpretation. Consider the previous discussion of the meaning of an implication (chap. 10). "If an electric current flows through the wire the magnetic needle will be deflected". We believe that the *if-then* relation has a meaning for this individual event: that the electric current necessarily produces the deflection of the needle. Logical analysis shows us that this interpretation is mistaken, that the necessity of the implication merely derives from its generality, and that all we mean by the necessary connection of the two events is the fact that if one event happens, the other one will always occur. In an individual instance we forget about this analysis and believe we can speak of an implication concerning this instance alone. It is not easy to get away from this interpretation. "If I turn on this faucet, the water will run". It appears so obvious that we speak about nothing but the individual instance, that turning on this faucet produces the running of the water. When the logician explains to us that there is a reference to generality involved in the statement, that we are speaking about all faucets in the world, we are unwilling to believe him—and yet, we have to accept his interpretation if our words are to have any verifiable sense.

Of the same kind is the interpretation of the probability statement. We believe it has a meaning that there is a 75 per cent probability that Mr. X will live; yet all that is said refers to a class of persons having a similar disease. We might wish very much to know something about the individual case. But Mr. X will either live or not live—it makes no sense to attach a degree of probability to an individual event, because one event is not capable of being measured by degrees. Assume Mr. X survives his illness—does that fact verify the prediction which referred to a probability of 75 per cent? Obviously not, because a probability is compatible with the happening as well as with the nonhappening of the event. If we consider a great number of events, the fraction of 75 per cent is expressible and therefore testable through observation. But an individual event cannot occur to a degree. A statement about the probability of a single event is meaningless.

Yet such statements are not as unreasonable as might appear after this logical analysis. It may be a good practice to attach a meaning to a probability statement about a single event, if daily experience supplies us with a number of similar cases. The man who believes that if he turns on the faucet, the water *must* flow, has developed a good habit in so far as his belief will lead him to correct statements about the totality of such events. Similarly, the man who believes that a probability of 75 per cent applies to a single case has developed a good habit, because his belief will induce him to say that of a great number of similar cases 75 per cent will have the result referred to. This consideration applies even when our daily experience does not supply us with similar events, but with a number of events of various kinds and various degrees of probabilities. We may be confronted today by a case of disease for which there is a 75 per cent probability of survival, tomorrow by a prediction of good weather of 90 per cent probability, the day after tomorrow by a prediction of 60 per cent probability concerning the stock market—if in all these cases we assume the more probable event to happen, we will be right in the greater number of cases. The many events of everyday life constitute a series, inhomogeneous as it may be, which admits of the frequency interpretation of probability. To speak of a meaning of probability for a single event is a harmless or even useful habit, because it leads to a correct evaluation of the future as soon as this language is translated into a statement about a series of events.

Linguistic habits of this kind need not make the logician unhappy. He has means to allot to such habits a place in logic. He regards expressions of this type as having a fictitious meaning, as representing an elliptic mode of speech, which has acquired an apparent life of its own, but which is meaningful only because it can be translated into a statement of a different kind. The logician allows the mathematician to speak of the infinitely distant point at which two parallels intersect, because he knows that all the statement means is that the two lines do not intersect at a finite distance. The logician will also allow a man to speak of a necessary implication in a single case, or of a probability in a single case, and regard such mode of speech as representing a fictitious meaning. Using a technical term he speaks of a *transfer of meaning* from the general to the particular case. Whenever linguistic habits are useful, the logician will always be able to account for them.

Differences arise, not in the language of everyday life, but when we speak about the meaning of such statements. These differences concern philosophy. The logician, who sees that probability statements refer to a frequency, arrives at a peculiar evaluation of probability statements, which differentiates them from other statements. I should like to explain this difference more closely.

Suppose somebody casts a die and you are asked to predict whether or not face "six" will turn up. You will prefer to predict that face "six" will not turn up. Why? You do not know it for certain; but you have a greater probability, namely of ⅚, for "nonsix" than for "six". You cannot claim that your prediction must come true; but it is advantageous for you to make this prediction rather than the contrary one, because you will be right in the greater number of cases.

A statement of this kind I have called a *posit*. A posit is a statement which we treat as true although we do not know whether it is so. We try to select our posits in such a way that they will be true as often as possible. The degree of probability supplies a *rating* of the posit; it tells us how good the posit is. Such is the only function of a probability. If we have the choice between a posit of the rating ⅚ and one of the rating ⅔, we shall prefer the first, because this posit will be true more often. We see that the degree of probability has nothing to do with the truth of the individual statement, but that it functions as an advice how to select our posits.

The method of positing is applied to all kinds of probability statements. If we are told that the probability of a rain tomorrow is 80 per cent, we posit that it will rain, and act accordingly; for instance, we tell the gardener that he need not come tomorrow to water our garden. If we have information that the stock market will probably go down, we sell our stock. If the doctor tells us that smoking will probably shorten our lifetime, we stop smoking. If we are told that we shall probably get a job with higher pay by applying for a certain position, we make the application. Although all these statements about what will happen are only maintained as probable, we treat them as true and act accordingly; that is, we employ them in the sense of posits.

The concept of posit is the key to the understanding of predictive knowledge. A statement about the future cannot be uttered with the claim that it is true; we can always imagine that the contrary will happen, and we have no guarantee that future experience will not present to us as real what is imagination today. This very fact is the rock on which every rationalist interpretation of knowledge has been wrecked. A prediction of future experiences can be uttered only in the sense of a trial; we take its possible falsehood into account, and if the prediction turns out to be wrong, we are ready for another trial. The method of trial and error is the only existing instrument of prediction. A predictive statement is a posit; instead of knowing its truth we know only its rating, which is measured in terms of its probability.

The interpretation of predictive statements as posits solves the last problem that remains for an empiricist conception of knowledge: the problem of induction.

Empiricism broke down under Hume's criticism of induction, because it had not freed itself from a fundamental rationalist postulate, the postulate that all knowledge must be demonstrable as true. For this conception the inductive method is unjustifiable, since there exists no proof that it will lead to true conclusions. It is different when the predictive conclusion is regarded as a posit. In this interpretation it does not require a proof that it is true; all that can be asked for is a proof that it is a good posit, or even the best posit available. Such a proof can be given, and the inductive problem can thus be solved.

The proof requires some further investigation; it cannot be given simply by showing that the inductive conclusion has a high probability. It requires an analysis of the methods of probability and must be based on considerations that are themselves independent of such methods. The justification of induction is to be given outside the theory of probability, because the theory of probability presupposes the use of induction. The meaning of this maxim will be made clear presently.

The proof is preceded by a mathematical investigation. The calculus of probability has been constructed in an axiomatic form, comparable to the geometry of Euclid; this construction shows that all the axioms of probability are purely mathematical theorems and thus analytic statements, if the frequency interpretation of probability is accepted. The only point where a non-analytic principle intervenes is the ascertainment of a degree of probability by means of an inductive inference. We find a certain relative frequency for a series of observed events and assume that the same frequency will hold approximately for further continuation of the series —that is the only synthetic principle on which the application of the calculus of probability is based.

This result is of greatest significance. The manifold forms of induction, including the hypothetico-deductive method, are expressible in terms of deductive methods, with the sole addition of induction by enumeration. The axiomatic method supplies the proof that all forms of induction are reducible to induction by enumeration: the mathematician of our time proves what Hume took for granted.

The result may appear surprising, because the method of constructing explanatory hypotheses, or of indirect evidence, looks so different from a simple induction by enumeration. But since it is possible to construe all forms of indirect evidence as inferences covered by the mathematical calculus of probability, these inferences are included in the result of the axiomatic investigation. By means of the power of deduction, the axiomatic system controls the most remote applications of probability inferences, like the engineer who controls a remote missile by radio waves; even involved inferential structures employed by the detective or by the scientist can be accounted for in terms of the axioms. These structures are superior to a simple induction by enumeration because they contain so much deductive logic—but their inductive content is exhaustively described as a network of inductions of the enumerative type.

I should like to illustrate how enumerative inductions can be combined into a network. For centuries Europeans had known white swans only, and they inferred that all swans in the world were white. One day black swans were discovered in Australia; so the inductive inference was shown to have led to a false conclusion. Would it have been possible to avoid the mistake? It is a matter of fact that other species of birds display a great variety of color among their individuals; so the logician should have objected to the inference by the argument that, if color varies among the individuals of other species, it may also vary among the swans. The example shows that one induction can be corrected by another induction. In fact, practically all inductive inferences are made, not in isolation, but within a network of many inductions. A biologist once told me that he had tested the heredity of an artificial mutation through many generations and thus was sure that it was a genuine mutation. When I asked him how many generations he had used for the test, he answered that he had examined fifty generations of flies. The number would appear small to an insurance statistician, who is accustomed to deal with millions of cases before he makes an inductive inference. What is a large number? The answer can be given only on the basis of other inductions, which inform us how large a number must be in order that we can expect an observed frequency to persist. For a test of heredity, fifty generations is a large number. When a doctor gives a Wassermann test to a patient, checking him for syphilis, he makes only one observation; so the number one is here a large number for an inductive inference. That it is, is shown by other inductive inferences, which have established the fact that, if one test is positive or negative, so will be all further tests. When I say that all inductive inferences are reducible to induction by enumeration, I mean that they are expressible through a network of such simple inductions. The method by which these elementary inferences are combined can be of a much more complicated structure than the one employed in the preceding examples.

Since all inductive inferences are reducible to induction by enumeration, all that is required for making inductive inferences legitimate is a justification of induction by enumeration. Such a justification is possible, when it is realized that inductive conclusions are not claimed to be true statements, but are uttered merely in the sense of posits.

When we count the relative frequency of an event, we find that the percentage found varies with the number of observed cases, but that the variations die down with increasing number. For instance, birth statistics show that of 1,000 births 49 per cent were boys; increasing the number of cases, we find 52 per cent boys among 5,000 births, 51 per cent boys among 10,000 births. Assume for a moment we know that going on we shall finally arrive at a constant percentage—the mathematician speaks of a limit of the frequency—what numerical value should we assume for this final percentage? The best we can do is to consider the last value found as the permanent one and to employ it as our posit. If the posit on further observation turns out to be false, we shall correct it; but if the series converges toward a final percentage, we must eventually arrive at values which are close to the final value. The inductive inference is thus shown to be the best instrument of finding the final percentage, or the probability of an event, if there is such a limiting percentage at all, that is, if the series converges toward a limit.

How do we know that there is a limit of the frequency? Of course, we have no proof for this assumption. But we know: if there is one, we shall find it by the inductive method. So if you want to find a limit of the frequency, use the inductive inference—it is the best instrument you have, because, if your aim can be reached, you will reach it that way. If it cannot be reached, your attempt was in vain; but then any other attempt must also break down.

The man who makes inductive inferences may be compared to a fisherman who casts a net into an unknown part of the ocean—he does not know whether he will catch fish, but he knows that if he wants to catch fish he has to cast his net. Every inductive prediction is like casting a net into the ocean of the happenings of nature; we do not know whether we shall have a good catch, but we try, at least, and try by the help of the best means available.

We try because we want to act—and he who wants to act cannot wait until the future has become observational knowledge. To control the future—to shape future happenings according to a plan—presupposes predictive knowledge of what will happen if certain conditions are realized; and if we do not know the truth about what will happen, we shall employ our best posits in the place of truth. Posits are the instruments of action where truth is not available; the justification of induction is that it is the best instrument of action known to us.

This justification of induction is very simple; it shows that induction is the best means to attain a certain aim. The aim is predicting the future—to formulate it as finding the limit of a frequency is but another version of the same aim. This formulation has the same meaning because predictive knowledge is probable knowledge and probability is the limit of a frequency. The probability theory of knowledge allows us to construct a justification of induction; it supplies a proof that induction is the best way of finding that kind of knowledge which is the only sort attainable. All knowledge is probable knowledge and can be asserted only in the sense of posits; and induction is the instrument of finding the best posits.*

---

* In his book *Human Knowledge* (New York, 1948) Professor Bertrand Russell has criticized my theory of probability and induction. I have always admired Professor Russell's critical judgment; but in this case I can regard his objections only as the result of misunderstandings. For instance, he does not see (pp. 413–414) that in my theory good grounds are given to treat a posit as true, and that my rule of induction cannot be shown to be invalid by constructing instances where the inductive conclusion is false. The answers to his objections are all given in my book *The Theory of Probability* (Berkeley, 1949), although this book does not ex-

This solution of the problem of induction will be clarified if it is confronted with the rationalist theory of probability. The principle of indifference, which occupies a logical position similar to that of the principle of induction because it is used for the ascertainment of a degree of probability, is regarded by the rationalist as a self-evident principle of logic; he thus arrives at a *synthetic self-evidence,* at a synthetic a priori logic. Incidentally, the principle of induction by enumeration is often also regarded as a self-evident principle; this conception represents a second version of a synthetic a priori logic of probability. The empiricist conception of inductive logic is essentially different. The principle of induction by enumeration, which constitutes its only synthetic principle, is not regarded as self-evident, or as a postulate which logic could validate. What logic can prove is that the use of the principle is advisable if a certain aim is envisaged, the aim of predicting the future. This proof, the justification of induction, is constructed in terms of analytic considerations. The empiricist is allowed to use a synthetic principle, because he does not assert that the principle is true or must lead to true conclusions or to correct probabilities or to any kind of success; all he asserts is that employing the principle is the best he can do. This renunciation of any truth claim enables him to in-

---

plicitly refer to Russell's objections, since it was printed before his book was published. But this presentation of my theory in the English language is more explicit in its formulations than the original, which was published in German in 1935 and on which Russell's criticism is based. It is to be regretted seriously that Bertrand Russell, who has contributed so much to the elimination of the synthetic a priori from mathematics, has apparently become the advocate of a synthetic a priori in the theory of probability and induction. He believes that induction presupposes "an extra-logical principle not based on experience" (p. 412). But if knowledge is interpreted as a system of posits, no such principle is needed. I should like to express the hope that Professor Russell, after reading my above mentioned presentation, will revise his views.

corporate a synthetic principle in an analytic logic and to satisfy the condition that what he *asserts* on the basis of his logic is analytic truth only. He can do so because the conclusion of the inductive inference is not asserted by him, but only posited; what he asserts is that positing the conclusion is a means to his end. The empiricist principle that reason cannot make other than analytic contributions to knowledge, that there is no synthetic self-evidence, is thus fully carried through.

The quandaries of empiricism, formulated in David Hume's skepticism, were the product of a misinterpretation of knowledge and vanish for a correct interpretation —such is the outcome of a philosophy grown from the soil of modern science. The rationalist had not only presented the world with a series of untenable systems of speculative philosophy; he had also poisoned the empiricist interpretation of knowledge by inducing the empiricist to strive for unattainable aims. The conception of knowledge as a system of statements that are demonstrable as true had to be overcome by the evolution of science, before a solution of the problem of predictive knowledge could be found. The search for certainty had to die down within the most precise of all sciences of nature, within mathematical physics, before the philosopher could account for scientific method.

The picture of scientific method drafted by modern philosophy is very different from traditional conceptions. Gone is the ideal of a universe whose course follows strict rules, a predetermined cosmos that unwinds itself like an unwinding clock. Gone is the ideal of the scientist who knows the absolute truth. The happenings of nature are like rolling dice rather than like revolving stars; they are controlled by probability laws, not by causality, and the scientist resembles a gambler more than a prophet. He can tell you only his best posits—he never knows beforehand whether they will come true. He is a better gambler, though, than the man at the green table, because his statistical methods are superior. And his goal is staked higher—the goal of foretelling the rolling dice of the cosmos. If he is asked why he follows his methods, with what title he makes his predictions, he cannot answer that he has an irrefutable knowledge of the future; he can only lay his best bets. But he can prove that they *are* best bets, that making them is the best he can do— and if a man does his best, what else can you ask of him?

15.

Interlude: Hamlet's Soliloquy

TO BE, OR NOT TO BE—that is not a question but a tautology. I am not interested in empty statements. I want to know the truth of a synthetic statement: I want to know whether I shall be. Which means whether I shall have the courage to avenge my father.

Why do I need courage? It is true, my mother's husband, the king, is a powerful man and I shall risk my life. But if I can make it plain to everybody that he murdered my father, everybody will be on my side. If I can make it plain to everybody. It is so plain to me.

Why is it plain? I have good evidence. The ghost was very conclusive in his arguments. But he is only a ghost. Does he exist? I could not very well ask him. Maybe I dreamed him. But there is other evidence. That man had a motive to kill my father. What a chance to become king of Denmark! And the hurry with which my mother married him. My father had always been a healthy man. It's a good piece of indirect evidence.

But that's it: nothing but indirect evidence. Am I allowed to believe what is only probable? Here is the point where I lack the courage. It is not that I am afraid of the present king. I am afraid of doing something on the basis of a mere probability. The logician tells me that a probability has no meaning for an individual case. How then can I act in this case? That is what happens when you ask the logician. The native hue of resolution is sicklied over with the pale cast of thought. But what if I should start thinking after the deed and find out I should not have done it?

Is the logician so bad? He tells me that if something is probable I am allowed to make a posit and act as though it were true. In doing so I shall be right in the greater number of cases. But shall I be right in *this* case? No answer. The logician says: act. You will be right in the greater number of cases.

I see a way out. I shall make the evidence more conclusive. It is really a good idea: that show I shall put on. It will be a crucial experiment. If they murdered him they will be unable to hide their emotions. That is good psychology. If the test is positive I shall know the whole story for certain. See what I mean? There are more things in heaven and earth than are dreamt of in your philosophy, my dear logician.

I shall know it for certain? I see your ironical smile. There is no certainty. The probability will be increased and my posit will have a higher rating. I can count on a greater percentage of correct results. That is all I can reach. I can't get away from making a posit. I want certainty, but all the logician has for me is the advice to make posits.

There I am, the eternal Hamlet. What does it help me to ask the logician, if all he tells me is to make posits? His advice confirms my doubt rather than giving me the courage I need for my action. Logic is not made for me. One has to have more courage than Hamlet to be always guided by logic.

16.

The Functional Conception
of Knowledge

I N THE preceding chapters, a number of results of
scientific philosophy have been presented; in addition, the two major tools of knowledge, deductive and inductive logic, have been reviewed in
their methods and results. I should like to give in this
chapter a summary of the most general parts of scientific
philosophy, in which a new conception of knowledge has
been developed and the problem of physical reality has
been given a scientific solution. To make the nature of
this conception clear I will compare it with the conception of knowledge which is more or less openly adhered
to in the traditional philosophical systems.

Speculative philosophy is characterized by a *transcendental* conception of knowledge, according to which
knowledge transcends the observable things and depends
upon the use of other sources than sense perception. Scientific philosophy has constructed a *functional* conception of knowledge, which regards knowledge as an instrument of prediction and for which sense observation
is the only admissible criterion of nonempty truth. I
should like to explain both views more fully in order to
confront the one with the other.

The transcendental conception of knowledge has
found its classical symbolization in Plato's parable of the

cave. Plato depicts a cave in which several persons live, who were born there and never have left it; they are chained to their places so that they face the back wall of the cave and cannot turn their heads. In front of the entrance of the cave there is a fire, which throws rays of light into the cave and upon the back wall. Between the fire and the entrance people are walking and their shadows fall upon the back wall of the cave; the inhabitants of the cave see these shadows, but will never see the people outside, because they cannot turn their heads. They will think that the shadows are the real things and will never know that there is a world outside, of which they see only the shadow. Of this kind, says Plato, is the knowledge of the physical world which human beings possess. The perceptible world is like the shadows on the wall of the cave. Thought alone can reveal to us the existence of a higher reality, of which visible objects are but poor images.

For two thousand years the parable of the cave has symbolized the attitude of the speculative philosopher. It expresses the view of a man deeply dissatisfied with the results of sense experience, who wishes intensely to go beyond the observables and what can be inductively inferred from them. It represents empirical knowledge as a poor substitute for a better knowledge accessible to mental vision alone and reserved to the mathematician and the philosopher. It is transcendentalism in its purest form. It introduces a line of philosophic thought which finally culminates in the distinction between things of appearance and things-in-themselves. The outcome of Kant's masterly synopsis of rationalism repeats the dichotomy into a world of this side and a world of the "beyond", by which rationalism began its triumphal march through western civilization—and which is psychologically so closely related to the religious dichotomy into the earthly life here and the heavenly life to come.

To those who cannot give up this dichotomy, scientific philosophy has not much to say. Rationalism is an emotional bias toward a world of imagination, a discontent with physical reality that springs from other than logical motives and must be cured by other than logical means. The logician of today can show that the aim of rationalism is unattainable, that knowledge derived from reason alone is empty, that reason cannot tell us the laws of the world. But to abandon the desire for the unattainable requires a revision of emotional weights. The symbol of the rationalist idealist is not the man who discovers the unobservable causes of observable phenomena—for that is what the scientist does, who, if he were chained in Plato's cave, would soon find out through the method of indirect evidence that the shadows observed have outside causes.* To go beyond the observables by means of scientific inference is the legitimate method of the empiricist. The symbol of the idealist is the man who resorts to daydreaming because he is unable to enjoy reality in all its moral and aesthetic imperfections. Idealism is the philosophical brand of escapism; it has always flourished in times of social catastrophies which have shaken the foundations of human society. Difficult as it is to overcome the narcotic wish-fulfillment of dreams, there are ways to get away from the rationalistic belief in things-in-themselves, disporting, unobserved, behind the façade of appearance. Such an emotional readjustment can sometimes be achieved by the study of positive sciences, by the experience of the emotional satisfaction originat-

* A study of methods of this type, by means of which Plato's cavemen could have inferred the existence of the external world, is presented in my book *Experience and Prediction* (Chicago, 1938), § 14. Reference is made to this book for a more elaborate exposition of a modern theory of knowledge.

ing from the control of observable things and the success-ful prediction of their behavior. But sometimes it re-quires the intervention of the psychoanalyst.

It was the historical mission of empiricism to counter-act the rationalist dichotomy. Ever since the days of the ancient atomists and skeptics it has endeavored to create a philosophy of this world, refusing to recognize a "be-yond". It could not be successful before science itself had stripped off its rationalist disguise. The mathematical analysis of nature, originally the apparent triumph of ra-tionalist methods, has eventually turned out to be the instrument of a knowledge which bases its truth claims on sense perception, an instrument only, not a source of truth. The nineteenth and twentieth centuries, to which we owe this development, have thus become the cradle of a new empiricism that not only attacked rationalism, but also had the means to overcome it. Because of its use of the methods of symbolic logic for the analysis of knowl-edge, it is also called *logical empiricism*.

In contrast to the transcendental conception of knowl-edge, the philosophy of the new empiricism may be called a *functional conception of knowledge*. In this interpre-tation, knowledge does not refer to another world, but portrays the things of this world so as to perform a func-tion serving a purpose, the purpose of predicting the future. I should like to discuss this conception, which has become a principle of logical empiricism.

Human beings are things among other things of na-ture, and they are affected by other things through the mediation of their sense organs. The affection produces various kinds of reactions of the human body, among which the linguistic reaction, the production of a sign system, is most important. Signs are spoken or written down; the written form, though perhaps for the purposes of life not as important as the spoken one, is superior in that it follows a stricter system of rules and exhibits more precisely the cognitive content of language.

What is this cognitive content? It is not something that is added to the sign system; it is a property of the sign system. Signs are physical things, such as ink mounds on paper, or sound waves, which are used in a correspondence relation to other physical things; the correspondence, which does not rest upon any similarity, is based on a convention. For instance, the word "house" corresponds to a house, the word "red" to the property of redness. Signs are combined in such a way that certain sign combinations, called sentences, correspond to states of affairs of the physical world. Such sign combinations are said to be true. For instance, when the sentence "the house is red" corresponds to an actual state of affairs, it is called true. Certain other sign combinations, which by the addition of the sign "not" can be transformed into true sentences, are called false. A sign combination which can either be shown to be true or be shown to be false is called meaningful. This concept is important because we are often concerned with sign combinations whose truth or falsity cannot be determined at present, but can be determined at some later time. Any unverified statement, like "it will rain tomorrow", is of this type.

The reference to verifiability is a necessary constituent of the theory of meaning. A sentence the truth of which cannot be determined from possible observations is meaningless. Although rationalists have believed that there are meanings in themselves, empiricists at all times have insisted that meaning hinges on verifiability. Modern science is a documentation of this view. In the foregoing analysis of space, time, causality, and quantum mechanics, the dependence of meaning on verifiability was obvious; without an adherence to this view modern physics would remain incomprehensible. The *verifi-*

ability theory of meaning is an indispensable part of a scientific philosophy.

Instead of saying "the sentence has a meaning" it would be preferable to say "the sentence is meaningful"; this version shows more clearly that meaning is a property of signs, and not something added to them. The meaningful sign combinations are important because they allow us to speak about happenings unknown to us, in particular, the happenings of the future. The widening of language from true sentences to meaningful sentences allows for the theoretical use of language; that is, this widening enables the sign user to describe various possible happenings and select among his formulations the one which it appears most advisable to regard as true.

Sentences can be verified in various ways. The simplest form of verification is through direct observation; but only a narrow group of sentences is thus verifiable, such as "it rains", or "Peter is taller than Paul". If an observation sentence refers to the past, we regard verification as possible even if there was no observer; for instance, the sentence "it snowed on Manhattan island on November 28, A.D. 4" is verifiable and thus meaningful because there might have been an observer. Other sentences cannot be directly verified. That there was a time when dinosaurs inhabited the earth and no human race existed, or that matter consists of atoms, can only be indirectly verified by the help of inductive inferences based on direct observations. Such sentences are meaningful because they admit of an indirect verification. The rules for this kind of verification are given by the calculus of probability. The sentence thus verified is uttered in the sense of a posit. If it concerns the future, it may be used as a guide for actions. The sign system constructed on this definition of meaning is so devised that it can be employed as an instrument of prediction—that is its function for the sign user. If it serves this purpose, it is called knowledge.

The objection has been raised that meaning is of a subjective nature; that nobody can tell a man what he means; and that everyone should be allowed to use his words in meanings which appear suitable to him. According to this objection, it is an unjustifiable imposition upon the use of language if the scientific philosopher insists that unverifiable sentences should be ruled out, or that verification should always be based on sense observation in combination with inductive or deductive inferences. This objection, however, misunderstands the logical nature of the verifiability theory of meaning. This theory is not intended to be a sort of moral command. The scientific philosopher is tolerant; he allows everyone to mean what he wants. But he tells him: if you use unverifiable meanings, your words cannot account for your actions. What you do is always oriented toward the future; and statements about the future can be translated into possible experiences only inasmuch as they are verifiable. The empiricist theory of meaning does not supply a description of a person's subjective meanings. It is a rule proposed for the form of language and advisable for good reasons: it defines the kind of meaning which, if assumed for a person's words, makes his words compatible with his actions. This latter property is all that can be reasonably required of a theory of meaning. Those who accept the verifiability criterion of meaning speak a language consistent with their behavior; for them, language performs a function indispensable for the pursuit of activities, and is not an empty system unrelated to the world of experience.

The functional conception deprives knowledge of all the mysteries that two thousand years of rationalism have carried into it. It makes the nature of knowledge very

simple—but the simple solution is often the most difficult one to find. The theory of knowledge had first to be
freed from the ballast of a synthetic a priori, the remnant
of a mystical trend toward a world of entities behind the
observable things, before it could proceed to a clear statement of knowledge as functional. And the proof that
knowledge is functional, that it is the best instrument for
making predictions, could not be given before a satisfactory interpretation of probability was found. As long
as empiricism was unable to account for the use of inductive inferences and probabilities, it was a program
only and not a philosophic theory. The program of empiricism, the principle that all synthetic truth derives
from observation and that all contributions of reason to
knowledge are analytic, could not be carried through before the science of the nineteenth and twentieth centuries had prepared the necessary means. Our time is the
first to see a consistent empiricism.

The verifiability theory of meaning is the logical tool
by means of which empiricism overcomes the dichotomy
into a world of things of appearance and things-in-
themselves. It eliminates the things-in-themselves because it makes it meaningless to speak about things
which are unknowable in principle. Instead of unknowable things, the empiricist speaks of unobservable things;
but such things are accessible to knowledge and can be
talked about in a meaningful way. Statements about unobservable things have meaning inasmuch as they are
derived from observations; they acquire meaning by
transfer, that is, by their relation to observable things.
These relationships were discussed in Chapter 11 with
reference to problems of quantum physics. They must
now be studied in more detail and with reference to all
forms of knowledge.

The problem of reality, the question whether the

world is real, arises from a familiar psychological experience: the distinction between dreaming and waking. This distinction, of course, is meaningful; but it is necessary to state more explicitly its meaning and its origin in order to overcome the many false conclusions which philosophers have drawn from it.

Imagine a man who is not aware of the difference between dreaming and waking and who writes down reports of everything he observes. He would write down sentences like "there is a dog", "Peter came to see me", "the car did not start", "Marion stood in the tomato soup", and so on. The last report, obviously, refers to what we call "dream"; but in the diary of this man there would be no explicit indication of dreaming. There could be no such indication because dream phenomena, while being experienced, do not differ in quality from actual observations; in other words, while dreaming nobody knows that he dreams. A perfect diary of this kind, which collects reports of all our observations, but does so without criticism and abstains from inferences going beyond what is actually experienced, may be regarded as the logical basis of human knowledge. To study the build-up of knowledge, the philosopher has to consider the inferences which lead from this basis to statements about physical objects, dreams, and all kinds of scientific construction, such as electricity or galaxies or a guilt complex. Let us therefore imagine a man who tries to construct a system of knowledge from the report sentences which he finds in his perfect diary.

He would try to construct an order into these sentences by arranging them in groups and formulating general laws holding for them. For instance, he would discover the law: whenever there is a sentence reporting that the sun shines, there is a later sentence that it gets warmer, which result he then formulates as a relation between things: whenever the sun shines it gets warmer. He would soon discover, however, that a certain group of sentences, like the one about Marion in the tomato soup, must be isolated from the others; he cannot include them into the ordered system, since they do not lead to correct predictions and thus not to general laws. For instance, he would find a report that whenever he put his finger into a bowl of soup it got wet; but apparently Marion's legs did not show this effect after she stepped out of the tomato soup. This group of reports, which forms a logical island, he would call dreams.

The difference between dreaming and waking is verifiable through structural differences within the collection of reports: that is the logical result of this analysis. It is a meaningful difference because it is translatable into verifiable relationships; dreams do not supply us with observations that permit the prediction of further experiences. This result leads to a classification of report sentences into those which are *objectively true* and those which are merely *subjectively true*. In order to have a name which applies before this distinction is made, I will call all report sentences *immediately true;* that is, it is assumed that they are not lies. Immediate truth divides into objective and subjective truth as a result of procedures of internal ordering, that is, of an ordering that does not go beyond the sentences listed in the perfect diary.

From sentences we proceed to things: reports that are objectively true are said to refer to *objective things,* reports that are merely subjectively true are said to refer to *subjective things.* So we have now two kinds of things; all of them are *immediate things,* but only the first are objective, or real things. What are the others?

In order to deal with them, we invent the concept "my body". We say that among the physical objects there is one, called "my body", which is causally affected by other physical things and thus put into a certain physiological state. Whenever there is an objective thing reported in the diary, my body is in a certain state; but it may even be in that state when there is no objective thing. In such a case we speak of a subjective thing. Thus subjective things, though having no reality, indicate real things of another kind: they indicate states of my body.

The last statement looks like a logical fallacy: if something nonexistent indicates something existent, it must also exist. In order to overcome this paradox, we must be more careful in the wording of our inferences. This is achieved by going back to the sentences of the diary. We found that not all of these sentences are objectively true. What we find now is that if a report sentence is not objectively true, we may infer, not that there is a corresponding physical object, but that there is a state of our body such as would also occur if there were a corresponding object. By speaking of sentences we avoid terms like "subjective things". Conversely, since this translation into a language that speaks about sentences is possible, it is also permissible to use such terms. We may therefore say that subjective things have a subjective existence, thus using a fictitious existence. Such expressions are permissible for the very reason that they can be eliminated.

The division of the world of experience into objective and subjective things is thus achieved by means of valid inferences and expressed in a legitimate mode of speech. Assuming that all report sentences are objectively true, we find that some are not; this is a valid inference of a type which the logician calls *reductio ad absurdum*. This means: The assumption that all report sentences are objectively true is "reduced to an absurdity". In order to incorporate those report sentences which are not objectively true into a consistent physical world, we introduce the assumption of the human observer, whose body can be in observation states without there being objective things. The dream sentences are thus connected with the waking-state sentences through relations of order; we can construct physiological laws which explain dreams, and psychoanalysis has developed methods which connect dream experiences causally with previous experiences in the waking state. The groups of dream sentences thus lose their island character and are incorporated into the total system; however, the interpretation thus given to them differs greatly from that of the other sentences.

The human observer and his bodily states are thus introduced by means of a physical hypothesis. The inferences leading to this hypothesis must be examined more closely. When we attempt to construct a consistent system of laws for physical things, we are often compelled to introduce the assumption that there are certain other physical things that cannot be observed directly. For instance, in order to account for electrical phenomena we introduce the assumption that there is a physical entity, called electricity, which flows through wires or travels as waves through open space. What we observe are phenomena such as the deflection of a magnetic needle or the music coming from a radio receiver; electricity is never observed directly. For such physical entities I use the name *illata,* meaning "inferred things". They are distinguished from the *concreta* that make up the world of observable things. They are also distinguished from *abstracta,* which are combinations of concreta and are not directly observable because they are comprehensive totalities. For instance, the term "prosperity" refers to a totality of observable phenomena, of concreta, and is used as an abbreviation which sums up all these observables in their interrelationship. The illata are not combinations of concreta, but separate entities inferred from concreta, whose existence is merely made probable by the concreta.

The internal states of the human body are illata, because we can observe only the reactions of the body, but not its internal conditions, including the different states of the brain. To characterize these states we use an indirect mode of speech; we say, for instance, "the state which would occur if the person saw a dog". This mode of speech has been called *stimulus language*. We characterize a bodily state by describing the kind of stimulus which would produce this state.

This sort of language may be illustrated by a physical example. The speedometer measures the speed of a car by the deviation of a needle. For this purpose, the revolving wheels of the car are connected through gears and a flexible shaft with the needle in such a way that greater speed corresponds to greater angular deviation of the needle. For every position of the needle, the corresponding speed is written on the dial. What the needle indicates directly is an internal state of the speedometer; but indirectly it thus indicates a speed, which acting as a "stimulus" puts the instrument into this state. Instead of using the figures on the dial as a measure of the speed of the car, we could also use them to indicate the internal states of the speedometer. Assume that someone takes the instrument out of the car and moves its shaft; then the speedometer is in a certain internal state. Looking at the figures on the dial, we may say "the speedometer is in the state sixty miles per hour". We thus characterize the state of the instrument indirectly in stimulus language.

This illustration will help to clarify the nature of subjective things. The things seen in a dream have the kind of existence which the speed of sixty miles has in the example of the speedometer taken out of the car. To speak here of existence is justifiable as a mode of speech, but physical existence is restricted to the states of the speedometer which are thus described indirectly. The duality of the dream state and the waking state offers no difficulties to an empiricist philosophy. It does not require the introduction of things "beyond" the realm of physical things; and it does not open the path to transcendentalism. It can be accounted for entirely in a "this-world philosophy". The meaning of statements about things existing in a dream is translatable into the meaning of statements about objective things.

This analysis permits us to clarify the meaning of the question whether the world is real. This question can be interpreted to mean: are we now in a waking state or in a dream? That is certainly a meaningful question. In fact, we have experienced dream situations in which we did ask this question, answered by the conclusion that we were awake, and later discovered that we were mistaken, that is, that we were still dreaming. Could the same thing happen now? We cannot exclude the possibility that, some time later, we shall discover that we were now dreaming. We feel pretty sure that this will not happen; but we have no absolute guarantees that it will not occur.

Returning to the logical device of the perfect diary, we can formulate this consideration as follows. The dream islands among our report sentences could be distinguished from the remainder because the remaining totality admitted of an order in terms of causal laws. But we cannot claim for sure that this ordering will always be possible. Imagine you have studied the first 500 sentences of the diary, discovered some islands of altogether 30 sentences among them, and succeeded in ordering the remaining 470 sentences reasonably. You now say: "I am awake". Then the diary is continued, and you find an additional 1,000 sentences which cannot be put together with the 470 previous sentences, but can be ordered reasonably among themselves. You will conclude that the 470 sentences were an island, that is, that you were dreaming; only now you are really awake. Are you now sure it will not go on like that? What if another 2,000 sentences were to turn up which compel you to regard your present status as a dream? And what if the same devastating experience would always repeat itself?

Let us be happy that such experiences do not occur. But we cannot exclude them through logical argument. Therefore, we cannot say that such experiences are impossible. If they did occur, if the thread of ordered experiences would break, and though spun anew, would always break again, we could not speak of an objective physical reality. Thus the statement that there is an objective physical world can only be maintained as highly probable, and not as absolutely certain. We have good inductive evidence for the existence of a physical world —but that is all we can maintain. And it is meaningful to speak about an objective physical world because statements about such a world are inductively derivable from observations.

Note that the language in which we speak about the physical world is not uniquely determined by observations. It is subject to the ambiguities discussed in Chapter 11 with reference to an imaginary Protagoras. There is a plurality of equivalent descriptions, and the usual realistic language in which we describe the physical world is merely one among these descriptions; it is the one which I have called the *normal system*. Inductive inferences can establish the usual form of statements about an external world only after the rule of identical laws

266

for observables and unobservables has been laid down. This rule has the nature of a definition determining the form of language; it may be called an *extension rule* of language, because it supplies the means to extend language to a wider domain of objects, including unobserved objects. But that the rule can be carried through, that there is a normal system for the description of the physical world of everyday life, is an empirical fact; more precisely speaking, a fact derived by means of inductive inferences. In this sense, it is an inductively well-confirmed hypothesis that there is a physical reality.

To put it in other words: the statement "there is a physical world" can be very well distinguished from the statement "there is no physical world", because we can depict experiences which would make the one statement probable and the other improbable. The two statements differ as to their predictive content. The functional conception of knowledge allots verifiable meaning to the hypothesis of the physical world.

I should like to compare this analysis with the traditional discussion of *solipsism*. According to the philosophical theory of solipsism, all we can assert is that we have experiences; but we can never go beyond this assertion and prove that there is an objective reality. Though this conception has scarcely ever been actually maintained, there have been some philosophers who developed it as a philosophical system; among them, G. Berkeley and M. Stirner may be mentioned. When I say that even these men did not actually adhere to this theory, I refer to the fact that they wrote books setting forth their theory, which fact can scarcely be explained if they did not believe there were other persons who could read these books. It has often been argued that although the theory of solipsism is utterly unreasonable, we have no logical arguments against it, because all that our experiences prove is that we have experiences, and not that there is a physical world.

I do not think the situation is that hopeless. The solipsist makes a fundamental mistake: he believes he can prove the existence of his own personality. But the discovery of the *ego*, of the personality of the observer, is based on inferences of the same kind as the discovery of the external world. The islands of the diary are interpreted as bodily states of the observer in the same way that the remaining sentences are regarded as evidence for a physical world; in fact, the islands are thus incorporated into an all-embracing physical interpretation, since the observer is a part of the physical world. It was said above that through the hypothesis of the observer and his bodily states, the sentence islands lose their island character and are made descriptive of the physical world, in that they are regarded as describing the observer. Thus if we can prove the existence of the *ego*, we can also prove the existence of the physical world, including the existence of other persons. The solipsist overlooks this parallelism of inferences. He introduces the *ego* and its experiences as absolute knowledge and then has trouble in deriving the external world—but his troubles stem from poor logic.

The correct analysis of the situation was given above: we have no absolutely conclusive evidence that there is a physical world and we have no absolutely conclusive evidence either that we exist. But we have good inductive evidence for both assumptions. Using the results of the analysis of inductive inference, we can say: we have good reasons to *posit* the existence of the external world as well as that of our personalities. All our knowledge is posits; so, our most general knowledge, that of the existence of the physical world and of us human beings within it, is a posit.

16. FUNCTIONAL CONCEPTION OF KNOWLEDGE

The incorporation of the human observer into the physical world is one of the fundamental characteristics of an empiricist philosophy. The transcendental conception of knowledge makes a cut between physical reality and the human mind and thus arrives at unsolvable problems, like the problem of how we can infer reality from mental data. Though mental existence is usually called an ideal existence and is distinguished from the world of dream, the psychological origin of idealism is to be sought in the experiences of dreaming and of images which we can visualize at will in the waking state. It is the incorrect logical analysis of these images that leads to the conception of the mind as an independent entity, as some sort of substance comparable to physical substance but having a reality of its own. The answer to the speculative philosophers of the idealist brand is given by an empiricist philosophy which, equipped with the tools of modern logic, construes knowledge as a system of inductive posits based on immediate report sentences. It is thus the functional conception of knowledge, the reduction of meaning to verifiability, which eliminates the traditional controversy of idealism versus realism, or materialism.

Strangely enough, the idealistic conception of the ego as builder of the physical world has recently found a new support by certain interpretations of quantum physics, which make an impermissible use of Heisenberg's disturbance through the act of observation and Bohr's complementarity. According to these interpretations, Heisenberg's indeterminacy leads to the conclusion that it is impossible to draw a line of separation between observer and physical object; as the observer changes the world through the act of observing, we cannot say what the world is, independent of the human observer. The analysis above (chap. 11) shows that this is a misinterpretation of quantum mechanics. The indeterminacy of unobservables exists only for the transition from macro-world to micro-world; but no such indeterminacy occurs when the transition from observed objects of our environment to unobserved macro-objects is considered. For this latter transition, there exists a normal system, which allows us to speak of an external world in the usual realistic language. The quantum-mechanical indeterminacy has nothing to do with the relationship between human observer and his environment. It begins to play a part only on a later step, when the world of smallest objects is to be inferred from that of larger objects.

This fact is made quite clear when we assume all instruments of observation to be constructed as registering instruments, which present the results of measurements in the form of numbers printed on a strip of paper. When the observer looks at the paper strips, he certainly does not disturb them, because this observation is a macroscopic affair. So he can infer in the usual way that there are certain measuring processes going on. The indeterminacy enters his computations only when he proceeds to infer from the working of the instruments that certain minute occurrences are happening, which he can interpret either as particles or as waves. This very simple consideration rules out all idealistic interpretations of quantum physics. It shows that empiricism has nothing to fear from the discoveries of the physicist and that modern relapses into philosophic idealism find no support in modern physics—if only the analysis of physics is freed from vague language and carried out with the precision of modern logic.

After discussing the inferences that lead to the construction of the ego from the basis of immediate reports, it will be useful to discuss in some detail how the concept of mind is dealt with in a functional conception of knowledge, which applies the postulate of verifiability to statements about the mind.

Imagine that scientists had succeeded in constructing a perfect robot. The machine would talk, answer questions, do what it is ordered to do, and give all kinds of information wanted; for instance, one could send it to a grocery store, have it ask the grocer how much the eggs are today, and it would return with the answer. It would be a perfect machine, but without a mind. How do you know it has no mind?

Because, you say, it does not react like human beings in other respects. It does not tell you that it is fine weather today, nor does it ever complain of toothache. What if it did? Assume that its behavior equaled that of human beings in every respect—could you still maintain that it has no mind?

The question may also be asked in the following way. Suppose you could take away temporarily the mind from a human being; during some periods it has a mind and behaves as usual, during other periods it has no mind, but behaves just as before. I do not mean a Dr. Jekyll and Mr. Hyde, because Mr. Hyde behaves very differently from Dr. Jekyll; I mean a Dr. Jekyll who is temporarily without a mind, but remains always the same Dr. Jekyll. How would we know that in these periods he has no mind?

According to what was explained about the meaning of sentences, the question is obviously meaningless. It is of the type of the question whether all things, including our bodies, became ten times larger as we slept last night. There is no verifiable difference between the two states of the person, and if we assume he has a mind in one state, we have also to admit the mind for the other state. The mind is inseparable from a certain state of bodily

organization. It follows that mind and bodily organization of a certain kind are the same thing.

We may also say that the word "mind" is an abbreviation denoting a bodily state that shows certain kinds of
reactions. To believe that the mind is more than that,
reminds one of the man who had a 130 h-p car and was
deeply disappointed when he took the engine apart and
did not find the 130 h-p. The belief in the independent
existence of a mind is a fallacy evolving from the misunderstanding of abstract terms. An abstract term is
translatable into very many concrete terms, and the object denoted by it is nothing but the aggregate of all the
concrete objects involved. The question of the existence
of the mind is a matter of the correct use of words but not
a question of facts.

The conception of an independent existence of the
mind is the backbone of transcendentalism; it regards
mental phenomena as instances of a nonphysical existence, and it is an easy step from this interpretation to the
belief in a higher reality, of which visible objects are
mere shadows. But the mind-body problem is a philosophical issue only because its usual formulation suffers
from linguistic difficulties, which have led the philosopher into a logical mess. The language in which we describe mental and emotional phenomena is a language
which was not made for this purpose and serves it only
by the use of rather involved logical constructions. The
language of everyday life—and that is the language we
use for psychological descriptions—has grown from a
reference to concrete objects around us and admits only
of an indirect description of psychological phenomena.
It is a stimulus language, in the sense explained above.
We say we have the picture of a tree in our mind; but
both the words "picture" and "tree", in their original
meanings, refer to concrete objects and lend themselves

only to an indirect expression of what we mean. In a more precise version we would have to say that our body is in a state of the kind which would result if light rays emitted from a tree fell into our eyes, although in this particular case there is no tree and no light ray. Our language has no terms which directly refer to bodily states, and we must use an indirect description in terms of external objects.

The wording of psychological reports must be carefully translated before philosophical questions about the mind can be answered. If that rule is forgotten, pseudoproblems arise. For instance, it is argued that we do not see our bodily states, but see a tree in a dream, although there is no tree. But no logician would claim that we see a bodily state. The word "see" is so coined that it refers to external physical objects, and what the logician maintains is that the total sentence "I see a tree" is equivalent to the sentence "my body is in a certain physiological state". Modern logic has means of dealing with equivalences of this type.

Another pseudoproblem is presented by the question: if light rays hit the human eye and nervous impulses are transmitted from the retina to the brain, how and where are the impulses transformed into the sensation *blue?* This question is based on a mistaken presupposition. Nowhere are the impulses transformed into a sensation. The impulses generate a physiological state of the brain; the person whose brain is in this state sees *blue,* but the *blue* is neither in the brain nor elsewhere in the body. "Seeing blue" is an indirect way of describing a bodily state; this state is the causal product of the light rays and the subsequent nervous impulses, but there is no causal product *blue.*

To give an illustration of these logical relationships, assume that a man takes 2,000 dollars in bills to a bank and opens an account. He now owns 2,000 dollars in the form of a bank account. Where are these 2,000 dollars? They do not consist in bills. The original bills have meanwhile traveled through many hands, and most of them, perhaps, are no longer in possession of the bank. As their causal product, there are figures written down in the files of the bank in combination with the man's name; but figures on paper are not dollars, and they belong not to the man but to the bank, which owns the stationery. So where are the 2,000 dollars that the man owns? They are "intangible things of another sphere of reality", and yet they seem to be the product of the original dollar bills, which were concrete things. How can something impalpable be causally produced by something palpable? In this case, everyone sees that the question is nonsensical and results from a confusion of modes of speech. There exists a state of affairs consisting in figures written down in bank files and causally produced by the passing of dollar bills from the man's hands into the hands of a cashier. This state of affairs is characterized indirectly by the statement "the man owns 2,000 dollars". These abstract 2,000 dollars owe their existence merely to a mode of speech. In the case of sense perceptions, however, many a philosopher has asked questions of this kind and advanced the thesis that there are insoluble problems, transcending the comprehension of the human mind. Philosophical worries of this kind can be allayed only by a lesson in logic.

The functional conception of knowledge need not be abandoned when knowledge of psychological phenomena is concerned. That a bodily system can talk about itself is no stranger than that a photographic camera can photograph itself by means of a mirror. The poor state of traditional logic is the chief cause of the extraordinary confusion with which these problems have been treated in traditional philosophy. This is one of the points where scientific philosophy has had the help of modern logic in its striving for clarity and scientific analysis. By such methods, a theory of knowledge has been built up which has taken the place of the discipline of the same name that the systems of speculative philosophy pretended to have elaborated.

I have presented this theory of knowledge only in its outlines; for further studies I must refer to the existing literature. The logician has discovered that the construction of a detailed theory of knowledge is by no means easy and requires a great deal of technical work. Our system of knowledge is a strange mixture of languages, of physical language, subjective language, immediate language, and metalanguage; and the connection and interrelation of these languages is to be explored with the help of the technique of a symbolic logic which includes expressions for probability relations. The student of philosophy who attends a modern class on theory of knowledge is usually surprised to find himself presented with logical formulas, which have taken the place of the picture language of speculative systems. But the presence of formulas indicates that philosophy has made the step from speculation to science.

17.

The Nature of Ethics

THE EXPOSITION of the second part of this book has so far been concerned with questions of knowledge; it was shown, in particular, how the synthetic a priori was eliminated in the cognitive field. The present chapter will be concerned with a similar analysis of the field of ethics. The idea of a synthetic a priori has been applied not only to knowledge but also to ethics; in fact, the program of an ethico-cognitive parallelism is one of the sources from which the idea of a synthetic a priori sprang. A historical study of the fallacious line of thought deriving from this parallelism was given in Chapter 4. It is the problem of the present chapter to replace the cognitive and aprioristic conception of ethics by a conception compatible with the results of scientific philosophy.

One conclusion can be immediately drawn from the analysis of modern science. If ethics were a form of knowledge it would not be what moral philosophers want it to be; that is, it would not supply moral directives. Knowledge divides into synthetic and analytic statements; the synthetic statements inform us about matters of fact, the analytic statements are empty. What kind of knowledge should ethics be? If it were synthetic, it would inform us about matters of fact. Of this kind is a descriptive ethics which informs us about the ethical habits of various peoples and social classes; such an ethics is a part of sociology, but it is not of a normative nature. If ethics were analytic knowledge, however, it would be empty and could not tell us what to do, either. For instance, if we define a virtuous man as a man who always chooses the maxim of his actions in such a way that it could be made the principle of a general legislation, we would know what we mean by the term "virtuous man", but we could not prove that we should aspire to be virtuous men. The phrase a "virtuous man", when so defined, is merely an abbreviation for the long-winded Kantian formulation about the maxim of actions, and could be replaced by any other name, for instance, by the term "Kantian"; but why should we try to be Kantians? If ethical statements are analytic, they are not moral directives.

The modern analysis of knowledge makes a cognitive ethics impossible: knowledge does not include any normative parts and therefore does not lend itself to an interpretation of ethics. The ethico-cognitive parallelism renders ethics a bad service: if it could be carried through, if virtue were knowledge, ethical rules would be deprived of their imperative character. The two-thousand-year-old plan to establish ethics on a cognitive basis results from a misunderstanding of knowledge, from the erroneous conception that knowledge contains a normative part. It is chiefly the misinterpretation of mathematics that is responsible for this error. We saw that from the time of Plato to that of Kant mathematics was conceived as a system of laws of reason that control the physical world; from such a synthetic a priori there was only a short step to the conception that reason can dictate to us moral directives which have an objective validity, such as was assumed for the laws of mathematics. If it turns out that mathematics is not of this kind, that it does not supply laws of the physical world but merely formulates empty relations that hold for all possible worlds, there is no longer any space left for a cognitive ethics. Knowledge cannot provide the form of ethics because it cannot provide directives.

I explained above (chap. 4) that the source of the cognitive interpretation of ethics is presumably to be found in the use of logic and knowledge for the derivation of ethical implications. If you want this aim you must also want this and that—implications of this kind are accessible to cognitive proof. By cognitive proof I mean a proof employing the laws of logic in combination with the laws of physics, or sociology, or other sciences. Thus if you wish to reap you have to sow; this implication is proved with the help of the laws of botany. A great many ethical controversies are concerned with such implications; that may be the reason for the erroneous conception that all ethical considerations are of the cognitive type. It seems as though during an ethical discussion we sharpen and deepen our ethical insight, in the same way that, in the opinion of Plato and Kant, we sharpen and deepen our insight into the nature of space through geometrical analysis. But the development of geometry has shown us that the latter conception is mistaken, that there is no insight into the nature of space, that different forms of space are possible and that a geometrical demonstration merely derives *if-then* statements, or relations between axioms and theorems. There is no geometrical necessity, only a logical necessity concerning the consequences that follow from a given set of axioms; the mathematician cannot prove the axioms to be true.

Had Spinoza foreseen this result of the modern philosophy of mathematics, he would not have attempted to construct his ethics after the pattern of geometry. He would have been horrified at the idea that non-Spinozistic ethics could be constructed which would possess the same kind of cogency that his own sytem possessed, and that if his axioms were of the nature of geometrical axioms, they could not be given a demonstrative proof. It would not have helped him to turn them into results of experience, like the axioms of geometry, for empirical truth is not what he wanted. He wanted to establish ethical axioms that are unquestionable. He wanted axioms that are *necessary*.

But if the word "necessary" is to mean anything comparable to logical necessity, then there can be no moral necessity. When we feel that during an ethical discussion our insight is sharpened and deepened, such achievement must not be regarded as proving the existence of an ethical insight. What we see better after an analysis of ethical problems is the relation between ends and means; we discover that if we want to satisfy certain fundamental aims we must be willing to pursue certain other aims, which are subordinate to the first in the sense of the means to an end. Such a clarification is of a logical nature; it shows that, in view of physical and psychological laws, the end logically requires the means. This argument is not merely parallel to logical proof—it *is* logical proof. Philosophers who speak of ethical insight confuse the logical evidence of the implication between ends and means with a supposed self-evidence of the axioms.

And yet, when decisions are to be made, implications between ends and means are not sufficient to determine our choice. We must first decide for the end. For instance, we may be able to prove the implication: if stealing were permitted, there would be no prosperous human society. In order to derive the conclusion that stealing should be forbidden, we must first decide that we want a prosperous human society. For this reason, ethics needs moral premises, or moral axioms, which state primary goals, whereas means represent secondary goals. When we call

279

them axioms, we think of ethics as an ordered system which is derivable from these axioms, whereas the axioms themselves are not derivable in the system. When we restrict the consideration to a specific argument, we use the more modest term "premise". There must be at least one moral premise for an ethical argument, that is, one ethical rule which is not derived by this argument. This premise may be the conclusion of another argument; but going farther up this way, we remain at every step with a certain set of moral premises. If we succeed in ordering the totality of ethical rules in one consistent system, we thus arrive at the axioms of our ethics. This analysis can be summed up in the thesis: logical necessity controls merely the implications between moral axioms and secondary moral rules; but it cannot validate the moral axioms.

But if the axioms of ethics are not necessary or self-evident truths—what then are they?

The ethical axioms are not necessary truths because they are not truths of any kind. Truth is a predicate of statements; but the linguistic expressions of ethics are not statements. They are directives. A directive cannot be classified as true or false; these predicates do not apply because directive sentences are of a logical nature different from that of indicative sentences, or statements.

An important kind of directive is given by imperatives, which we use for the direction of persons other than ourselves. Consider the command "shut the door". Is this imperative true or false? We need only pronounce the question in order to see that it is nonsensical. The utterance "shut the door" does not inform us about matters of fact; nor does it represent a tautology, that is, a statement of logic. We could not say what would be the case if the utterance "shut the door" were true. An imperative is a linguistic utterance to which the classification true-false does not apply.

What then is an imperative? An imperative is a linguistic utterance which we use with the intention of influencing another person, of making the other person do something we want to be done, or not to do something we want not to be done. It is a matter of fact that this aim can be reached by the use of words, though that is not the only way to reach it. Instead of saying "shut the door" we could seize the man's hands and guide them in such a way that the door would be shut. However, that would not only be impolite but it would also be inconvenient for us, since it would be easier to do the thing ourselves. We therefore prefer to make use of the fact that our fellow men are conditioned to respond to words as instruments of our will. The imperative mood of the command makes it clear that even grammatically speaking the command is not a statement. Not all commands, however, are articulated in the imperative mood. The statement in the indicative mood "I should be glad if the door were shut" may be uttered by me in the sense of a command and, in fact, may represent a better instrument of achieving my aim than would the sentence in the imperative mood; politeness is not only a policy of diplomats but is also recommended for the little diplomacies of everyday life. Our utterance is a command disguised as a statement.

But is not the utterance "I should be glad if the door were shut" a statement concerning my wishes? It is; only in this case it is employed as a command. However, it is true that whenever an imperative is uttered there exists a *correlated statement* which informs us about the will of a person. Thus to the imperative "shut the door" corresponds the indicative statement: "Mr. X wishes the door to be shut". This statement is true or false and can be

281

verified like other psychological statements. Sometimes the correlated statement is used in place of the command. For the purpose of logical analysis it is convenient always to express imperatives in the imperative mood and thus to distinguish them grammatically from statements.

Although imperatives are neither true nor false, they are understood by other persons and therefore have a meaning, which may be called an *instrumental meaning*. It is to be distinguished from the *cognitive meaning* of statements, defined in the verifiability theory of meaning (chap. 16). Moreover, every imperative possesses a *cognitive correlate,* given by the correlated statement.

Like imperatives, directives concerning our own actions are expressions of volition, which as such are not true or false and therefore belong among volitional utterances. Acts of volition may concern various objects; we want food, shelter, friends, pleasure, and so forth. That we find in ourselves acts of volition, is a matter of fact; they are distinguished from perceptions or logical laws in that they appear as products of our own in a situation leaving us choice. I may go to the theater or I may not; it is my will to go. I may help another man or I may not; it is my will to help him. Whether it is true that we have a freedom of choice is a different question; for the definition of an act of volition it is sufficient that we at least believe that we have the possibility of choice. For this definition it is therefore irrelevant where volitions come from, and we do not ask, at the moment, whether we are conditioned to our volitions by the milieu in which we grow up, or whether our volitions flow from certain fundamental urges, like the sexual urge or the urge for self-preservation. Let us simply acknowledge the psychological fact that we make volitional decisions which direct our behavior.

Only if the volitional decision concerns actions to be

done by other persons does it assume the form of an imperative. Sometimes the imperative is uttered with the threat of enforcement through power; for instance, the power of the governmental authorities, or of the authority of the officer; it then is called a command. Other imperatives are wishes, which are also expressed in the imperative mood. Thus we say, "Please give me a cigarette".

If a command is directed or a wish addressed to us, in other words, if we are on the receiving side of the imperative, we may respond positively or negatively. A positive response consists in an act of volition on our side directed toward carrying out the imperative and may even include a readiness to give corresponding imperatives to other persons. A negative response consists in an act of volition directed against carrying out the imperative. This alternative is expressed through the words "right" and "wrong". Thus if I am told "you should go and see Paul", I may answer "that is right", and then start with preparations for a visit to Paul. The positive response to an act of volition expressed through an imperative thus consists in a secondary act of volition of a similar kind generated in the receiver. If the response is negative, the secondary act of volition is opposed to the first. Linguistic usage does not always draw this clear distinction between the alternatives yes-no and right-wrong, but employs them interchangeably. It may appear justifiable, however, to regard the distinction explained as a proper interpretation of the terms.

Whereas we have for directives referring to other persons the grammatical form of the imperative, we have no such linguistic form for the directive addressed to ourselves. For this reason we express such directives in the form of an indicative sentence reporting about the setting up of the directive, as in the sentence "I will go to the theater". Sometimes we address ourselves as though we were talking to a different person, applying the imperative mood; thus we say to ourselves, "Old fellow, do write that letter". By means of this rather schizoid method it is possible to transfer to ourselves the notation applying to the receiving side of an imperative, and to speak of secondary acts of volition raised in ourselves through an imperative which we give to ourselves.

These considerations will clarify the difference between cognitive sentences and directives. If I am given a cognitive sentence, or statement, and I agree with it, I say "yes", meaning that I regard the statement as true. For instance, if you tell me that it is a long way to Tipperary, I say "yes", meaning I, too, regard it as true that it is a long way to Tipperary. If you tell me, however, that stinginess is bad, I express my agreement by saying "that is right". What you mean is a directive and thus an expression of your will, namely, you say: I wish that there were no stinginess. My answer is a corresponding directive; it means I, too, wish that there were no stinginess. The positive answer to a directive is not an affirmation of the cognitive kind; it consists in a secondary act of volition, expressed in an utterance indicating that the listener shares the will of the speaker.

The considerations so far given refer to directives of all kinds. Let us now study those directives which are called *moral directives,* or moral imperatives.

It is a characteristic mark of a moral directive that we regard it as an imperative and feel ourselves to be on the receiving side of it. We thus regard our act of volition as a secondary one, as a response to an imperative given by some higher authority. What the higher authority is, is not always clearly known. Some persons claim it is God, others contend it is their conscience, or their daemon, or the moral law within them. These are, obviously, interpretations in picture language. Psychologically speaking, the moral imperative is characterized as an act of volition accompanied by the feeling of an obligation, which we regard as applying to ourselves as well as to other persons. Thus we regard it as our obligation, and as the obligation of everybody, to support the needy where that is possible. Volitional aims other than moral are not accompanied by the feeling of obligation. If a man wants to become an engineer, he will usually not feel obliged to decide for this aim, nor does he wish that all others have the same aim as he. It is the feeling of general obligation which distinguishes moral imperatives from others.

How can we explain the fact that moral volitions appear to us as secondary volitions, as the expression of an obligation? I think the explanation is that these volitions are imposed upon us by the social group to which we belong, in other words, that they are originally group volitions. This origin accounts for their superpersonal dignity and for the feeling of subordination with which we make the moral decision. Psychologically, this origin is understandable. The rules not to steal, not to kill, and so forth, were rules the enforcement of which was necessary for group preservation. As generations passed, individuals were conditioned to these rules; and in our own education we were subject to a conditioning process of the same kind. No wonder, then, that we feel ourselves on the receiving side of the moral imperatives; in fact, we are. If a feeling of duty is regarded as characteristic for moral aims, such a conception mirrors the fact that moral aims were instilled into us forcibly, whether through the authority of the father or of the teacher or by the pressure of the group in which we lived.

If ethics is social in its origin, how is it possible that there are antisocial ethics?

An ethics which we regard as antisocial can still be a group ethics. Thus criminals have an ethics of their own class; within their class they do not steal or kill, but they oppose their class to the larger class of what we call a civilized society and disregard all moral obligations with respect to this wider class. Students of a high-school class may regard their class as a group opposed to the teacher and find it their moral right to deceive and harass him. Conversely, there are teachers who are highly esteemed by the students and are seldom deceived; such a teacher has succeeded in making the students incorporate him into their group. The working class has an ethics of its own; so has the class of big capitalists, or the aristocracy of countries that have not yet eliminated the remnants of feudalism. Even the Nazi ethics was a group ethics, tailored to the needs of the so-called master race. The completely individualistic ethics of Nietzsche's superman or of Machiavelli's prince is an extreme case in which all moral rights are reserved for one man. Such ethical systems have never been carried through except on paper. They represent a strange mixture in which the authority psychologically derived from group will is transferred to one man, who is regarded as the only individual whose will is to be respected.

The ethics of our social and political life is a conglomeration of group ethics of various strata. Nations have grown through fusion of states and merging of social groups; they have taken over the ethical rules of older times, especially through the codified law, which perpetuates the moral systems of the Romans, of feudalism, and of the Church. No wonder that the result is no consistent system. The obedient citizen who attempts to satisfy all moral rules of a nationwide society soon finds himself confronted by ethical conflicts. Should he support the needy or attempt to get hold of their pennies by the methods of good business? Should he work for the welfare of the nation by contributing to the suppression of strikes, or by supporting labor in its fight for better economic conditions? Should he stand for freedom of speech or support the government of a state that does not tolerate the teaching of Darwin's theory of evolution in its universities? Should he honor the teachings of the Bible or demand that the offspring of the people that wrote the Bible be excluded from public offices? Should he advocate equal rights for all races or uphold regulations which provide for segregation of streetcar passengers who have abundant pigmentation in their skin? It is not an easy matter to work one's way through the muddle of moral rules of present-day society.

Where, then, is the ethics that answers all our questions? Can philosophy provide such a system?

It cannot. That is the answer we should frankly give. The attempts of philosophers to fashion ethics as a system of knowledge have broken down. The moral systems thus constructed were nothing but reproductions of the ethics of certain sociological groups; of Greek bourgeois society, of the Catholic Church, of the Middle Class of the preindustrial age, of the age of industry and the proletarian. We know why these systems had to fail: because knowledge cannot supply directives. Who looks for ethical rules must not imitate the method of science. Science tells us what is, but not what should be.

Does that mean resignation? Does it mean that there are no moral directives, that everybody may do what he wants?

I do not think so. I think it is a misunderstanding of the nature of moral directives to conclude that if ethics is not objectively demonstrable everybody may do what he wants.

To inquire into this problem let us go into a detailed study of the volitional nature of moral directives by a grammatical analysis of the phrase "he should", which can be regarded as the grammatical form of a moral directive. (For our purposes, the phrase may be regarded as synonymous with "he shall" and with "he ought to".) We saw that the phrase cannot mean there is an objective moral law from which the imperative is derivable. What, then, does it mean? There remain two different possible meanings of the phrase.

The first is an *implicational meaning:* we know that the person referred to has adopted a certain aim, and we wish to say that this aim implies the action under consideration. For instance, we say "Peter should not smoke", meaning that from the aim of being healthy it is derivable, because of Peter's physiological constitution and by the use of the laws of physiology, that he should not smoke. In other words, the decision not to smoke is entailed by the decision to live in good health; it therefore is called an *entailed decision*. The obligation of the entailed decision is of the implicational type and represents not a moral, but a logical obligation.

The second is the meaning of a *subjective imperative* on the part of the speaker: I, the speaker, wish that he do this or that. According to this interpretation, moral directives include an indispensable reference to the speaker; they are expressions of a volitional decision by the speaker. If this conception is assumed, it is impossible to eliminate the speaker from the meaning of a moral directive; the phrase "he should" includes, in a hidden form, the phrase "I will", and we thus arrive at a *volitional ethics.*

The logical nature of this conception can be analyzed as follows. The use of such expressions as "he should not lie", or "lying is morally bad", represents a pseudo-objective mode of speech; what is expressed is actually an attitude of the speaker. The phrase "he should" is comparable to terms such as "I" and "now", which refer to the speaker, or the act of speech, and convey different meanings in the mouths of different persons. Such terms are called *token-reflexive*. The word "token" denotes an individual instance of a sign; if two persons utter the same word, each of them utters a different token, or instance of the word. Usually, the different tokens have the same meaning. However, if the terms are token-reflexive, each of the tokens has a different meaning. If each of two persons says "President Franklin D. Roosevelt", the two tokens denote the same person. But if each of them says "I", the two tokens denote different persons. The word "reflexive" indicates this reference of the meaning to the token.*

Both the implicational and the token-reflexive meaning are employed. But the implicational meaning of the phrase "he should" cannot be used for moral premises, or moral axioms, since these premises do not express implications, but are directives. They thus contain the phrase "he should" in a token-reflexive meaning. This meaning of the phrase is transferred from the premises through the derivation to every ethical rule. To understand this transfer, we may think of derivations in the cognitive field, which transfer the truth of the premises to the conclusion. If the premises were not asserted, neither could the conclusion be asserted. Likewise, if the ethical premises were not advanced as directives, that is, in the meaning of a nonimplicational and thus token-reflexive "he should", neither could the ethical conclusion have the character of a directive.

It may happen that the two meanings of the phrase "he should" are combined; then an implicational "should"

---

* For a further discussion of token-reflexive terms see the author's *Elements of Symbolic Logic* (New York, 1947), p. 284. Since imperatives are token-reflexive, they are not equivalent to their cognitive correlates; two identical imperatives, uttered by different persons, have different cognitive correlates.

is asserted which refers to a premise advanced with the token-reflexive "should". This double meaning must be clearly recognized. The implicational "should" then assumes a moral connotation; but it does so only because the directive assumed as the premise of the person referred to is a moral imperative supported by the speaker. Thus we say "the President should open this country to displaced persons", meaning that from the aim of helping the displaced persons, which we know the President adheres to and which we support, it is derivable that immigration to this country is the only available means of reaching this aim. A moral connotation of "should" in the implicational meaning is therefore reducible to the use of "should" in the volitional meaning. If the directive is not shared by the speaker, the "he should" loses its moral character. Thus we say "instead of conquering Paris, Hitler should have invaded England". We mean that it would have been in the interest of Hitler to invade England, and thus mean an implicational obligation; but since we do not share Hitler's aims, the word "should" is not used as a moral imperative. This illustration makes it clear that the reference to the speaker is inseparable from the moral meaning of the phrase "he should". The recognition that the phrase "he should" in its moral meaning is a token-reflexive term is the indispensable basis of a scientific analysis of ethics.

With the intention of escaping the subjective reference of ethical terms, a third interpretation of the phrase "he should" is sometimes attempted. According to this interpretation, the phrase means as much as "the group wishes that he do this or that". This meaning seems to eliminate the subjectivity from moral obligations. However, this interpretation is not tenable. When group will is concerned, we use the phrase "he should" only if its meaning is reducible to one of the first two interpretations. First, we use it when the action follows from the will of the person concerned, in whose interest it is to honor the group will; then the phrase has the implicational meaning of the first interpretation. Second, we use the phrase when we share the group will; and only in this case is the phrase meant to express a moral obligation. For instance, if a criminal betrays his accomplices, we know that his group condemns such a behavior; a member of the group, therefore, would say "he should not have talked". When *we* utter this sentence, we might use the implicational "should" and express the opinion that being silent would have been in the interest of the criminal, who perhaps is exposed to acts of vengeance by the group. However, if we utter the sentence in the sense of a moral judgment, we wish to say that we regard it as a moral obligation of the man to protect his group; then the phrase is token-reflexive and includes an expression of the will of the speaker.

We arrive at the result that moral directives are of a volitional nature, that they express volitional decisions on the part of the speaker. This result may at first sight appear disappointing; it looks as though we have no longer any solid ground on which to establish our volitions. Is it necessary, however, that we be on the receiving side of an imperative in order to feel entitled to follow it, and in order to demand that others follow the same imperative? It was the feeling of obligation resulting on the receiving side of a group will that was misconstrued by philosophers as an analogue of cognitive necessity, as the compulsion of a law of reason or of an insight into a world of ideas. As we have discovered that the analogy breaks down, that the feeling of obligation cannot be transformed into a source of the validity of ethics, let us forget about the appeal to obligation. Let us throw away the crutches we needed for walking, let us stand on our own feet and trust our volitions, not because they are secondary ones, but because they are our own volitions. Only a distorted morality can argue that our will is bad if it is not the response to a command from another source.

You answer: "If moral directives are volitional decisions, it appears justified that everyone set up his own moral directives. But how can someone demand that others follow his directives? You appeal to us to trust our own volitions and not to feel ourselves on the receiving side of an imperative; at the same time, you demand the right for everyone to set up imperatives for others. Is not that a contradiction? The volitional interpretation of imperatives seems to lead to the conclusion that everybody may do what he wants, that is, to anarchism".

Let us first study the inference expressed in your last statement. Assume that I set up the imperative that a certain person behave in a certain way. You answer: "No, he may do what he wants". Obviously, the phrase "may do" in your answer is the opposition to my imperative; you wish to say that although I am entitled to set up my own imperatives, I am not entitled to set up universal obligations, that is, imperatives for others. The clause "Mr. X is not entitled" is not a cognitive sentence; it is an imperative, meaning "Mr. X should not do this or that". So you have answered me by an imperative; you command that I should not set up imperatives for others. What is the title on which you base your imperative? You set your will against my will; and I do not see why I should recognize your will and renounce setting up directives for others.

The problem represented by your inference is important enough to be given a closer examination. Let us first consider the clause "everybody has a right". It can mean, first, that the legal authorities do not restrict the activities of any person. That is a cognitive statement, but it is not what you mean by your conclusion. To make my point clear, let us insert the assumed meaning of the clause into the total statement. The statement "if a moral directive is a matter of a volitional decision, the legal authorities will not restrict the activities of any person" is of questionable truth and is not what you wish to say. Second, the clause "everybody has a right" can mean that no one's activities should be restricted. The word "should" indicates an imperative; according to the previous analysis, it can have two meanings. The first is that of an imperative given by the speaker, which is you; your sentence then means: "If a moral directive is a matter of a volitional decision, I insist that there be no restrictions upon the activities of any person". If that is what you want to say, you do not establish a logical relation, but merely pronounce a volition of your own and thus do not arrive at an inference. The second meaning of "should" is that of a logical implication leading to a derivable imperative for the person referred to. So what you mean is: "If a man adheres to the principle that a moral directive is a matter of a volitional decision, it follows that he adheres to the imperative that there be no restrictions upon the activities of any person". But is that a valid inference? I do not see how such a conclusion can be derived logically, because it is perfectly consistent for a man to want certain aims and also want other persons to be restricted in those activities which would oppose these aims.

Let me state the last argument somewhat differently. You wish to show that I am logically committed to the entailed decision: "No person should be restricted in his activities". If this is to be a derivable imperative, it must be derived from other imperatives. But thus far I have not uttered any imperatives. I merely made the cognitive statement that moral directives are matters of volitional decision. From this cognitive statement you can not derive any imperative. You can derive imperatives from other imperatives, or from imperatives in combination with cognitive sentences, but never from cognitive sentences alone. So your inference is invalid.

You see that the volitional interpretation of moral directives does not lead to the consequence that the speaker should allow everybody the right to follow his own decision; that is, it does not lead to anarchism. If I set up certain volitional aims and demand that they be followed by all persons, you can counter my argument only by setting up another imperative, for instance, the anarchist imperative "everybody has the right to do what he wants". You cannot prove, however, that my system of a volitional ethics is inconsistent, that logic compels me to allow everybody the right to do what he wants. Logic does not compel me to do anything. The directives I set up are not consequences of my conception of ethics, either; nor does logic tell me what imperatives I should regard as obligatory for all persons. I set up my imperatives as my volitions, and the distinction between personal and moral directives is also a matter of my volition. Directives of the latter kind, you remember, are those which I regard as necessary for the group and which I demand everybody to comply with.

Now you are in complete despair. You retort: "Maybe what you say is true, logically speaking; but do you really think—you, the author of a book on scientific philosophy —that you are the man to give moral directives to the whole world? Why should we follow you"?

I am sorry, friend. I did not intend to convey this impression. I was looking for the path of truth; but for this very reason I am not going to give you moral directives, which by their nature cannot be true. I have my moral directives, that is true. But I shall not write them down here. I do not wish to discuss moral issues, but to discuss the nature of morality. I even have some fundamental moral directives, which, I think, are not so very different from yours. We are products of the same society, you and I. So we were imbued with the essence of democracy from the day of our birth. We may differ in many respects, perhaps about the question of whether the state should own the means of production, or whether the divorce laws should be made easier, or whether a world government should be set up that controls the atom bomb. But we can discuss such problems if we both agree about a democratic principle which I oppose to your anarchist principle:

Everybody is entitled to set up his own moral imperatives and to demand that everyone follow these imperatives.

This democratic principle supplies the precise formulation of my appeal to everybody to trust his own volitions, which you regarded as contradictory to my claim that everybody may set up imperatives for other persons. Let me show now that the principle is not self-contradictory. Assume, for instance, I set up the imperative that if there is more than one room to each person in a house, the surplus rooms should be opened to persons who have no rooms of their own. You set up the imperative that no one should be compelled to open his house to other persons. You have a surplus room in your house and I demand that it be opened to a victim of the housing shortage; if I have the power to enforce my demand through the authority of the government, say by making my regulation a law through a referendum, I shall even do that. However, I leave you the right to demand that such law be repealed. It is therefore the difference between the right to act and the right to demand a certain action which saves my principle from being a contradiction.

I demand that you act in a certain way, but I do not demand that you renounce your demand to the contrary. That is good democracy; and in fact, it corresponds to the actual procedure in which differences of volition are fought out in a democracy.

I do not derive my principle from pure reason. I do not present it as the result of a philosophy. I merely formulate a principle which is at the basis of all political life in democratic countries, knowing that in adhering to it I reveal myself as a product of my time. But I have found that this principle offers me the opportunity to propagate and, in large measure, to follow my volitions; therefore I make it my moral imperative. I do not claim that it applies to all forms of society; if I, the product of a democratic society, were placed in a different society I might be willing to modify my principle. But let us examine this principle which for our society appears to be the most suitable one.

The principle is not an ethical doctrine, answering all questions of what we should do. It is merely an invitation to take active part in the struggle of opinions. Volitional differences cannot be settled by the appeal to a system of ethics constructed by some learned man; they can be overcome only through the clash of opinions, through the friction between the individual and his environment, through controversy and the compulsion of the situation. Moral valuations are formed in the pursuit of activities; we act, we reflect about what we have done, we talk to others about it, and act again, this time in what we regard as a better way. Our actions are trials to find out what we want; we learn through error, and often we know only after our action is done whether we wanted to do it. Volitional aims usually do not come to us with the clarity of a vision, but more often constitute the subconscious or semiconscious background of our attitudes;

and those which do appear clear and bright, like stars showing our paths, often lose all their attractiveness as soon as they are reached.

Whoever wants to study ethics, therefore, should not go to the philosopher; he should go where moral issues are fought out. He should live in the community of a group where life is made vivid by competing volitions, be it the group of a political party, or of a trade union, or of a professional organization, or of a ski club, or a group formed by common study in a classroom. There he will experience what it means to set his volition against that of other persons and what it means to adjust oneself to group will. If ethics is the pursuit of volitions, it is also the conditioning of volitions through a group environment. The exponent of individualism is shortsighted when he overlooks the volitional satisfaction which accrues from belonging to a group. Whether we regard the conditioning of volitions through the group as a useful or a dangerous process depends on whether we support or oppose the group; but we must admit that there exists such group influence.

How, then, is it possible that volitions are modified and harmonized in a group? What is the process that conditions volitions?

There can be no doubt that this process, to a great extent, is the learning of cognitive relations. I said above that implications between imperatives are accessible to logical proof. The part played by such implications is much greater than is usually assumed. We are often mistaken about the relations between our aims. If some fundamental aims are the same, quite a few moral issues are transformed into logical issues. For instance, the question whether private property is sacred is no longer a moral question, once we recognize the aim that a minimum of adequate living conditions should be guaranteed

297

to all citizens. It then is a matter of sociological analysis whether this aim is better reached through private enterprise or through state ownership of the means of production. The difficulties in this case result from the imperfect state of the science of sociology, which cannot give us unambiguous answers, comparable to the answers given by physics. Among the adherents of a democracy, most political issues are reducible to cognitive controversies. It is our hope, therefore, that such issues will be settled through public discussion and peaceful experiments rather than by resort to war.

Most volitional decisions we are confronted with are entailed decisions, that is, decisions entailed by more fundamental aims which we set for ourselves. It is for this reason that cognitive clarification is of so great an import for moral questions. Apart from political questions, we may mention questions of education, health, sex life, the civil law, the criminal code, and the punishment of criminals. Thus the question whether a sentenced criminal should be put into a penitentiary is not a moral, but a psychological question for all those who are agreed that the jurisdiction of the state should attempt to produce as many socially adjusted citizens as possible. That persons released from penitentiaries are usually conditioned to the contrary of this aim is borne out by too many experiences.

It is a psychological fact, however, that even when a cognitive clarification is reached it is difficult to change volitional attitudes. We may know that since we want a certain fundamental aim we must also accept a certain other decision, and yet we hesitate to do so. Thus we may be convinced that a criminal should not be punished, but should be put into an environment that offers him possibilities of a readjustment. Nevertheless, it may be difficult for us to overcome the call for punishment, the desire for revenge, that has dictated so many of our regulations for criminals. Again, the ethics of sex relations is filled with so many taboos that it is extremely difficult to overcome habitual prejudices even when psychological considerations have made it clear that we must change some of our traditional valuations if we want happier and healthier men and women. In all such cases, the cognitive result has to be supported by a readjustment of our volitional attitudes. It is in this respect that education through the group plays an indispensable part. Only through living in an environment in which the new valuations are carried through do we learn that we can accept them; do we acquire the force to will what logical derivation has shown to be a consequence of our fundamental aims. The psychology of volitional attitudes is not settled by logical argument; it is logic in combination with group influence that helps us to organize our volitional setup.

Are all moral questions answerable through a reduction to common fundamental aims? The fact that we are all human speaks for such an assumption, since it appears plausible that the physiological similarities between men include a similarity of volitional aims. Other facts speak against the assumption, since certain groups, such as the nobility in feudal states, or the capitalists in the capitalist state, or the members of the party in control of a one-party totalitarian state, enjoy a definite advantage from maintaining the privileges of their class.

I think the answer to the question is not so very important. We saw that knowledge of an implication between aims does not *eo ipso* change volitional attitudes; that is to say, if such knowledge is to lead to a revision of decisions, it must be accompanied by a conditioning of volitions. If such conditioning is necessary and possible, it does not matter so much whether it concerns fundamen-

299

tal or entailed decisions. Even fundamental volitions are accessible to group influence, and will change under the suggestive power of an environment that exemplifies other volitions and their consequences.

Such adjustment to the necessities of the group is often made difficult by adherence to an absolute ethics. If a person has been indoctrinated in the theory that moral rules constitute absolute truths, he will be greatly inhibited from abandoning such rules and may remain unamenable to the conditioning by the group. Conversely, if a person knows that moral rules are of a volitional nature, he will be ready to change his goals to some extent if he sees that otherwise he cannot get along with other persons. Adaptation of goals to those of other persons is the essence of social education. Naïve egoism encounters resistance if it is set against the egoism of others, and the egoist will soon discover that he fares better when he coöperates with the group. The give and take of social coöperation offers much deeper satisfaction than does obstinate refusal to abandon one's goals. Thus the person educated in an empiricist approach to ethics is better prepared than the absolutist to become an adjusted member of society.

This is not meant to imply that the empiricist is a man of easy compromise. Much as he is willing to learn from the group, he is also prepared to steer the group in the direction of his own volitions. He knows that social progress is often due to the persistence of individuals who were stronger than the group; and he will try, and try again, to modify the group as much as he can. The interplay of group and individual has effects both on the individual and on the group.

Thus the ethical orientation of human society is a product of mutual adjustment. The recognition of relations between various goals plays only a limited part in this process. The greater part is played by psychological influences of a noncognitive kind, emanating from individuals to other individuals, from individuals to the group, and from the group to individuals. The friction between volitions is the propelling force of all ethical development. It may therefore be admitted that power plays a leading part in the change of moral valuations—if power is measured by any form of success in asserting one's volitions against those of other persons. This widest meaning of the word is not restricted to the power of arms. Other forms of power can be equally or even more efficient: the power of social organization, the power of a social class that has discovered its common interests, the power of coöperative groups, the power of speech and writing, the power of the individual that shapes the pattern of a group through exhibiting outstanding behavior. Yes, it is power that controls social relationships.

We should not commit the fallacy of believing that the struggle for power is controlled by a superhuman authority that leads it to an ultimately good end; nor should we commit the complementary fallacy of believing that the good is to be defined as that which is the most powerful. We have seen too many victories of what we regard as immorality, too much success of mediocrity and class egoism. We try to pursue our own volitional ends, not with the fanaticism of the prophet of an absolute truth, but with the firmness of the man who trusts in his own will. We do not know whether we shall reach our aim. Like the problem of a prediction of the future, the problem of moral action cannot be solved by the construction of rules that guarantee success. There are no such rules.

And there are no rules by means of which we could discover a purpose, or a meaning, of the universe. There is some hope that the history of mankind will be progressive and lead to a better-adjusted human society, although there are strong tendencies to the contrary. To believe that the physical universe is progressive in the human sense, is absurd. The universe follows the laws of physics, not moral commands. We have been able to a certain extent to employ the laws of physics to our own advantage. That some day we shall control larger parts of the universe is not impossible, though none too probable. It is more likely that finally the human race will die with the planet on which its life began.

Whenever there comes a philosopher who tells you that he has found the ultimate truth, do not trust him. If he tells you that he knows the ultimate good, or has a proof that the good must become reality, do not trust him, either. The man merely repeats the errors which his predecessors have committed for two thousand years. It is time to put an end to this brand of philosophy. Ask the philosopher to be as modest as the scientist; then he may become as successful as the man of science. But do not ask him what you should do. Open your ears to your own will, and try to unite your will with that of others. There is no more purpose or meaning in the world than you put into it.

18.

The Old and the New Philosophy: A Comparison

I SHOULD like to summarize the philosophic results grown from the analysis of science and to compare them with the conceptions developed by the philosophy of speculation.

Speculative philosophy sought to acquire a knowledge of generalities, of the most general principles that govern the universe. It was thus led to the construction of philosophic systems including chapters that we must regard today as naïve attempts at a comprehensive physics, a physics in which the function of scientific explanation was assumed by simple analogies with experiences of everyday life. It attempted to account for the method of knowledge by a similar use of analogies; questions of the theory of knowledge were answered in terms of picture language rather than by logical analysis. Scientific philosophy, in contrast, leaves the explanation of the universe entirely to the scientist; it constructs the theory of knowledge by the analysis of the results of science and is aware of the fact that neither the physics of the universe nor that of the atom can be understood in terms of concepts derived from everyday life.

Speculative philosophy wanted absolute certainty. If it was impossible to foretell individual occurrences, at least the general laws controlling all occurrences were regarded as accessible to knowledge; these laws were to be derived by the power of reason. Reason, the lawgiver of the universe, revealed to the human mind the intrinsic nature of all things—a thesis of this kind was at the basis of all forms of speculative systems. Scientific philosophy, in contrast, refuses to accept any knowledge of the physical world as absolutely certain. Neither the individual occurrences, nor the laws controlling them, can be stated with certainty. The principles of logic and mathematics represent the only domain in which certainty is attainable; but these principles are analytic and empty. Certainty is inseparable from emptiness: there is no synthetic a priori.

Speculative philosophy strove to establish moral directives in the same way that it constructed absolute knowledge. Reason was considered the giver of the moral law as well as of the cognitive law; ethical rules were to be discovered by an act of vision, analogous to the vision revealing the ultimate rules of the cosmos. Scientific philosophy has abandoned completely the plan of advancing moral rules. It regards moral aims as products of acts of volition, not of cognition; only the relations between aims, or between aims and means, are accessible to cognitive knowledge. The fundamental ethical rules are not justifiable through knowledge, but are adhered to merely because human beings want these rules and want other persons to follow the same rules. Volition is not derivable from cognition. Human will is its own progenitor and its own judge.

Such is the balance of a comparison between the old and the new philosophy. The modern philosopher renounces very much; but he also gains very much. What a difference between the science built on the basis of experiments and the science derived from reason alone! How much more reliable, in spite of their uncertainty, are the predictions of the scientist than those of the philosopher who claimed to have an immediate insight into the ultimate laws of the universe! How superior is an ethics not bound by rules allegedly dictated by a higher authority, when new social conditions emerge, unforeseeable for older ethical systems!

And yet, there are philosophers who refuse to acknowledge scientific philosophy as a philosophy, who wish to incorporate its results into an introductory chapter of science and claim that there exists an independent philosophy, which has no concern with scientific research and has direct access to truth. Such claims, I think, reveal a lack of critical judgment. Those who do not see the errors of traditional philosophy do not want to renounce its methods or results and prefer to go on along a path which scientific philosophy has abandoned. They reserve the name of philosophy for their fallacious attempts at a superscientific knowledge and refuse to accept as philosophical a method of analysis designed after the pattern of scientific inquiry.

What is required for a scientific philosophy is a reorientation of philosophic desires. Unless the aims of speculative philosophy are recognized as unattainable, the achievements of scientific philosophy cannot be understood. The language of pictures is the natural mode of expression for the poet; but the philosopher must renounce the use of suggestive pictures for explanations if he wants to understand scientific philosophy. The desire for absolute certainty may appear to us as an aim of admirable grandeur, but the scientific philosopher must avoid the fallacy of regarding conditioned habits as postulates of reason and must learn that probable knowledge is a basis solid enough to answer all questions that can reasonably be asked. The desire to establish moral directives by an act of moral cognition appears understandable; but the scientific philosopher must forego the quest for moral guidance, which misled others to conceive morality as a form of knowledge acquired through an insight into a higher world. Truth comes from without: the observation of physical objects tells us what is true. But ethics comes from within: it expresses an "I will", not a "there is". Such is the reorientation of philosophic desires required of the scientific philosopher. Those who are able to control their desires will discover that they gain much more than they lose.

The gain, in fact, is impressive if compared with the results of the traditional philosophical systems. Let me emphasize again that I will not deny the historical merits of these systems. It is a long way from the first vision of a problem to its clear formulation, and another long way from there to its solution. Many of our present-day solutions can be traced back to origins in the analogies and the picture language of some ancient philosopher. Yet nothing is more dangerous to a critical understanding of philosophy than regarding those pictures and analogies as prophetic anticipations of modern discoveries. The first vision of a problem often springs from naïve astonishment rather than from insight into its far-reaching implications. The labor and ingenuity invested in the development that led to the modern solution can be as great, can even be much greater than the contribution of those who started this development. Due respect to the ancients should not make us blind to the achievements of our own time. It takes independence of judgment and acuity of critique to discover the few genuine problems among the collections of vague concepts and dogmatic verbiage bequeathed to us by traditional philosophy. Only a thorough understanding of modern scientific method can equip a philosopher with the tools necessary to solve those problems.

18. THE OLD AND THE NEW PHILOSOPHY

The present book has tried to give an account of answers which modern scientific philosophy has given to problems that have played a part in traditional philosophy ever since its inception in Greek thought. There is the question as to the origin of geometrical knowledge answered in the distinction between physical geometry, which is empirical, and mathematical geometry, which is analytic. There is the question of causality and a general determination of all physical occurrences, which has received a negative answer: causality is an empirical law and holds only for macroscopic objects, whereas it breaks down in the atomic domain. There is the question as to the nature of substance and matter, which was answered by the duality of waves and particles, a conception more amazing than any brand of fiction ever developed in philosophic systems. There is the question as to the controlling principle of evolution, which principle was found in a statistical selection in combination with causal laws. There is the question as to the nature of logic, which discipline was shown to be a system of laws of language that does not restrict any possible experiences and thus does not express any properties of the physical world. There is the question as to predictive knowledge, answered through a theory of probability and induction, according to which predictions are posits, are the best instruments available to predict the future if such prediction is possible. There is the question of the existence of the external world and of the human mind, which is found to be a question of correct use of language rather than a question of a "transcendental reality". And there is the question as to the nature of ethics, which was answered by the distinction of goals and implications between goals, an answer which makes only these implications accessible to cognitive judgment and leaves to primary goals the status of volitional decisions.

This is a collection of philosophic results which have been established by means of a philosophic method as precise and dependable as the method of science. The modern empiricist may quote these results when he is invited to supply evidence that scientific philosophy is superior to philosophic speculation. There is a body of philosophical knowledge. Philosophy is no longer the story of men who attempted in vain to "say the unsayable" in pictures or verbose constructions of pseudological form. Philosophy is logical analysis of all forms of human thought; what it has to say can be stated in comprehensible terms, and there is nothing "unsayable" to which it has to capitulate. Philosophy is scientific in its method; it gathers results accessible to demonstration and assented to by those who are sufficiently trained in logic and science. If it still includes unsolved problems subject to controversy, there is good hope that they will be solved by the same methods as those which, for other problems, have led to solutions commonly accepted today.

Drawing the balance between old and new philosophy, one is astonished at the fact that there is still so much opposition to the new philosophic method and its results. I should like to discuss the possible psychological causes of this opposition.

The first is that there is much technical work to do in order to understand the new philosophy. The philosopher of the old school is usually a man trained in literature and history, who has never learned the precision methods of the mathematical sciences or experienced the happiness of demonstrating a law of nature by a verification of all its consequences. Our high-school instruction does not lead further than into the lobby of mathematics and the sciences, and who can judge about the theory of knowledge if he has never seen knowledge in its most successful form?

18. THE OLD AND THE NEW PHILOSOPHY

The usual argument of the defense is that scientific philosophy is too much oriented toward the mathematical sciences and does not do justice to the social and historical sciences. This argument is but a new demonstration of a misunderstanding of the program of scientific philosophy. The scientific philosopher would welcome any attempt to deal with the social sciences by a philosophic method analogous to the one carried through, with so much success, in the natural sciences. What he refuses to accept is a philosophy which draws a line of demarcation between social and natural sciences and which claims that such fundamental concepts as explanation, or scientific law, or time, have different meanings in the two fields. Such claims originate frequently from a misunderstanding of the mathematical sciences. In fact, the analysis of causality carried through in physics brings that science much closer to sociology than it was ever before; the recognition that physical laws are probability implications, and not dictates of reason, should encourage the sociologist to formulate laws even when his laws hold only for a majority of instances. The extreme complexity of social conditions, which makes it impossible to see a sociological law realized in an ideal case, recalls the similar condition of the physical science of meteorology. In spite of the fact that strict meteorological predictions are impossible, no physicist doubts that the weather is controlled by the laws of thermodynamics and aerodynamics. Even if it is so difficult to forecast the political weather, why must the sociologist refuse to believe in the existence of sociological laws?

The argument that sociological happenings are unique and do not repeat themselves breaks down because the same is true for physical happenings. The weather of one day is never the same as that of another day. The condition of one piece of wood is never the same as that of any

309

other one. The scientist overcomes these difficulties by incorporating the individual cases into a class and by looking for laws that control the different unique conditions at least in a majority of cases. Why should the sociologist be unable to do the same thing?

The contention of an unbridgeable gap between social and natural sciences looks very like an attempt to create, in the philosophy of the social sciences, a reservation for philosophers who are afraid of the logical and mathematical technique without which a theory of knowledge can no longer be built up. Fortunately, there also exists a group of social scientists who look to scientific philosophy for help in their struggle for the understanding of the method of their science, and who recognize that a good deal of house-cleaning is necessary before a philosophy of the social sciences can be constructed. I should like to express the hope that scientific philosophy of the future will attract men from all fields of knowledge, who have turned from researches in their special fields to philosophic inquiry.

The help of unprejudiced collaborators from the nonmathematical sciences is welcome for further reasons. Although mathematical and logical research has greatly contributed to building up the new philosophy, such work is in itself not necessarily associated with a critical philosophical attitude. There are mathematicians, and even mathematical logicians, who have never felt the need of extending the precision of their methods to the logical analysis of empirical knowledge, or who believe that any such extension has to be supplemented by an appeal to a superempirical insight, that is, an insight into a nonanalytic absolute truth. They regard philosophy as a sort of guesswork which can never lead to serious results; or they consider the convictions of common sense to be unavoidable presuppositions of philosophy and deny the possibility of a criticism of such convictions; or they believe that the vague and fanciful language of the speculative philosopher offers the only means to deal with philosophical problems. Mathematical training is no guarantee for an understanding of the problems and methods of the modern theory of knowledge. And even if the problems are seen, the solutions might still be sought along those paths which an age-old tradition has glorified and which the student of our universities, in the formative years of his scientific training, has usually not learned to criticize.

The line of demarcation between the old and the new philosophy does not set off mathematics from speculative philosophy. It severs the man who feels responsible for every word he says from the man who uses words for the conveyance of intuitive guesses and unanalyzed conjectures; the man who is willing to adjust his conception of knowledge to attainable forms of knowing from the man who cannot renounce the belief in superempirical truth; the man who regards analysis of knowledge as accessible to logical precision methods from the man who thinks of philosophy as an extralogical domain, free from the restriction by logical controls and open to the satisfaction that flows from the use of picturesque speech and its emotional connotations. The separation of these two types of mentality is an inescapable consequence of the new philosophy.

The second possible cause of opposition against scientific philosophy is the view that the scientific philosopher has no understanding of the emotional side of life, that logical analysis deprives philosophy of its emotional import. Many a student of philosophy goes into philosophic lectures in the search for edification; he reads Plato as he reads the Bible, or Shakespeare, and is disappointed by a class in philosophy where he has to listen to an exposition of symbolic logic or the theory of relativity. All I can say with regard to such an attitude is that those who wish edification should go to lectures on the Bible, or on Shakespeare, and should not expect to find it in a place where it does not belong. The scientific philosopher does not want to belittle the value of emotions, nor would he like to live without them. His life may be as rich in passion and sentiment as that of any literary man—but he refuses to muddle emotion and cognition, and likes to breathe the pure air of logical insight and penetration. If I may be permitted a more earthly comparison: the taste of logical analysis resembles that of oysters, in so far as one has to learn to like it. But as the man who eats oysters will gladly accept a glass of wine, the student of logic need not renounce the wine of emotional experiences offered by less logical pursuits.

It is a myth that a mathematical and logical mind cannot appreciate the value of art. A famous mathematician has edited the writings of a lyrical poet; many a famous physicist plays the violin in his hours of leisure; and a famous biologist was a painter, his artistic talent being visible in the drawings of his microscopic observations. Art and science do not exclude each other; but they should not be identified. "Truth is beauty and beauty is truth"—that is a beautiful statement, but not a true one, and thus disproves its own thesis.

My argumentation will perhaps be judged as not to the point. The personal attitude of the scientific philosopher, so it might be objected, is not under discussion, and no one will deny that the scientific philosopher may have good taste and be open to sentiment. What is held against him is that he assigns no place to art and emotion in his philosophical system. The speculative philosophers allotted to art a dignified position by putting art on a par with science and morality; truth, beauty, and the good were for them the triple crown of human searching and longing. It appears that the crown of the scientific philosopher possesses only one point. Why did he break off the two others?

Because, I would answer, the relation between truth and beauty is not a matter of crowns or dignity. The question of how to classify art is a logical question and thus a question concerning truth. It is the question of the logical nature of valuation, the answer to which must not be given in terms of valuations. Whether or not the answer satisfies our emotional desires is irrelevant.

Art is emotive expression, that is, aesthetic objects serve as symbols expressing emotional states. The artist as well as the person who looks at, or listens to, the works of art inserts emotive meanings into physical objects consisting in paint spread on canvas or sounds produced by musical instruments. The symbolic expression of emotive meanings is a natural goal, that is, it represents a value which we aspire to enjoy. Valuation is a general characteristic of human goal-activities, and it is advisable to study its logical nature in full generality, not restricting the analysis to art.

In some sense, every human activity serves the pursuit of a goal, whether it consists in the performance of a job necessary for making one's living, or in the attendance of a political meeting through which one wants to contribute to certain political decisions, or in a visit to an art gallery where one wants to see landscapes or portraits or abstract form through the eyes of an artist, or in having a dance and enjoying the erotic stimulus of rhythmic motion and music. In all such activities, however, there are moments where a choice is to be made; it is here that behavior exhibits valuation. The valuation need not be explicitly stated, nor achieved through reflection and comparison; it may be performed in the spontaneous impulse which drives us to read a book or to see a friend or to attend a concert. But in the decisions made we express our preferences and thus indicate through our behavior the valuational order which constitutes the background of our actions.

The explicit elaboration of this valuational order is studied by the psychologist. He knows that this order is not always the same, that preferences vary with momentary conditions, with environment, and with age. He can try to construct a sort of average order, to be inferred from statistics of goal-behavior. He can proceed to classify goal-behavior into different kinds. There is the physiological urge for food, sex, rest. There is the urge toward social recognition and social influence, or even social power. There is the creative impulse driving a man to write a book or to make his own fence for his garden. There is the desire to play, or to see others play a football game. There is the urge to emotive expression found in listening to a string quartet or gazing into the flaming colors of the setting sun. There is the urge to know, satisfied through studying scientific books or making scientific experiments. Any classification of this kind will be imperfect, and the attempts at constructing a neat logical order will be baffled by the overlapping of various goals in every action.

One common feature, however, can be stated for all goal activities. The decision for a goal is not an action comparable to the recognition of truth. There will be cognitive implications involved; for instance, the goal of making one's living may require the endurance of vocational drudgery. But the choice of the goal is not a logical act. It is the spontaneous affirmation of desires, or volitions, which come upon us with the compulsion of inescapable urges, or the animation of prospective satisfaction, or the smooth naturalness of unquestioned habits.

18. THE OLD AND THE NEW PHILOSOPHY

There is no point in asking the philosopher to justify valuations. And he cannot supply a scale of valuational order, distinguishing between higher and lower values. Such a scale is in itself valuational, not cognitive. As a man of education and experience, he may be able to give good advice for valuations, that is, he may influence other persons to accept more or less his valuational scale. But men of other professions may be just as good as he in this educational function. If they are trained educators or psychologists, they might even be better qualified.

The scientific philosopher does not regard problems of valuation as irrelevant; they are as relevant for him as for any other person. But he believes that they cannot be solved by philosophical means. They belong in psychology, and their logical analysis is to be given along with the logical analysis of psychological concepts in general.

The third possible cause of an opposition against scientific philosophy is the fact that no moral guidance can be derived from its results. The clear-cut distinction between ethics and knowledge, between volition and cognition, has frightened away many a student from the teachings of scientific philosophy. The old-style philosopher gave maxims advising him how to live and promised him that through sufficient study of philosophical books he would know what is good and what is bad. The scientific philosopher tells him pretty frankly that he has nothing to expect from his teachings if he wants to know how to lead a good life.

The refusal of scientific philosophy to give moral advice is mitigated by its encouragement to use cognitive thinking for the study of the relations between various moral aims. The implications between ends and means, and between primary and secondary aims, are of a cognitive nature; and one should not forget that this fact settles a great deal of ethical controversy. Most of the moral

315

decisions by which we are confronted do not concern primary aims, but secondary aims; and all they require is an analysis of the contribution which the decision under consideration will make to the realization of some fundamental aim. Political decisions are virtually all of this type. For instance, whether the government should control prices is a question to be answered by economic analysis; the ethical aim of producing as many goods as necessary for as low a price as possible is not under discussion. But in classifying moral implications as cognitive the scientific philosopher eliminates the discussion of such relations from the domain of philosophy and allots to them a place within the social sciences. The logical analysis of ethics shows that just as in physics, many questions which had been regarded as philosophical are to be answered by an empirical science. The history of philosophy demonstrates over and over again that questions asked of the philosopher were passed on to the scientist. The answer can thus only become more profound and more reliable. Those who ask the philosopher for guidance in life should be grateful when he sends them to the psychologist, or the social scientist; the knowledge accumulated in these empirical sciences promises much better answers than are collected in the writings of the philosophers. The ethical systems of speculative philosophy are often built on the psychological conditions and the social structure of times past, and, like the theoretical systems, present as philosophical results what is no more than the product of a temporary stage of knowledge. The scientific philosopher keeps clear of such errors in reducing his contribution to ethics to a clarification of its logical structure.

Although the scientific philosopher refuses to give ethical advice, he is willing, in following his program, to discuss the nature of ethical advice and thus to extend his method of clarification to the study of the logical side of this human activity. Ethical advice can be given in three forms. In the first form, the adviser attempts to persuade a person to accept the moral aims which he, the adviser, regards as good. In the second form, the adviser asks the person what his aims are and then tells him implications suitable to help him reach his aims. In the third form, the adviser acquires information about the aims of the person not by asking him, but by observing his behavior and inferring from it what goals the person pursues. He then puts these goals into words and tells the person, as before, implications pertinent for the attainment of these goals.

Of the first form is the advice offered by politicians, by representatives of religions, and by other advocates of an authoritarian ethics. In the second form, the adviser assumes the function of a psychological technician, like a vocational adviser, who answers questions about the ways of preparation for the various vocations. In the third form, the adviser takes upon himself the task of interpreting a man's behavior. Since men are often none too clear about their goals and do many things without reflecting about their own intentions, the adviser may sometimes be able to tell a man what he "really wants". This means he can give a consistent interpretation of the man's behavior and induce him to desire openly something that so far he had not desired explicitly. The adviser can thus become of great influence for the person's psychological setup and help him clarify his volitions, a function analogous in some respects to the clarification of meanings achieved through logical analysis. This form of advice is the most efficient one and requires high qualifications on the side of the adviser, demanding psychological understanding as well as extensive knowledge of sociological conditions.

Only in the first form is the subjective component of the advice openly visible; but in the second and third form, a subjective component is usually present also. The adviser will be ready to inform a person about means to reach his aims only if he approves of these aims, at least to a certain extent. For instance, the advocate of a democratic ethics would not be willing to advise a totalitarian government about means to achieve its aims, unless he "sells his soul"—a kind of job which most people would regard as immoral. Conscientious advice is therefore never purely objective; the adviser is bound to be an active participant in the formation of goals, an agent of morality, and he assumes an operative function in addition to the cognitive part of his work.

It is sometimes argued that the advice is objective because the client, once he has accepted the advice and realized it in his personal life, often admits that he knows now what he wants and feels happier than before. Such a result is no proof of objectivity, however. Human personalities are malleable, and if the person had been under the influence of advisers who guided him to very different goals, he might just as well have endorsed their advice by feeling happy and illuminated. The followers of a totalitarian society are often as happy and self-reliant as those of a democratic society, and yet it is highly probable that any of them would have accepted the opposite goals had he been brought up in a corresponding environment. Ethical advice cannot be justified by its psychological success. The adviser should know that he induces the person to do something he, the adviser, regards as right, that the responsibility is with the adviser, and that there is no escape from the commitment to one's own volitions into an objective morality, to be revealed through psychological studies of human behavior. Psychology can tell us what men want, but not what men *should* want, if the word "should" is meant in a nonimplicational sense—and the implicational "should" cannot establish an objective morality because it cannot validate primary goals.

The solution which scientific philosophy offers for the problem of ethics resembles in many respects the solution found for the problem of geometry. This solution was explained in Chapter 8: whereas the older mathematicians regarded the whole of geometry as a mathematical necessity, the mathematicians of today restrict the necessary character to the implications between axioms and theorems and exclude the axioms themselves from the domain of mathematical assertions. Similarly, the scientific philosopher distinguishes between ethical axioms, or premises, and ethical implications, and he regards only the implications as capable of logical proof. There is, however, a fundamental difference. The axioms of geometry can be made true statements when they are regarded as physical statements, based on coördinative definitions and proved through observation; they then possess empirical truth. The axioms of ethics, in contrast, cannot be made cognitive statements at all; there is no interpretation in which they can be called true. They are volitional decisions. When the scientific philosopher denies the possibility of a scientific ethics, he refers to this fact. He will never deny that social sciences play an important part in all applications of ethical decisions. And he does not wish to say that the so-called axioms are invariable premises, holding for all times and all conditions. Even general ethical premises may change with the social environment, and when they are called axioms this term means only that for the context considered they are not questioned.

Ethics includes both a cognitive and a volitional component, and cognitive implications can never eliminate volitional decisions completely, though they can reduce the number of such decisions to a small number of basic decisions. The logical relationship between decisions and implications may be made clear by the following analysis. Suppose a man wants both the goals A and B. The social scientist proves to him that A implies not-B. Is he now committed to abandon B? Certainly not. He might as well abandon A and decide for B. He will do so if B appears to him the preferable goal. An ethical implication does not tell a man what he should do; it merely confronts him with a choice. The choice is a matter of his volition; and no cognitive implication can relieve him from this personal choice.

For instance, a man wants peace among nations; but he also wants freedom from dictatorship. He finds out that under certain conditions a dictatorship can be overthrown only by the force of arms. Does it follow that, if these conditions obtain, he should advocate war against the dictator? This conclusion would be erroneous. What follows is that he cannot have both peace and freedom. Which of these goals he should prefer is up to him. The cognitive implication "freedom implies war" merely compels him to make his choice, but does not tell him what to choose.

This analysis will also make it obvious that there are no absolute goals, that is, goals that are pursued under all circumstances. Every goal can be judged in terms of its consequences. If a goal requires the use of a means which we regard as detrimental to certain other goals, and if these other goals rank higher with us than the first, we shall abandon the first goal. The end justifies the means—yes, but conversely, the means can call for the rejection of the end. The end-means implication does not supply a proof that the means must be adopted; it merely proves an either-or; it proves that we either have to apply the means or to give up the end. This choice is to be made by everyone for himself.

Sometimes it will help to know further implications. If a choice is to be made between A and B, it may be useful to know that A is required for a goal C, and B is required for a goal D. Instead of weighing A against B, one may then weigh C against D. For instance, a man is offered a well-paid position which, however, would commit him to advocate political opinions he has so far strongly rejected. Now he needs the money in order to give a college education to his children; but if he becomes a political renegade, he will lose self-esteem and the esteem of his friends. The original choice between the well-paid position and the adherence to his political opinions is thus reduced to the choice between having the means to give his children a college education and maintaining his personal integrity. This illustration offers an example where the reduction of decisions scarcely alleviates the difficulty of the choice; in other instances, it may be easier to select between the goals C and D than between the goals A and B. It is obvious, however, that any such reduction will leave us with a choice which cannot be settled by cognitive means. Our volition is the ultimate instrument of our decision.

I should like to express the hope that my formulation will open the path to an understanding with pragmatist philosophers, who maintain the existence of a scientific ethics. The difference between their formulation and mine is merely verbal when the term "scientific ethics" is meant to denote an ethics that uses scientific method for the establishment of implications between ends and means. Perhaps that is all that pragmatists want to say; and yet I should be very glad if I could find, in the writings of pragmatists, a clear statement in which all attempts at validating primary goals by cognitive means

321

are openly denounced as unscientific. The pragmatist speaks of human needs; but that men have needs does not prove that needs are good. If needs, or goals, are inferable from man's behavior, it can be very helpful to state such goals explicitly; but he who gives advice intended to clarify and satisfy needs indicates through *his* behavior that he regards such needs not only as existent, but as good. If it is clearly seen that the word "good" used here means that the adviser endorses the goals he has uncovered, the pragmatist is welcome in the function of ethical adviser.

Admitting this interpretation openly, an adviser may insist, for instance, that a physician adhere to professional secrecy, since the physician's goal of curing patients would be impaired if the patients could not be sure that their personal histories would remain confidential. Or he may argue that scientific research, though purely cognitive in its method, constitutes a pursuit of goals which carry social implications with them. The search for truth promises success only in a milieu of freedom and honesty, and the scientist who is not willing to stand up for these ethical postulates counteracts the interests of his own work. This argument does not mean that scientific theorems imply moral imperatives, but that the ethical goals indicated by the activity of the scientist imply such imperatives.

Constructing a social ethics of this kind is a significant contribution to the functioning of the social organism. It uses the science of sociology for the elaboration of rules of conduct appropriate to a man's place in human society. I would not object to calling such an ethical system a scientific ethics if there is agreement that it is not a science. It is scientific in the same sense that medicine and machine industry are scientific; it is a form of social engineering, that is, it is an activity by means of which the results of cognitive science are utilized for the pursuit of human goals. These goals themselves are not validated through cognition, or through science. They express volitional decisions, and no scientist can relieve anyone from listening to his own will. The scientist cannot even give moral advice without listening to *his* own will. In assuming the function of ethical adviser, he goes beyond the boundaries of science and joins the work of those who shape human society after a pattern they judge to be right.

A scientific philosophy cannot supply moral guidance; that is one of its results, and cannot be held against it. You want the truth, and nothing but the truth? Then do not ask the philosopher for moral directives. Those philosophers who are willing to derive moral directives from their philosophies can only offer you a sham proof. There is no use in asking the impossible.

The answer to the quest for moral directives is therefore the same as the answer to the quest for certainty: both are demands for unattainable aims. In pointing out that these aims cannot be attained for logical reasons, modern scientific philosophy has arrived at a cognitive result which is of greatest significance for human orientation in face of traditional philosophical goals. It demands to renounce these goals. But renouncing the impossible does not mean resignation. The negative truth calls for the positive directive: adjust your aims to what is attainable. This directive follows from the volition to reach one's aims; it expresses the trivial implication: if you want to reach your aims, do not strive for aims that cannot be reached.

In the temple of Delos in ancient Greece there was a golden altar of a very precise cubical shape. Once there was a pestilence, and the Delians, consulting the oracles, were told that in order to satisfy their god they had to double exactly the volume of the golden altar, giving it again the shape of a cube. The priests asked the mathematicians how to figure out the length of the edge of a cube whose volume is twice that of a given cube; but the mathematicians were unable to find a strict solution to the problem. I have always thought the god might have been satisfied with a cube of approximately the double volume; a Greek goldsmith would certainly have been able to attain a high degree of approximation. But the Greek mathematicians would not have accepted such a makeshift solution; they wanted the truth, and nothing but the truth. It took two thousand years to find the true answer; and the answer is negative—it is impossible to exactly double the volume of a cube by geometrical methods in the usual sense. Should the Greek mathematicians have refused to accept this answer because it is negative? He who wants the truth must not be disappointed when the truth is negative. It is better to know a negative truth than to demand the unattainable.

It is impossible to have a knowledge of the world that has the certainty of mathematical truth; it is impossible to establish moral directives that have the impelling objectivity of mathematical, or even of empirical, truth. This is one of the truths that scientific philosophy has uncovered. The solution of the problem of absolute certainty, as well as that of the problem of constructing an ethics by analogy with knowledge, is negative; this is the modern answer to an age-old quest. If someone argues that he is disappointed with scientific philosophy because it does not provide certainty, or does not supply moral directives, tell him the story of the Delian cube.

◆　　◆　　◆

The comparison between the old and the new philosophy is a matter for the historian and will be of interest to all those who were brought up in the old philosophy and wish to understand the new one. Those who work in the new philosophy do not look back; their work would not profit from historical considerations. They are as unhistorical as Plato was, or Kant, because like those masters of a past period of philosophy they are only interested in the subject they are working on, not in its relations to previous times. I do not wish to belittle the history of philosophy; but one should always remember that it is history, and not philosophy. Like all historical research, it should be done with scientific methods and psychological and sociological explanations. But the history of philosophy must not be presented as a collection of truths. There is more error than truth in traditional philosophy; therefore, only the critically minded can be competent historians. The glorification of the philosophies of the past, the presentation of the various systems as so many versions of wisdom, each in its own right, has undermined the philosophic potency of the present generation. It has induced the student to adopt a philosophic relativism, to believe that there are only philosophical opinions, but that there is no philosophical truth.

Scientific philosophy attempts to get away from historicism and to arrive by logical analysis at conclusions as precise, as elaborate, and as reliable as the results of the science of our time. It insists that the question of truth must be raised within philosophy in the same sense as in the sciences. It does not claim to possess an absolute truth, the existence of which it denies for empirical knowledge. Inasmuch as it refers to the existent state of knowledge and develops the theory of this knowledge, the new philosophy is itself empirical and is satisfied with empirical truth. Like the scientist, the scientific philosopher can do nothing but look for his best posits. But that is what he can do; and he is willing to do it with the perseverance, the self-criticism, and the readiness for new attempts, which are indispensable for scientific work. If error is corrected whenever it is recognized as such, the path of error is the path of truth.

Index